PEOPLE AND PLACES

Other books by the author

Roman Mornings 1956 (Heinemann Award)
Earls of Creation 1962
St Peter's 1967
Another Self 1970
Ancestral Voices 1975
Prophesying Peace 1977
Harold Nicolson 1980–1 (Heinemann Award)
Caves of Ice 1983
The Last Stuarts 1983
Midway on the Waves 1985
The Enigmatic Edwardian 1986
The Bachelor Duke 1991

PEOPLE AND PLACES

*Country House Donors
and the National Trust*

JAMES LEES-MILNE

JOHN MURRAY
Albemarle Street, London

A catalogue record for this book is available from the British Library

ISBN 0–7195–6202 3

Typeset in 10½/13pt Baskerville by
Wearset, Boldon, Tyne and Wear
Printed and bound in Great Britain by
St Edmundsbury Press Ltd, Bury St Edmunds, Suffolk

CONTENTS

ILLUSTRATIONS

(Between pages 152 and 153)

Illustrations are reproduced by kind permission of the following: Bromyard and District Local History Society, 1; National Trust, 2 (East Anglia Regional Office), 3, 4, 6, 12 (Mercia Regional Office), 13, 14 (Ellen Terry Memorial Museum), 19 (Northumbria Regional Office), 8, 15, 16; Rachel Morris, 9; Whitworth Art Gallery, University of Manchester, 10; Sir Edmund Fairfax-Lucy, Bt., 11; Lady Hilaria Gibbs, 17; Lord Sackville, 20; Sotheby's, London, 21; Prinknash Abbey Archives, 22; *Country Life*, 23.

ACKNOWLEDGEMENTS

I am greatly indebted to the National Trust's archivists for allowing me to comb through and quote from relevant files at the Trust's London Headquarters, 36 Queen Anne's Gate, SW1. Indeed the National Trust's staff in London and the regions have enabled me to write this book. I am grateful for their help and kindness in guiding my faltering steps back to some ancient haunts of yesteryear and allowing me to bore them with questions when we got there. Some even had me to stay the night for which I thank them. In particular I wish to thank Martin Drury, Merlin Waterson, Jeffrey Hawarth, Emma Ferry, Julian Gibbs, Belinda Cousens, Anthony Mitchell, Dudley Dodd, Mrs Weare (curator of Smallhythe Place), Christopher Wall, Hugh Dixon and Christopher Rowell.

To Lady Harrod, Michael Trinick, Nigel Nicolson and Hugh Massingberd I am grateful for much-needed transport and hospitality in Norfolk, Cornwall, Kent and Lincolnshire.

To Ariane Goodman's encouragement and Grant McIntyre's painstaking editorship I owe more than I can adequately express. Gail Pirkis too has done wonders in seeing my text through to the printers. Once again I am beholden to Douglas Matthews for his masterly indexing; and to John Kenworthy-Browne for help. Lastly, to James Fergusson is due the credit – if credit it becomes – of having suggested to me the subject of *People and Places*.

J.L-M. 1992

In mem.
Eardley Knollys

INTRODUCTION

I N the New Year of 1936 I was without a job. After coming down from Oxford I became private secretary to the statesman Lord Lloyd, whom I admired and liked, and then assistant secretary to Sir Roderick Jones, the chairman of Reuters, whose insolent personality and aggressive conduct I intensely disliked. Neither politics nor journalism held me in thrall. As a boy I had nurtured a mild enthusiasm for architecture of the romantic sort. It was fostered by the magical beauty of the university city in which I learned to detect the reflection of our national history and culture. There, quite suddenly, mild enthusiasm received a positive jolt into fervour. It was occasioned by my witnessing an act of deliberate vandalism for which afterwards I felt partially responsible through my sheer feebleness in not having remonstrated. I had been taken by some fellow undergraduates to a dinner party at Rousham Park, a lovely house set in William Kent's incomparable grounds on the banks of the infant river Cherwell. After dinner, in an orgy of inebriation, our host with a hunting crop slashed the family portraits, which were not his own for the house was rented, and with a rifle fired at the garden statues. The ductile guests sat and cheered. To my eternal shame I remained silent, although aghast. I have never got over this flagrant exhibition of iconoclasm. It aroused in me some deep atavistic compassion for ancient architecture so vulnerable and transient, and some paternal instinct to protect and safeguard all tangible works of art. Most adults' priority is for flesh and blood. Mine was for stones and mortar. The country houses of England, I became increasingly convinced, were our most precious secular shrines just as the cathedrals were their sacred counterparts. In a naïve way I longed to devote myself to their protection; how exactly I could not then foresee. I had a friend working for the Council for the Preservation of Rural England who somehow managed to survive on a minute salary

1

supplemented by a minute allowance from his parents. I had not even a minute allowance. I confided my pitiable ambition in hardly a soul beside my mother. But Vita Sackville-West was one.

Vita had a friend whom I never knew called Hilda Matheson. Hilda worked at the BBC. She had a brother called Donald MacLeod Matheson, who was secretary of the National Trust. She told Vita that there was a vacancy on the Trust's staff relating to country houses. I could hardly believe my ears when Vita suggested that I should apply. I did so and was interviewed by two members of the Executive Committee, of whom one was Rob Holland-Martin of Overbury Court – he was a neighbour and friend of my parents in Worcestershire – and MacLeod Matheson. Whether the fact that Mr Holland-Martin happened to be in the National Trust boardroom when I presented myself had any influence upon the outcome I am not sure. At the time I supposed it might have gone against me in that he alone would know how indifferent my qualifications were. I was proved wrong, and duly appointed Country Houses secretary. Ever since I have favoured a mild nepotism as opposed to a strict dependence upon paper attainments.

The National Trust for Places of Historic Interest or Natural Beauty was founded in 1895. In the first forty years of its existence far less attention was directed to the places created by man than to those by nature. Until the 1930s the Trust owned, apart from a handful of small and fairly insignificant buildings such as dovecotes, inns, chapels, barns and priests' houses, only two country houses, both in Somerset, namely Barrington Court acquired in 1907 as a ruin and Montacute House. The first had been let on a 99-year lease to a rich tenant who more or less rebuilt it; the second was totally empty of contents. On the other hand the Trust had much to show by way of stretches of beautiful landscape, notably in the Lake and the Peak districts. It was upon scenic open spaces that the Trust's founders concentrated towards the close of Queen Victoria's reign; England's great country houses hardly entered their minds.

Today it may seem strange that until the 1930s there was so little overt concern about their future. Successive governments had shown none and the preservation societies certainly did not express any. Nevertheless there were individuals who foresaw that with rising taxation, notably death duties, rates, high costs of maintenance and the diminishing band of domestic servants, the landed gentry would eventually find difficulty inhabiting large premises in the manner to which from time immemorial they had been accustomed. One of those individuals who remarked the cloud on the horizon was Philip Kerr,

11th Marquess of Lothian. He was a man who looked ahead of his time and appreciated the importance to the nation of its finest domestic architecture. By invitation of the National Trust's chairman the Marquess of Zetland, who at the time was Secretary of State for India, he delivered in July 1934 a speech, now famous in the Trust's annals, at the annual meeting of its members. He outlined to them the perils confronting historic houses, their collections, gardens and parks. He exhorted the Trust to consider how to save some of the best of these repositories of the arts. In the chapter headed Blickling Hall I shall be dealing with the contribution of this remarkable man to the general problem as well as the preservation of his own country house and estate in Norfolk.

Inspired by Lord Lothian's speech the National Trust consulted *Les Demeures Historiques* of France and Belgium. These societies, already in fairly successful operation in the two countries, were not holding bodies. Their members were owners of historic *châteaux* who had banded together, rather like their English counterparts after the last war within the Historic Houses Association, a sort of trades union of aristocrats. The *Demeures Historiques* had managed to wring some reluctant concessions for *châteaux* owners out of the respective French and Belgian governments and reductions of rates out of their local authorities in return for a limited amount of public access. Early in 1936 the founder president of *La Demeure Historique* in France, the Duc de Noailles, owner of the Château de Maintenon in Eure-et-Loir, addressed a gathering of English country house owners and members of the Trust committees, at a reception held in his honour in the Royal Geographical Society's rooms in London. The Duke exhorted the Trust to adopt similar measures in England to those of his society. In fact, because conditions in the two countries were so dissimilar England adopted far different, and as they turned out rather more positive, measures.

Lord Zetland instantly set up a special department within the National Trust to investigate methods and means of maintaining the continuity of landed families and their houses in England, Wales and Northern Ireland (Scotland already had its own separate National Trust) while granting access to the public. This necessitated much dialogue with government departments over how, along with country houses, agricultural land or capital funds to pay for their upkeep could be transferred to the Trust by owners without their involvement in taxation, especially death duties. For although the National Trust was exempt from taxation, the law forbade donors of land or capital from deriving financial benefit from what was transferred. The Trust had absolutely no money of its own for the purchase of country houses, could not provide funds for their upkeep and management, and yet wished the donors to go on living in them. Unless the government relaxed their punitive tax claims in return for public access donors naturally enough would not give their houses and estates.

The outcome of Lord Zetland's deliberations with the government was the two National Trust Acts of Parliament of 1937 and 1939 which granted the Trust further statutory powers to those it enjoyed already. Some particulars of the gradual process are outlined in the differing cases of country houses recorded in this book.

Our office was a cramped and stuffy house in Buckingham Palace Gardens, a dreary late nineteenth-century terrace in sub- 'Pont Street Dutch' style facing the high blank wall which conceals the shunting yard of Victoria station. Notwithstanding the high-powered chairmen of its committees the National Trust was then a very small affair compared to what it has become. Within the fifth decade of its existence its membership was under 5,000 and the total acreage of its properties about 40,000. The entire male staff consisted, beside secretary Matheson, of deputy-secretary Christopher Gibbs, Bruce Thompson, whose role and home was in the Lake District, and me. Shortly before the outbreak of war we were joined for a short while by Gordon Wordsworth, a great-grandson of the poet, as assistant to Gibbs. When peace returned new staff were enrolled in considerable numbers.

MacLeod Matheson was a strange man, sandy-haired, bearded, extremely bright, a product of Balliol, and a disciple of the Russian-born guru P.D. Ouspensky whose teaching seemed to have brought him not so much enjoyment of the higher consciousness as a marked *goût* for tortured self-martyrdom. Matheson would go out of his way to court unnecessary disasters like skidding off his motor-cycle in an empty road in broad daylight, and at night holding a torch in his mouth in lieu of a headlamp. He would linger in the office until midnight re-writing minutes and memoranda which his subordinates on the staff fancied they had drafted adequately. He was a jealous boss and a bad delegator of business. Needless to say he excelled the rest of us in grasping the most recondite problems, which was always annoying. His previous job of secretary to the Gas Light & Coke Company had not however made him an aesthete.

Christopher Gibbs was a true blue. A Wykhamist with the benevolence and dedication to duty of a scout-master, he pursued every task to its end with terrier-like persistence. He walked with a springy gait which was all optimism and good intentions. Yet his personality was far from obvious. His craggy and slightly severe face would fragment into guffaws of unexpected laughter. He had the slender fingers of a man who could manipulate delicate instruments and situations. Having trained at an agricultural college he was equipped to deal with those local committees and local estate agencies which managed our distant properties. As for Bruce Thompson, he was a gentle giant of a Norseman. He spent little time in London where his diffident advice was always welcome. He could hardly bear to be away from the Lake District where he knew everyone, rich and poor, exalted and humble. Not a landowner, farmer, or shepherd did not know and love him, and for thirty years or more he devoted his life to promoting the Trust's interests amongst the hills and fells of his native region.

In addition to us four males in the office there was the usual complement of lady clerks and typists presided over by a saintly nanny figure, Florence Paterson. She had come as a girl to take down in longhand the few daily letters dictated by Matheson's predecessor, S.H. Hamer, usually at half-past eleven in the morning for his signature after a protracted luncheon at half-past three. Hamer was a shy, lethargic individual, who had been editor of *Little Folks* in the 1890s, a close friend of John Bailey, man of letters and former chairman of the National Trust. He was a member of the recently founded Publicity Committee when I came, and anyone less equipped for PR work could hardly be imagined. I remember him at meetings with his eyes shut, blandly sucking at an old pipe and emitting little smoke.

Certainly No. 7 Buckingham Palace Gardens was a friendly and close-knit community. It has been described as having 'a cosy family atmosphere'. Each of us enjoyed, especially when delicate Mr Matheson was away sick, a generous quota of independence. We were entirely free from the bureaucratic stranglehold which, by the time I left the staff, was beginning to tighten its grip. We could take decisions on our own and were not obliged to submit half a dozen carbon copies of each draft letter for the approval of every Tom, Dick and Harry of the amenity world before posting it. A fairly happy-go-lucky and jolly atmosphere prevailed. Certainly we felt privileged to be working for the National Trust. It was not a career – we were paid next to nothing – but a dedication like nursing or being in Holy Orders. We were united by a strong missionary zeal to proselytize the caring and acquire more properties. The announcement of a new one was the cause of tremendous jubilation. I daresay in our eagerness we recommended and the Executive Committee accepted a few properties, whether open spaces or buildings, which today would be considered below par.

Although National Trust press announcements seldom made the hottest news for journalists, the public, or rather a vociferous minority of the public, applauded our efforts. Very few – and there were some, especially amongst the landowning class – regarded the Trust in the way high-born Romans of the Empire regarded the early Christians, as a sinister little group of left-wing dissidents edging a way towards wholesale take-over of private property. Friends and allies would spring up from unexpected quarters. A group of local desperadoes, calling themselves Ferguson's Gang, kept us on our toes. An invasion of the office without warning by a member of the gang, the Bloody Bishop, Red Biddy, Sister Agatha or Bill Stickers, appropriately disguised, would throw our old caretaker Lovell who opened the front door into paroxysms of alarm. The intruder, brushing Lovell aside, would burst into the secretary's room or, if there were a solemn meeting in progress, into the boardroom, and roughly deposit with a dreadful imprecation a large spotted handkerchief stuffed with pound notes and coins. Lord Zetland's face endeavouring to frame itself into a suitable grimace of amusement and gratitude was always worth observing. Such events were instantly announced to the press and followed by very acceptable publicity.

On 12 March 1936 the first Country Houses Committee of the Trust met. Lord Zetland took the chair and the founder members consisted of Nigel Bond (who had been the Trust's secretary from 1901 until 1911 when Hamer took over), a rugged, beetle-browed Dorset squire of great kindliness who sometimes between committee meetings gave me luncheon at the Grosvenor Hotel, and in tipping the waiter 6d. would ask if I thought it too much, Oliver Viscount Esher, Sir Alexander Lawrence (one-time solicitor to the Treasury), Lord Methuen (artist owner of Corsham Court, Wiltshire), R.C. Norman (one-time chairman of the LCC and the BBC, and surely the most charming and most handsome man who has ever existed), and Major Michael Peto (owner of Iford Manor, Wiltshire), with the secretary of the Trust and myself, the newly appointed secretary of the committee, in attendance. The chairman reported recent inconclusive negotiations he had had with the Chancellor of the Exchequer Neville Chamberlain, the Treasury and the Office (in 1940 to become the Ministry) of Works about tax concessions to affiliated owners and to donors of country houses to the Trust. The sole positive outcome of these talks was that the government wished to know which country houses the Trust considered either worthy of help if in private hands, or of acceptance if offered as gifts. So the committee set up a sub-committee to draw up a list of houses of 'undoubted merit'. W.A. Forsyth (architect), Christopher Hussey (editor of *Country Life*), Sir Charles Peers (retired chief inspector of Ancient Monuments) and Lord Gerald Wellesley (architect) were nominated to undertake this exacting task.

Within three weeks the sub-committee met under the chairmanship of Lord Esher. He was a shrewd, genial, irreverent and witty man – in fact the funniest I have ever met. In temperament he was the very opposite of Lord Zetland who, though enthusiastic and tireless in the Trust's service, was a dry stick, aloof, magisterial and humourless. The memory of Lord Zetland standing on the pavement outside the office, wearing a neat trilby set squarely over a poker face, turning neither to left nor right, but brandishing aloft a furled umbrella as though it were the sceptre on offer to his sovereign in Westminster Abbey and intoning the long drawn-out word, 'Cab!' still reduces me to a nervous tremor. Lord Esher may be described as a cultured landowner in that he never worked for his living or held public office. Yet he dedicated his easy-going life to patronage and salvation of the arts and architecture in a prominent way. To be in his company was a delight; to witness his handling of committees was an education. With infinite merriment he always got what he wanted, and what he wanted was invariably right. For years he was also chairman of the Society for the Protection of Ancient Buildings, an even older foundation than the National Trust. The SPAB had been the brainchild of Ruskin and William Morris and its vaunted formula was *anti-scrape*, that is, no 'restoration' and the minimum of repair of old buildings. To its carefully trained architects we looked for advice and the treatment of the Trust's historic architecture. I soon became a member of the SPAB Committee and a sort of working link between the society and the Country Houses Committee. My job brought me very close to Oliver Esher as the years went by. He was a most loyal boss and friend who supported me through thick and thin in whatever argument or tiff I might be engaged in with what he termed the 'mangel-wurzels' of this world.

The sub-committee drew up a list of 230 houses. It was probably the first attempt at a general register and of course there were many more important buildings unknown to almost everybody, let alone the four nominated members of the sub-committee, left out. Raw and ignorant though I was, and distinguished and knowledgeable though they were, I had at the time a good deal of misgiving about this hastily compiled and definitive list. I only knew that England was crammed with wonderful country houses, many of which we must have overlooked, and several of which, little regarded in 1936, might be highly esteemed by the next generation. After all, men's tastes changed with fashion as well as scholarship. Lord Esher was far too wise a chairman not to have been well aware of the fact also, for he was always opposed to inflexible opinions and rules. He would caution committees against laying down portentous conditions which sooner or later they would feel bound to contravene.

On 27 April of this same year the Country Houses Committee, to which Sir Edgar Bonham Carter (a retired judicial officer and adviser to various Indian provinces) and the 4th Marquess of Salisbury, Tory leader in the House of Lords, had been co-opted, met for the second time. They readily approved the sub-committee's list to which they made but one addition, namely Holland House, resolving that it 'be deemed to be a country house'. Country or urban it was totally destroyed by bombs in the forthcoming war. The committee decided to recommend the list for the Office of Works' approval, with the submission that Works might advise whether extensively restored houses with beautiful exteriors like Hever and Herstmonceux castles, ought to be included or not. Works did approve the list (I remember going through it house by house with George Chettle, the whimsical chief inspector, ebullient of wry jests and often convulsed with laughter while holding one hand over rather toothless gums), but whether they deigned to elicit an opinion about ruins, which they very much regarded as their preserve, I do not recall, and somehow doubt. To extract a definite pronouncement from the academic officers of the Ancient Monuments section was always like wringing blood from a stone.

Nominally the Country Houses Committee was advisory to the Executive Committee which alone had the power of accepting or rejecting properties, and to which strictly speaking it could merely make recommendations and suggest policies. Yet so elastic was the Trust's constitution in those happy days that the Country Houses Committee never seemed fettered in word or deed. To the Executive Committee the Finance and General Purposes Committee was likewise subordinate. It was small and select, composed of the cream of the Executive Committee, and exercised a very great deal of authority. Its chairman was also Lord Esher. In addition there was the Estates Committee responsible for the management of all the Trust's properties other than country houses. Its chairman was the eminent historian Professor George Macaulay Trevelyan. The Estates Committee was of the same grade in the hierarchy as the newly founded Country Houses Committee.

The Country Houses Committee quickly decided to issue invitations to the 230 owners of the houses on their list to join one of the two schemes: either to hand over their houses to the Trust direct (Scheme 1), or to be affiliated in some way, as yet unspecified, in the hope that the government would grant concessions (Scheme 2). In either case a minimum of thirty days opening to the public in the year was deemed sufficient. We may laugh today at this figure. It did not imply any reluctance on the Trust's part to give access to its properties, which was of course the ultimate purpose of saving them. It merely indicated a fear that donors, who it was then assumed would continue inhabiting every room as of old, would not stand for more opening of their homes to be gaped at. Had the Trust demanded additional access it might not have been given the houses. As it happened several donors soon positively asked for more opening days, and got them.

A brochure outlining the advantages (in that the Trust was exempt from taxation) of Scheme 1 and the anticipated advantages of Scheme 2 was prepared, printed and circulated to the aforesaid owners before a response was vouchsafed from the Office of Works. Owners were offered the dubious pleasure of a visit from the Country Houses secretary if they were in any doubt as to the schemes' advantages, or in any need of further elucidation or persuasion. Accordingly I was launched upon the most enjoyable summer of my existence, visiting by train, bicycle or Shank's nag a succession of stately homes and their forbearing owners. I am amazed when I look back upon the friendliness and hospitality I received from the great majority. Occasionally embarrassment ensued to the very stateliest domains. It might be looked upon askance if I arrived to stay without a white tie. Old Lord Bath, the most distinguished and courteous of patricians, received me at Longleat in a frock coat. He had presumably just come down from London. At the conclusion of – I regret to say – a fruitless interview he rang the bell and ordered my motor-car to be brought round. He insisted on accompanying me to the front door. The steps to the drive were flanked on either side with a row of footmen in livery. In place of my uniformed chauffeur an extra footman wheeled my bicycle to the front of the steps. I shook my host's hand, descended the perron and mounted. At the end of a straight stretch of drive, having turned smartly to the right, I looked back for a last view of the glorious façade. Lord Bath, attended by his posse of open-mouthed and doubtless disdainful servitors, was in the old-world manner of true hospitality still standing at the top of the steps until his guest was out of sight. I gave a half-hearted wave, and pedalled ahead.

Embarrassment was occasioned at times to me. It would happen that an enthusiastic owner, fired by the prospect of the National Trust preserving for all time his ancestral seat and thus immortalizing him and his forebears, invited the Country Houses secretary to pay him a visit in remotest Wales or even Cumberland. The Country Houses secretary must stay a night, sometimes two, in order to allow adequate time to take in the architectural beauties of the house, the historic contents and the spectacular park and surroundings. The seat in question might not be on our list of 230 and, what's more, Christopher Hussey of *Country Life* might never have heard of it. Then it might happen that before dismounting from whatever vehicle had borne me 400 miles from Buckingham Palace Gardens one glance told me – the flat terrain, the immoderately restored façade or the lamentable Edwardian excrescences – that Colonel So-and-So's seat was totally unacceptable. Nevertheless I was still faced with forty-eight hours' examination of every nook and cranny, maybe a contained revulsion, and certainly the obligation to gush appreciatively. I had to answer a thousand questions relating to the anticipated acceptance of a property of no merit whatever. If directly asked whether or no Tantivy Towers was worthy I would reply that, charming though I found it, I dared not predict what might be the opinion of my committee. Even in favourable circumstances I always tried to be non-committal, though not always with success. My enthusiasm would get the better of me.

Yet I must confess that the larger a hideous country house was the more fascinating I found it. This sounds and is snobbish. But it was always interesting to speculate why and how Colonel So-and-So's father or grandfather became inspired either to build from scratch or to convert a perfectly decent old house on the site into such a monstrosity and to lavish so much money on it. It is always extraordinary how some people contrive to see their geese as swans.

Such occurrences as I have just outlined may have been fairly few and far between, though they were not rare. On the whole, owners had a just opinion of the merits of their houses and possessions. The majority had knowledge and taste. Two generations ago all hereditary owners formed a race apart, heirs to a long tradition of government, either national or local, and often both at once. And when I come to think of it, what form of government in our history has evinced fewer failings than the squirearchical? Until the last war the National Trust still accepted the squirearchical system if it did not proclaim it. That is why I once wrote that my loyalties were to the houses, the families and the National Trust (which I regarded as the instrument of the others' preservation) in that order; and received criticism from a younger generation for so doing. Were I still on the Trust's staff I would no longer do so because today the squirearchy is virtually extinct, and the families have all but gone. On the whole the Trust's donors were eminently civilized and delightful. To nearly all of those with whom I had dealings I became very attached. With many I made fast friends.

On 22 June 1936 the Country Houses Committee held its third meeting. By now Lord Esher was firmly in the chair, to remain there for twenty-five years. He informed the committee that the Office of Works had approved the list, subject to the addition of six houses and elimination of three. I do not remember which these houses were. The committee was however disappointed with the Office of Works' cautious redraft of the brochure (which had been prematurely dispatched) in the light of the Treasury's refusal to countenance certain tax concessions which the Trust had rashly anticipated. The committee, a trifle nettled, was emphatic that, if Scheme 1 was to work, donors must be given a guarantee that their houses would be let back to them or their families by the Trust.

On 26 October the committee considered the response of owners to the precipitate brochure. Alas, it was not very encouraging, and I feared my job would come to an abrupt end. The overtures of two owners of houses, both deemed insufficiently important, were turned down. The Treasury was to be informed that Scheme 2 was a total failure and urged to grant the concessions previously recommended by the Trust for Scheme 1, or it too would come to nothing.

By January 1937 the committee decided to drop Scheme 2 altogether, since the Treasury had now relaxed its original proviso that Scheme 1 must be conditional upon the carrying through of Scheme 2. Unlike the French and Belgians, the English owners could see no advantages in clubbing together. In those years they were dubious of any good coming out of a government department, and also suspicious of the Trust's much vaunted democratic principles. In July the first actual offer of a country house (it happened not to be on the sacred, definitive list of 230) came before the committee. Stourhead was unanimously pronounced acceptable. Then came a second, Corsham Court, negotiations for which dragged on abortively until Lord Methuen's death in 1974, and thirdly, Knole. That these three houses were all settled property presented considerable difficulties of acceptance. The difficulties could be overcome only by means of the National Trust Act of 1939 which enabled entailed estates to be conveyed in certain circumstances. Even so this Act left endowment funds liable to tax.

It cannot be claimed that the surviving country houses scheme started with a bang. Progress in the pre-war years was laboured. Momentum gathered during the war. Nevertheless the Trust had friends in high places. Lord Brocket, who had joined the committee, was on terms of intimacy with the Prime Minister, Neville Chamberlain. There is no doubt that he won the sympathy of the Prime Minister, who was a frequent and appreciative guest for shoots at Bramshill and Brocket, Lord Brocket's two houses (very definitely on the list), to the Trust's cause. In January 1938 Lord Brocket reported that he had had conversations with Chamberlain about it; and to show his goodwill and to stir up that of the Prime Minister, he gave the Trust restrictive covenants over Bramshill and Brocket. The committee, emboldened by these marks of favour, addressed a letter to the Prime Minister urging that death duties on agricultural land surrounding privately owned historic houses should be alleviated. Nothing immediately came of this particular plea.

Other events of the year 1938 were a decision to consult the Office of Works on the preparation of a supplementary list of country houses (the idea was to increase the number by about a hundred), the acceptance of offers of Herstmonceux Castle (which came to nothing) and Attingham Park, the request for an endowment of £17,000 (not granted) for Doddington Hall, Cheshire, from Sir Delves Broughton, and a visit to England of members of *Les Demeures Historiques* of France and Belgium.

A large and distinguished party of *châteaux* owners, based in Bath, were entertained at several important privately owned country houses already opened to the public, like Corsham, and not then open, like Badminton and Longleat. The next year, just before the outbreak of war, the Country Houses secretary took a party of English country house owners to Belgium, where they were hospitably received at a number of *châteaux*. They were also entertained by a famous hero of the First World War, Burgomaster Max, in Brussels, and by King Leopold at Laeken Palace. During a too prolonged tour round the Brussels town hall consternation was caused by one of the British guests, Lady Kennet of the Dene, a woman impatient of custodians' chatter and averse to ceremonial, taking a flying leap through an open window on to a garden bed at the feet of the Burgomaster and assembled officials in purple raiment and gold chains. Our visit to the royal palace was also marked by an incident which indelibly impressed upon me the pathetic snobbishness which members of the lower ranks of society can betray. We were lined up by a breeched and powdered courtier before an imposing doorway about to admit us to the royal presence in strict order of precedence, that is to say the earls, viscounts and lords at the head of the queue, the baronets and lesser gentry in the middle, and the *hoi polloi* at the end, with their respective spouses. Immediately in front of me, necessarily at the very tail, stood the Mayor of Bath and a benefactor of the National Trust, Major Benton-Fletcher. When the great doors were thrown open a scuffle ensued under my nose. The Mayor and the Major were locked together in a struggle for pre-eminence. The Major began expostulating, 'You are a nobody outside your own provincial city!' The Mayor retorted, 'But my father was a clergyman.' The combatants were eventually parted by a pacific baronet who offered to swop places with the shamefaced Major.

The first eighteen months of the war were a completely dead period in the Trust's annals. Younger members of committees and nearly all the staff were away on service of various sorts. Committee work was practically in abeyance. The Country Houses Committee held no meetings between July 1938 and March 1941. By that year, however, it became apparent that the National Trust's part in the future preservation of country houses would be paramount.

My last duty in September 1939 before leaving for war service was to help MacLeod Matheson move the Trust office from Buckingham Palace Gardens to the country for safety. In the desperate hurry the twin Lutyens pavilions at Runnymede were chosen for sanctuary. They were of course far too small, and room for the office files totally inadequate. Nevertheless, within two days the move was accomplished and during a few extremely uncomfortable months the secretary, Miss Paterson, Miss Ballachey and two typists were crammed together or seen flitting across the main road from one pavilion to the other. Through the intervention of Captain John Burrow Hill, a member of the Estates Committee and agent to Sir John Dashwood, the office was transferred to West Wycombe Park where it remained for three years. But in 1943, the Trust, greatly daring, moved back to the old London premises. By then I had rejoined the staff, having been invalided from the Army. Many a rowdy night was spent sleeping fully clothed below the area railings on a mattress during air raids, dashing into the street and applying a stirrup pump to neighbours' roofs. Luckily we entirely escaped fire bombs. Often after long expeditions into the country I would return on foot from, say, Paddington station, carrying my luggage for lack of public transport, not homewards to Chelsea, but straight to that lonely mattress to keep guard at Buckingham Palace Gardens. When the war was over the Trust was given two adjacent houses, built in 1704, in Queen Anne's Gate to which we soon moved our headquarters. The donor, a dear old lady, Mrs Murray Smith, was I think the widow or daughter of a canon and looked as though she had never stirred from the purlieus of Westminster Abbey. She somehow survived the war amongst piles of dust-strewn, semi-protected furniture, like a wraith in a deserted cemetery of memories.

After recovery from the initial shock of involvement in another world cataclysm, owners of historic houses began to look beyond the bleak years of requisitioning by evacuees, mental deficients and American troops. What were they to do with freezing staterooms and interminable bedroom wings when peace returned? How were they to heat them? How even clean them? How indeed were they to make both ends meet in the horribly brave new world that would surely dawn? Many who had rejected our advances in the 1930s turned in the 1940s to the National Trust as the only apparent solution to their problems. Lord Lothian, who died while ambassador to Washington, left the Blickling estate to the Trust in 1941. The important bequest of this superb Jacobean house and beautiful estate, together with Sir Charles Trevelyan's gift of Wallington Hall, was a turning point in the Trust's fortunes. Other owners followed suit. Sir Robert Throckmorton set in motion the slowly grinding wheels of the Chancery Court whereby the Coughton settled estate was eventually transferred. Often negotiations took several years, sometimes a decade, before the gift of a country house and estate was made absolute.

In 1941 the committee was belatedly informed that the Treasury declined to collaborate with the Trust in drawing up a supplementary list of approved houses. In future, they said, every house on offer ought to be considered on its individual merits. How right in fact they were. In 1942, Cliveden, which was not among the first 230 houses and doubtless would not have been included in the supplementary list, was accepted, ostensibly because of its majestic setting and grand garden above a stretch of the Thames, on the understanding that the son of the donor, Lord Astor, would be allowed to live in the house after his father's death, and virtually because of the handsome endowment offered. The grandson of the donor no longer lives there.

Meanwhile the transfer of Knole was held up. Knole was made a test case. The Treasury was informed that unless, with settled estates, exemption from tax on endowment monies was granted on the deaths of successive tenants for life, this most famous of all pre-classical palaces could not be saved by the Trust. The following year the Treasury's consent was obtained, and in due course Knole became National Trust property.

In February 1942 Lord Esher submitted a memorandum in which he warned the committee that unless the Trust was prepared in certain cases to accept from owners a minimum endowment to maintain houses on a caretaker basis in between lettings, they need not expect to receive many offers. It should, he suggested, be the families' responsibility to maintain houses at a standard to suit their inclination and purse, and if they left, then the Trust need merely keep the roof watertight and the dry rot at bay until a rich tenant was forthcoming. Somehow, although the honorary treasurer and other guardians of the Trust's finances were deeply shocked, the committee endorsed Lord Esher's memorandum. And on this understanding a few important houses, like Dyrham Park, were indeed taken with very inadequate endowment. In the immediate future trouble often ensued; but in the long run relief did come from unexpected legacies and gifts of money. So the risks had clearly been worthwhile. However, I need hardly say that today Lord Esher's recommendation would be looked upon by his successor in the chair with dismay. And, as things have turned out, it is because such stupendously large endowments are demanded that few country houses now come the Trust's way.

In 1942 the committee, influenced by Lord Esher's memorandum, agreed to take over beautiful Great Chalfield Manor in Wiltshire, leaving the donor to bear most of the maintenance costs. The committee undertook not to press him for more than thirty days a year opening of the house in his lifetime. At the same time it recorded that after the war more opening days must be exacted from future donors. Indeed they have been, and quite properly so. Today, in the majority of the Trust's houses wherein the families still reside, the principal apartments or staterooms are open six out of seven days like those of other houses owned and shown by government or corporation.

Before the war was over the following country houses, in addition to those already mentioned, had been given or bequeathed to the Trust: Packwood House, Dinton House and Hyde's House, West Wycombe Park, Lindisfarne Castle, Lacock Abbey, Speke Hall, Gunby Hall and Hatchlands. They were soon followed in 1946 by Lyme Park, Cotehele, Horton Court and Osterley; in 1947 by Petworth; and in 1948 by Ham House. Negotiations for all these houses had been proceeding during the last years of the war. Roughly speaking, another twenty-five had come by 1951, the year I retired as secretary of the Historic Buildings Committee, which the old Country Houses Committee had been renamed in 1945 because all the Trust's historic architecture was by then within its province. From 1951 until 1966 I worked on a half-time basis, being called Adviser on Historic Buildings, a cautionary rather than an administrative role.

Looking back on the pioneer days of the country houses enterprise two things strike me forcibly. One was the declared policy of the Country Houses Committee – in fact it was their solemn pledge given to donors – to encourage families to go on living in their old homes, even if that meant on reduced standards. They positively exhorted Lord Jersey and Sir Lyonel Tollemache to remain at Osterley and Ham, two huge country houses already engulfed by the London suburbs, vainly as it turned out. They believed that the families not only made the best caretakers but also breathed that ineffable spirit essential to the legendary purpose of country houses. The other thing was the committee's determination not to allow country houses to become museums unless it was absolutely unavoidable. In this regard they echoed the words of that staunch radical Lord Lothian: 'Nothing is more melancholy than to visit these ancient houses after they have turned into museums . . . If they are to be preserved, they must be maintained, save perhaps for a few great palaces, for the uses for which they were designed.' Melancholy was indeed the adjective which sprang to most people's minds when considering rural museums before the war. In the eyes of the committee members – most of whom, it must be borne in mind, were themselves country house owners – such places became inert when deserted by the ancient families; at best half alive when lived in by usurping parvenus; and wholly dead when inhabited by no one but a custodian.

These anxieties and misgivings will strike the present generation as grotesque, even risible. It is true that since 1945 a new art of presentation of country houses deprived of a family of any sort has arisen and developed in a surprisingly successful manner. Today's cultivated bourgeoisie are perfectly content to visit country house museums: the more the merrier. In fact they probably prefer them unencumbered with the unsightly bric-à-brac of everyday living – dog baskets, stinking ashtrays, drink trays, children's plastic toys and the master's old gumboots in the hall. Yet I cannot but regret the absence of these homely things. And in revisiting some old haunts it is easy to see in the suites of pristine Chippendale chairs and sofas ranged stiffly against walls the artificial hand of the metropolitan museum director. I remember our great chairman (David) Lord Crawford saying, with a sigh, to my colleague Christopher Wall and me in the long gallery at Hardwick Hall in the 1950s, 'Not one person of the next generation will have a clue how country houses were really lived in before the war.'

INTRODUCTION

Anyway, of the fourteen taken very much at random in the following
pages in only two do the old families live as of yore, and in only two
others does a lonely descendant perch in one corner for the odd
weekend or a consecutive fortnight in the summer.

I am sometimes asked what was the Trust's policy in the 1930s and
'40s on conservation of its country houses. In truth the Trust was wholly
pragmatic. In setting its face against hard and fast opinions and the
academic restoration of old buildings, which it regarded as the contrasting practice of the Office of Works (they sometimes rebuilt their ruined
castles from the ground upwards), and one to be deplored, it saw itself
as assuming the mantle, in so far as an institution could do such a thing,
of the squire. Relying like that superannuated personage on its communal good sense and on the good taste, formerly exercised by the
squire's lady, but now by a band of honorary representatives scattered
across the counties, and heeding or not heeding the advice of the SPAB,
the Georgian Group and the whole gamut of national museum officials,
it soldiered ahead in its amateur way while striving to preserve the
status quo and displaying the fruits thereof as often as it thought fit to
an appreciative public. When it came to redecorating rooms it employed whatever firm of artisans it found suitable, if it chose one at all.
It is not for me to pronounce whether it held its own in this respect or
failed dismally during those formative years. At all events I can claim
the credit of introducing John Fowler to the Trust in the 1950s. This
scholarly decorator, with his sure sense of history, was to leave an
indelible imprint upon many interiors of our grandest country houses.

It is not possible to overpraise the honorary representatives in the
counties. Peter Fleetwood-Hesketh in Lancashire, Charlie Brocklehurst
in Cheshire, Sir Gyles Isham in Northamptonshire, first Alec Penrose
and then Wyndham Ketton-Cremer in Norfolk, Peter Orde in Northumberland and Myles Hildyard in Nottinghamshire amongst others
were either country house owners or county historians and often both.
All busy and highly intelligent landowners they gave their services
gratis when asked to help in the arrangement of the Trust's new
acquisitions, in the choice of fabrics for furnishing and colours of walls
and ceilings as well as a hundred other matters to do with buildings and
gardens, not the least of which was smoothing out the sometimes
strained relations between the Trust's staff and donors. I was in
constant touch with them. They had me to stay and often motored me
miles across their regions. I can never forget their help. The memory of
the days spent in their company and their friendship is very precious to
me.

All now is, quite rightly, changed to keep pace with very different conditions. I merely record in these pages what happened during my period as secretary of the Historic Buildings Committee which ended over forty years ago. Soon afterwards it became clear that the Trust's rapidly increasing properties, responsibilities and visitors demanded the immense recruitment to the staff of an army of experts on every conceivable aspect of the arts and crafts – painting, furniture, porcelain, plate, books, textiles – as well as experts on horticulture, landscape, trees and agriculture. The story of the Trust's phenomenal growth within the past four decades is too well known to its two million members and, probably, to the fifty or more millions of our population who may not be active but are surely passive supporters, to need recapitulation here.

CHAPTER ONE

LUTLEY OF BROCKHAMPTON
Herefordshire

THREE months after the conclusion of the First World War
Constance Sitwell, looking through the window of the Worcester to Bromyard train, thought she was 'almost there'. As an old
lady, exquisite and beautiful, she recorded some memories of Brockhampton in *Smile at Time*, a poetic and nostalgic autobiography,
published in 1942. She went on, 'for now the well remembered line of
the common rising up through the woods came into view in the waning
light of an autumn afternoon, and a blur of lilac smoke trailed over the
little town. What fun this is going to be.' Her husband took down from
the luggage rack his shooting-stick, guns and cartridge-bag and her
heavy fitted dressing-case. She said to herself, it was to be a real party
again; all the best bedrooms would be in use; all the silver taken out of
the safe; pots of ruby amaryllis and white gloxinias from the greenhouses brought indoors; the best bunches of grapes and biggest apples
displayed on the sideboard. As a child she had frequently stayed with
her first cousin at Brockhampton – 'a nice Tory household'. This is
what it was; a far cry from the palatial Whig households. John Talbot
Lutley, retired Colonel in the Worcestershire Regiment, was the English squire incarnate, standing for Church and Crown, plain and
staunch like his forebears who in the Civil War had been royalists and in
the '45 may even have sympathized with Bonnie Prince Charlie.

Colonel Lutley was a man of few words either in speech or on paper.
On getting to hear about the National Trust's country houses scheme
he wrote a short letter explaining that he was a bachelor whose heirs
were remote cousins. He owned an estate in the Midlands. He might
possibly bequeath it to the National Trust in his will. Would the Trust
please send a member of its staff to see the place and let him know if
they would like to have it. I was duly instructed to take a train to

19

Bromyard where, not knowing how far Brockhampton was from the station, I hired a taxicab.

My first visit was on one of those tired days of mid-August 1938. Having passed a pretty Tuscan lodge, modelled it is said on Inigo Jones's barn-like church in Covent Garden, though in miniature, the taxi crawled down a bumpy drive over which sheep and cattle were straying. A park of idyllic enchantment, sleepy with ancient trees, rolled leisurely on my right down to a heavy glade of massed oaks and beeches with distant glimpses of the Vale of Worcester and the Malvern Hills to the south-east. It was lush, English Midlands country without flaw, tranquil, undramatic, seemingly defying time. There was not an offensive object within sight. Ahead, on the spur of a ridge separating Bromyard town from Brockhampton, and dominating the scene, stood the family house. Just as it should be the Hall was high, gaunt and plain to dullness; and for all that a seat of the lesser gentry. Of dun red brick it had a central porch and an attempt at a Venetian window on the floor above. Evidently its mid-Georgian architect had never bestowed any frills on it. From the distance it looked like a creditable water-colour done by a great-aunt. When I got closer I was sorry to see that the façade had been given hideous fanciful window surrounds and plate glass by a Victorian owner. The chimneys too had been treated to a ponderous titivation. Instantly I surmised that these alterations might rule out acceptance of the Hall by the National Trust on architectural merits. In those days I was a little too purist and intolerant of period disimprovements which can often denote interesting trends in the social history of country houses. However I am sure that aesthetically I was in this case right.

I don't remember much of the visit. I did not record it. But I have a clear vision of Colonel Lutley as a tall, ungainly, pipe-smoking countryman. Like many old bachelors of his generation he was shy, remote and rather gruff, albeit irreproachably polite. In the background I see the ghost of a sister – maybe there were two – hovering in black, and immensely distinguished. I do remember a sticky dinner and sitting alone with the Colonel over the port and nuts. Afterwards in the library he put to me a few questions about the National Trust, receiving my answers without comment. He remained non-committal throughout.

Next morning we perambulated the estate. The true squire's ancestral allegiance is nearly always to the estate before the house. The Colonel was justly proud of his land, particularly the woods. The Brockhampton trees are reckoned to be the finest in Herefordshire. On them he lavished infinite care. Plans exist for a local landscape gardener, by name George Leggett, to have improved the park *à la* Capability Brown in the mid-eighteenth century. I am rather glad they were not carried out. The result is that the park looks today absolutely natural in so far as any English landscape can be so described. In fact most English fields, woods, coverts and hedgerows were contrived by successive squires during that glorious age in a casual-seeming, non-artistic fashion. Before we got down to Lower Brockhampton Manor it became abundantly clear to me that the land itself would be a worthy acquisition for the Trust, even if the big house, in spite of being its nucleus, were to prove a liability. And if the Hall was the scenic nucleus, then the old manor-house was undoubtedly the historic core of the Brockhampton estate.

The Brockhampton estate had been inherited in direct descent, though twice through the female line, for 750 years at least. The Colonel's forebears had acquired the tiresome habit of switching the surname of Lutley to Barneby and back again from Barneby to Lutley, thus causing much confusion for those consulting the family tree. About 1555 Richard Barneby from Bockleton across the border in Worcestershire, married Mary, daughter and heir of Richard Habington of Brockhampton. The Habingtons, likewise an ancient Worcestershire family, were recusants with Popish Plot associations, and descended from the Brockhamptons who were the first recorded owners. Their memorial is a ruined twelfth-century chapel just outside the moat that surrounds the manor-house. The last of the original Barnebys, John, dying in 1731, left the estate to a sister's son, Bartholomew Richard Lutley, who took the old name and arms of Barneby. He was the builder of the Georgian Hall. It was his great-grandson, John Habington Barneby, who carried out the unsightly fenestration while resuming the Lutley name in 1864.

Lower Brockhampton lies at the bottom of a steep drive, or track, to the north of the Hall. I knew of its existence and picturesque appeal amongst orchards of damson and cherry from GWR photographs above the seats of railway carriages. It had long been a sort of textbook house beloved of medievalists and antiquarians. Indeed the bulk of it was built even before the Habingtons' inheritance, that is to say in the fifteenth century. It is hard to suppose that in those times anyone would lay siege to this flimsy, ramshackle-looking house any more than he would attack a pack of cards. Yet the wide moat, carpeted with fallen leaves and weed, suggests a defensive purpose. The narrowest arm of the moat is spanned by a picture-postcard gatehouse which dates from the sixteenth century during the Habington ownership. Between closely packed upright timbers which frame white plaster panels, a wide doorway gives entrance to what was once an open courtyard. Almost crushing and overlapping it so that the rickety timbers have had to be supported by curved brackets, is an upper storey, a primitive doll's-house sort of arrangement, stuck on precariously. It has casement windows and bargeboards elaborately carved with grape-vine. Some of the carved boards have had to be renewed in a commendably conservative manner by the National Trust.

Within the moat on which swans alight when they feel inclined, shorn grass slopes to the water's edge and a narrow flower-bed beneath the front and south elevations of the house is cultivated with the least pretentious plants.

Georgian Bartholomew Richard Barneby must have found the moated manor-house incredibly uncomfortable as well as in a barbaric style of architecture. Apart from the open hall, with high and draughty roof in a 'wealth of timbers' as the estate agents say (the whole lavishly restored, if not wholly reconstructed, by his great-grandson in the 1870s), the rooms are small and poky. Only one other, the parlour, is shown today. Even Constance Sitwell, who loved the place, admitted that 'with their tiny windows and uneven floors they seemed gloomy then and gloomy they remained.' No wonder Bartholomew Richard, in employing a regional architect, T.F. Pritchard, to construct a commodious brick edifice, chose for its site not a dip but an eminence. Pritchard's design was certainly conventional as befitted a country gentleman who was brought up in the age of Gibbs and Kent yet may just have heard of the famous metropolitan architect Robert Adam. To his brand-new Hall the squire would have moved his family portraits and but little of the furniture which struck him as incredibly primitive and out of date. He would have bought or had made by local craftsmen new furniture in what he considered the latest mode and suitable for a classical residence.

I do not think that after my 1938 visit Colonel Lutley had much commerce with the National Trust. He may have communicated his decision in correspondence with the secretary, Donald MacLeod Matheson. Of that I am not sure. Anyway, having survived the Second World War and watched his beloved estate deteriorate, he died in 1946. The National Trust found that he had indeed bequeathed to it the Georgian house, the moated manor-house and the whole property of nearly 1,700 acres, comprising five farms. About the two houses he expressed the wish that Lower Brockhampton should be appropriately furnished and shown to the public. As for the big house he imposed no conditions beyond a preference that one of his Barneby cousins might be given the option to reside there. He knew this was unlikely to happen because nearly all of the cousins had houses of their own in Hereford-shire where they had been long established through intermarriage with Herefordshire and Worcestershire gentry. This does not mean that several cousins were not greatly vexed by the Colonel's will when they learned its contents. It is perhaps a pity that the Colonel did not seem to care what happened to the contents of the Georgian house since he left their disposal to the National Trust's decision absolutely. These con-tents did not, it is certain, qualify as museum pieces, but they comprised much that was of a very decent, middling country house standard.

Two days after Christmas 1946, accompanied by my father (for I was staying with my parents in Worcestershire), I motored to Brockhamp-ton to meet Matheson the secretary, Colin Jones the regional agent and Edward, known as Ruby, Holland-Martin, the eldest of Rob's sons, who was the Trust's honorary treasurer and himself by then a Worcester-shire squire, to inspect our latest acquisition. It surprises me now that my father came with me because he resolutely ignored the National Trust's very existence, turning a blind eye upon its properties and functions. In fact whenever its name was mentioned in his hearing he would slightly purse his lips and move away. I fancy he resented it as an impertinence, an intrusion upon the hereditary rights of the English squirearchy. He was however greatly enamoured of half-timbered buildings, whereas classical and particularly Georgian architecture was to him anathema.

We all lunched, I recorded,

> in the cold, cold hall, and walked round the house where Colonel Lutley's personal belongings are left lying about since the day he died. Something poignant in a house which has suddenly ceased to exist with the last owner. Life arrested in old tobacco jars with the lids off, smelly old pipes, books turned face downwards on tables, the well-worn favourite chair with deep imprint of the late 'behind' and threadbare arms, and the mournful, reproachful gaze of dozens of forgotten ancestors on the walls.

Only the strips of coloured Victorian glass in the great stair window gave a semblance of warmth. I regret that some 'improver' has lately thought fit to remove them.

The following March I stayed several nights at the Hop Pole in Bromyard. This was a dank, frowsty inn, smelling of stale cider and tobacco, where the occasional commercial traveller would put up for an odd night. Bromyard, being a very small town off the beaten track, may not even have had a makeshift cinema, or bug-hole as it would be called locally, in which to relieve the tedium of long winter evenings. I hope I do not malign it. I do remember my bedroom being so cold that I could not feel to turn over the leaves of my book. At least there was no need to pile the hearth rug on my bed, a thing I had to do sometimes in war-time inns. I spent the days at Brockhampton, probate inventory in hand, marking those contents I deemed suitable for Montacute and other houses we were furnishing at the time since the Trust committees had decided that the Hall was not of sufficient architectural merit to be opened to the public. Yet it saddened me to be a party to the dispersal of a family's tables, chairs, beds, silver, books and pictures, apart from a handful of objects to commemorate the Barnebys in the moated house. I was haunted too by the mournful faces of Bakewell, the old butler, who spoke in whispers, and Mrs Hughes, the stately housekeeper, both of whom were extremely friendly, plied me with cups of tea and cakes at all hours and enjoyed gossiping about the Colonel. He had been a disciplinarian of the old school, but God-fearing and just. Bakewell, whose wife lived in one of the lodges, had spent every day and night of the last two years in the big house ministering to the Colonel, whom he bathed, dressed and undressed because he was crippled with arthritis. The worst chore, he confided, was cleaning his toes. For these services Bakewell received £2 a week wages and a cottage to which he was seldom free to retreat. Yet he spoke of his late master with respect and affection. 'Oh yes,' he said with a wry smile, 'I used to hear the bell wires creaking along the corridors before the ultimate jangle from the board outside my pantry.'

This visit is an unforgettable memory because I was marooned by drifts of snow, followed by floods, and could not leave. How I managed to get to and fro from Bromyard I can't remember. Bakewell and Mrs Hughes begged me to sleep in the house. 'You need not pull the bells,' they laughed. But I thought it better not. When the wind subsided and the sun came out the crystal clearness invested the place with a dream-like happiness, and the total isolation fostered the friendship I had formed with Bakewell and Hughes.

With the spring I was back again. Various ancient relations and cronies of the Colonel turned up like mendicants forewarned of possible bounties. Spry Mrs Hill (irreverently nicknamed Stinkie by one of my colleagues), an 85-year-old friend and neighbour of the Lutleys, shared my hard-boiled eggs, told me what things to throw away and what to keep as though it were her business, and went off with a small chair which she coveted and the Trust could well do without. At a later date the secretary and I distributed to a gathering of Barneby cousins several unimportant objects at their probate valuation which was practically nil. Some select pieces of family silver were offered them at the reserve price fixed by the auctioneers. And who were we in their eyes to be so condescending? A bunch of subfusc officials from London graciously dispensing a few trifling trinkets which had belonged to the Colonel and, but for a quirk or two of nature, might have passed with everything else to one of them. However, we prided ourselves that such largesse was justified and would not have been sanctioned by bureaucrats from the Ministry of Works had they become the beneficiaries.

Throughout 1947 I was frequently at Brockhampton, sometimes staying with my parents in the vicinity, more often at Bromyard's Hop Pole so as to be on the spot. Experts from London – George Wingfield Digby from the Victoria and Albert Museum to pronounce on the fabrics, Margaret Jourdain on the lace, Harold Clifford Smith and Ralph Edwards (also from the V & A) on the furniture, and Arthur Grimwade of Christie's on the silver – had to be met, buttered and entertained, for their services were rendered mostly free, only the poorer advisers being paid a pittance. Of these were Clifford Smith and Margaret Jourdain. The first, well in his late sixties, had retired from being Keeper of the Furniture Department at the V & A in 1936. I fancy he had a pretty meagre pension and difficulty in keeping up appearances and making both ends meet with his gentle mouse-like wife in their nice little house in Kensington High Street. His knowledge of antiques was pretty general, if not profound. His publication of *Buckingham Palace, Its Furniture, Decoration and History*, in collaboration with Queen Mary in 1931, had brought him much acclaim. I regret now that his friends, not excluding myself, laughed so immoderately at his superlative, but harmless snobbishness ('As Her Majesty said to me only yesterday'), his sleuth-like appearance at the break-up of every country house and lynx eye for a job, and his hesitancy of speech ('I have an infallible nose for an – um – er – seat.') He was indeed an egregious bore, but a very kindly old man. Margaret Jourdain, who mocked Clifford Smith mercilessly, could not be described as kindly, at least on the surface. Her manner was astringent, and yet she too was forward in helping young friends with advice and guidance. I got to know and like her very well, seeing much of her and her companion the novelist Ivy Compton-Burnett in their austere flat in Cornwall Gardens off the Gloucester Road. She was undoubtedly very poor indeed. She had been a contributor to the *Dictionary of Furniture* on nearly every aspect of furnishing besides lace. She had written several books on multifarious subjects. A formidable figure, she was square of build and dumpy. She usually wore a rather rakish hat with a large feather, which lent her a resemblance to Henry VIII. To a tiny porcine eye she would raise a gold-framed quizzing glass on a long gold chain and, without wasting more than an oblique glance at some antique submitted to her judgement, declare, 'I would get rid of that if I were you.' This oft-repeated pronouncement was made in a dead-pan voice such as the implacable monarch might have assumed in issuing a command to his axe-man. The words invariably sent a shiver down the interrogator's spine.

Those small Brockhampton items too precious to be entrusted to the removal vans – Jacobean velvet cushions, stumpwork mirrors, carriage clocks, plate and calf-bound books – were taken by me to their ultimate destinations by car. Rapidly the big house was being emptied. I resented the behaviour of the removal men who leapt from the vans and disrespectfully invaded the rooms with loud cries and oaths and stamped their cigarette butts on the floor-boards. I experienced how Muslims feel about infidels entering a mosque with their shoes on. By the end of the year all those surplus contents not needed by the Trust were sold in Worcester in the names of Colonel Lutley's executors so as not to invite criticism. And many a pretty bargain was picked up by local residents. A few things went which were overlooked by us and should not have gone. On Christmas Day while having tea with Matley Moore, a noted antiquary lately retired from dentistry, and his sister Elsie at the Greyfriars, Worcester, I found Elsie, who was a well-known restorer of church murals, repairing a large leather screen painted with birds and rabbits and dated by her around 1695. They had bought it at the sale for £10. It now belongs to the National Trust in the Greyfriars which they in turn bequeathed years later. 'Thus do we despoil the Lutleys' ancient heritage,' I wrote at the time. To be fair to the National Trust's committees they did not consider themselves justified in preserving intact a commonplace Georgian squire's house containing a hotchpotch of moderate contents at the expense of the nation's Exchequer. It is arguable that they were in too great a hurry to find a suitable tenant. And indeed no private tenant was ever forthcoming. For some reason, inexplicable to me, every applicant decided that the house was too isolated. Yet the Trust did not foresee what came to pass in 1985, that a tenant in the shape of an insurance company, Pioneer Mutual, would rent the house and actually put it into spanking (if a little too spanking) order. But what is almost too good to be true, this tenant has removed, with the Trust's connivance, the unsightly window dressings from the main front, reinserted the sash bars to the glazing and redecorated and even furnished decently, but of course and alas, with alien contents, a few of the downstairs rooms for use on official occasions. The rest are in use for offices. Before this happened the building, which in desperation the Trust felt obliged to let for years as a company's store or warehouse, had been allowed to deteriorate alarmingly.

Lower Brockhampton Manor has been no problem. At first the Trust offered to let it to the Youth Hostels Association, then withdrew. Instead they left the greater part of it as a farmhouse, to which use it was put in the mid-eighteenth century when the Barnebys bettered themselves. But with increasing numbers of visitors this became impractical. Farmer Freegard and his large family left, although they still rent the farm buildings alongside. The rear of the house is now lived in by the Trust's warden whose job is to supervise things like gates, stiles and classifiable farm buildings, animal, bird and plant life throughout the Severn region.

The great hall has been revivified by the Trust and is regularly open to the public. It houses the old Lutley-Barneby portraits, flintlocks, pewter, leather fire-buckets and some survivors of the oak furniture which doubtless belonged there originally and, somewhat incongruously, the fine Georgian dining-table from the Georgian house which the Victorian John Habington Lutley had banished to the stables. Lower Brockhampton has always been a place of pilgrimage, chiefly for walkers, approached only down what was formerly a rutted, grass-grown, gated track, and is now a metalled drive. The ethos of Lower Brockhampton lies in its isolation which has to be safeguarded. Its charm is enhanced by the farmyard activity beside it and the prevailing smell of pigs and manure. Long may it be possible to preserve these rural amenities.

One June evening of 1947 after a storm I walked down to Lower Brockhampton at dusk. The trees were dead quiet, not even whispering, and the undergrowth was steaming. A horizontal sunbeam from the west left the gatehouse in shadow. A middle-aged couple, whom I had not seen before, were leaning against the top gate. They were not speaking. 'A lovely evening!' I said fatuously. 'Yes,' they replied. They were still there when I returned. I asked them if they came often. They explained that they lived in Bradford, Yorkshire, and visited Brockhampton twice a year. With the Colonel's consent they had scattered the ashes of their son in the park. He had been a pilot in the RAF. 'After all,' they said with conviction, 'this must be the most beautiful place in England.'

CHAPTER TWO

LOTHIAN OF BLICKLING
Norfolk

T
HE bequest of the Blickling estate marked a turning point in the National Trust's fortunes. The country houses scheme (1) inaugurated in 1936 had hardly got off the ground before war came; for two years after the outbreak it was dormant. Country house owners were in a state of shock. The world they had reaccustomed themselves to in 1918 seemed to them for a second time about to disintegrate. They were incapable of looking to the bleak future. They were merely concerned with the immediate problem: what to do with the big house. Fill it with evacuees? Hospital beds? Schoolchildren? Museum treasures? Troops?

Philip Kerr, Lord Lothian, had died *en poste* as British ambassador to the United States in December 1940. His will was complicated and took months to unravel. His possessions were vast. In fact several years passed before his executors were able to dispossess themselves of the Blickling estate.

Philip Kerr was a distinguished statesman and man of letters. He was also an idealist with a first-class practical mind. Through his mother, a Fitzalan-Howard, he was born a Roman Catholic and educated at Cardinal Newman's Oratory School, Edgbaston. Under the influence of Bernard Shaw's writings he soon abandoned his faith and adopted that of Christian Science. But he remained all his life a devout Christian believer. Associating himself with Lionel Curtis's group of Leftist political idealists he went to South Africa where he became the youngest member of Alfred Milner's famous Kindergarten in working for federal union of the four self-governing South African colonies, and in 1919 editor of the *Round Table* magazine. He was fired by the Kindergarten's shared mission to introduce social reform and justice to imperial policy. As private secretary to Lloyd George from 1916 to 1921 he played an important role in dealing with the dominions. He was also

28

largely responsible for drafting the preface to the Treaty of Versailles which dictated Germany's immediate future. This was a factor in his career which after the rise of Hitler caused him much self-doubt and no little guilt. He felt that he had been partially responsible for a grave injustice done to Germany and in consequence must carefully weigh, longer than did less compromising observers, the unacceptable policies of the Nazi party before they turned to downright evils which had to be resisted.

Working with Lionel Curtis in the 1920s towards European unity and the federal movement on the Continent, he helped him create the Institute of International Affairs at Chatham House. In Ramsay MacDonald's coalition government of 1931–2 he was consecutively Chancellor of the Duchy of Lancaster and Under-Secretary of State for India. Before the outbreak of the Second World War his appointment to Washington indicated the high respect in which he was held for impartiality, tact and persuasion. His services, although cut short at such a critical moment of history, proved to have been of incalculable value to the war effort. He had played a decisive part in persuading the United States to enter the war.

In 1930 Philip Kerr inherited from a lunatic cousin the title of 11th Marquess of Lothian with large estates in Scotland and England, including Blickling. In addition to his political commitments he was suddenly confronted in middle age with the responsibilities and problems of landowning. Being the possessor of three historic country houses in Scotland and one in England he felt deeply the burden of his architectural and artistic inheritance. He believed that its future must first be assured and then enjoyed by the public. In 1934 he delivered the stirring speech at the National Trust's annual meeting on the perils facing England's great country houses. The outcome is well known. The National Trust established a special committee to concentrate on country house conservation. Behind the scenes Lord Lothian helped the National Trust chairman Lord Zetland persuade the Treasury to grant concessions to the Trust in the forthcoming National Trust Bill (of 1937). By 1935 he made known to the Trust his intentions regarding Blickling. He frequently called at the office and discussed them with secretary MacLeod Matheson with whose political views and somewhat arcane religious opinions he seemed to accord. He happened to be a friend of Hilda Matheson, MacLeod's sister who was the first Director of Talks at the BBC and a frequent visitor to Blickling. He advocated the Trust setting up a land management department because he foresaw a considerable amount of property coming into its hands.

Lord Lothian was of rather massive build, broad and chunky, with a genial face that conflicted with a severe demeanour. His manner was slightly sanctimonious and lacked everyday light-heartedness. At meetings of the Country Houses Committee, of which he was a founder member, he was usually silent and detached.

I did not go to Blickling until May 1942 for Matheson had been dealing with Lord Lothian's solicitors over the slow transfer of the estate. My first visit was with W.A. Forsyth, an austere architect member of the Estates Committee and a well-known 'anti-scrape' (Society for the Protection of Ancient Buildings) conservationist. We motored from London. On leaving Aylsham we were greeted on our right by a sea of Nissen huts obliterating the orangery and on our left by an amorphous brick NAAFI complex in direct view from the front door of the Hall. There was likewise a settlement of what were termed semi-permanent office buildings right up to the west elevation which we were shortly to come upon. But just past the church we were subjected, at the end of a straight drive, to the breath-taking view of the south front of high, fanciful gables, tall chimney stacks and central cupola between flanking square towers. The tight, vertical and regimented façade seemed almost to be advancing aggressively, enticed forward first by detached projecting wings and then by elephantine yew hedges in the vanguard. It certainly was a vision to make a man take notice. I gasped and gazed. The more I gazed the more I was impressed by the dowagerial majesty of this ancient pile; and then bewitched by its rosy brick complexion. The aggressive thrust turned into a benign embrace; and I was seduced.

That afternoon I was guided round the outside by Christopher Birkbeck, Lord Lothian's agent, a sort of woolly bear squire of nearby Rippon Hall and man of Norfolk to his finger-tips. We looked at the imposing spread of the east front, the deceptively Jacobean north front and the undeceptive 'Jacobethan' west front, a dull rebuild from funds rather touchingly left for the purpose by a 29-year-old Countess of Buckinghamshire in 1769, before we admired the sickle-shaped lake extending into a wooded distance. All was magnificent and glorious. We met Miss Muriel O'Sullivan, Lord Lothian's ex-secretary, now the Trust's resident guardian, who showed us round the inside of the house. In the staterooms all the furniture which had not been removed for safety was under dust-sheets, and the pictures were off the walls. The Royal Air Force were in occupation of the rest of the house, seemingly packed by the hundred into bedrooms and attics. The attendant risks from fire were ever present. The lusty young pilots were even more terrified of Miss O'Sullivan, whom they called 'the dragon', than they were of night flights over Germany. She mercilessly scolded them for consistently vandalizing the house and anything else they could lay their hands on. They smashed the old crown glass of the windows and broke open doors leading to the staterooms. Before my second visit in August a gang of them were to force a way into the mausoleum in the park by making a battering ram of a tree trunk against heavy iron doors. In search of the poor Countess's jewellery, which they erroneously supposed to have been buried with her, they prized open her marble sarcophagus. The situation created was a delicate one. Miss O'Sullivan's protective instincts were roused and she was out for retribution. But Birkbeck did not in the circumstances like to appear too disapproving of 'our brave boys' who were nightly risking their young lives on England's and our sedentary behalf.

By August I was already in love with Blickling. With Birkbeck I got to know the splendid woods and admire the new plantations which were his pride and joy. In spite of the RAF station Blickling seemed to me at the furthermost extremity of East Anglia, if not of the United Kingdom.

For nearly 340 years the estate had been owned by descendants of Sir Henry Hobart, an astute lawyer who having become Lord Chief Justice of the Common Pleas bought it in 1616. There was already a house within the surviving moat (now dry) which was dug about 1400. In the sixteenth century it belonged to the Boleyn family. The luckless Anne may – or may not – have spent part of her childhood there before marrying Henry VIII in 1533. But this is speculation. Between 1619 and 1625 Sir Henry rebuilt, practically from scratch on an ambitious scale which all but ruined him, one of the stateliest houses of King James I's reign. Being in the centre of national affairs with a foot in court circles the Lord Chief Justice was able to engage the services of Lord Treasurer Salisbury's 'surveyor', one Robert Lyminge who had already built Hatfield House for the Cecils. Blickling bears close resemblances to its archetype and vies with it in the variety of elaborate plaster ceilings worked by a stuccoist of genius until recently unrecognized, Edward Stanyan.

Sir Henry had been granted a baronetcy in 1611, the year in which James I instituted the new order of chivalry. And in 1625, the same year as his sovereign, he died. For the next hundred years and more Blickling remained the palatial pile of an impoverished family of baronets, rather looked down upon by the patrician owners of Norfolk's other great houses, Raynham, Holkham, Houghton and Oxnead, who had achieved political renown and prestige. The Hobart family's most glittering achievement was the 3rd Baronet's entertainment of Charles II and his Queen in 1671; and its greatest notoriety the death of the 4th Baronet in a duel which he had provoked and which reflected little glory on him.

In 1728 the 5th Baronet Sir John was created Baron Hobart and in 1746 Earl of Buckinghamshire, not for particular merits but through the influence of his sister Henrietta Howard, later Countess of Suffolk, with King George II whose mistress she reputedly was. This intellectual lady was the intimate friend of Lord Burlington, Horace Walpole and the poets and writers Pope, Gay and Swift, whom she entertained at the house she built for herself at Marble Hill, Twickenham, on the north bank of the Thames. The 1st Earl however left little mark on Blickling, not through lack of will but lack of funds, beyond converting the Jacobean long gallery into a vast library containing an enormous and important collection of books which he inherited from a cousin, Sir Richard Ellys of Nocton, Lincolnshire. Unfortunately Lord Lothian was obliged to sell some of the rarest in 1932 to meet death duties.

The 2nd Earl of Buckinghamshire was the next Hobart of note after the Lord Chief Justice and the second representative to leave a mark on the house. A picturesque and flamboyant figure, he was appointed ambassador to St Petersburg in 1762–5 and Lord Lieutenant of Ireland in 1777–80. In Russia he impressed Catherine the Great with his handsome appearance and *tenue*, receiving from her the vast tapestry panel of Peter the Great defeating the Swedes at the Battle of Poltawa, which he hung in the great chamber created for it. He introduced a Norwich family of architects and decorators, the Ivorys, to rebuild the west front and part of the north front, and to refashion Lyminge's theatrical staircase. Apart from the Peter the Great room and the adjoining state bedroom his alterations were not in the classical style. As he wrote to his aunt Suffolk about his intended alterations to Blickling, 'Gothick it was and more Gothick it will be in spite of all the remonstrances of modern improvers and lovers of Grecian architecture.' Of abounding charm the 2nd Earl was not a man of enduring substance. Horace Walpole called him 'the Clearcake: fat, fair, sweet, and seen through in a moment.'

On his death in 1793 without male issue his title went to a brother and the Blickling property to the second of four daughters, Caroline Lady Suffield. Thereafter for long periods at a time Blickling was the residence of widows. Lady Suffield lived there from 1793 to 1850. Dying childless she left Blickling to her elder sister Harriet's grandson who through Harriet's marriage to the 6th Marquess of Lothian became the 8th Marquess. But he reigned a mere twenty years, dying in 1870. He left the place to his widow Constance Lady Lothian who survived him by thirty-one years. She had strong artistic tastes which were imposed upon both the house and garden. But when she died in 1901 the family ceased to live at Blickling, the 9th Marquess being already dead and the 10th in custody. It was when the 10th departed in 1930 that his first cousin Philip Kerr succeeded.

The 11th Marquess as he became had less than a decade to enjoy Blickling. He was devoted to it but not a consistent resident, usually snatching hasty weekends from his political commitments to entertain friends who shared his Radical views like Leo Amery, Arnold Toynbee, Lord Halifax, W.L. Hichens, Lionel Curtis, the Astors and other members of the so-called Cliveden set. Often a party amounting to thirty guests might stay in the house at the same time. Nor were they by any means all politicians. Ralph Vaughan Williams gave an address to the Norfolk Rural Music School in the long gallery. The scientist Julian Huxley, the golf champion Joan Wethered, the garden designer Norah Lindsay, who reconstituted the great east parterre, were frequent visitors. For nearly two autumn months of 1936 when the Abdication crisis was looming Lord Lothian lent Blickling as a retreat to the Prime Minister Stanley Baldwin and his wife Lucy.

Being a bachelor he allowed a sister, Lady Minna Butler-Thwing, to supervise for him redecoration of several rooms. This she usually did in the safe beige or pea-green taste of the 1930s. An exception was the south drawing-room where Lady Minna ventured upon flesh-pink walls and stripped the Jacobean chimneypiece down to the bare woodwork. It was in this favourite room that so many political consultations took place among the intimate coterie. Brother and sister considered the house he had inherited horribly gloomy and stuffy. Together they swept away much Victorian decoration and furniture, some of it more interesting than what replaced it. Lord Lothian would never do anything to thwart the national war effort so when in 1939 Blickling was selected by the Air Ministry as suitable eastern headquarters for the RAF he complied without demur.

Throughout 1942 and the ensuing years of RAF occupation and then those of the post-war tidying-up operations, followed by the reassembly from divers hiding-places and rearrangement of the house's contents, and a token redecoration with minimum funds available in the face of maximum spending restrictions imposed by the government, I paid many visits. I stayed with the kind Birkbecks or Miss O'Sullivan, whose flat was in the detached west wing, or at the Buckinghamshire Arms inn close to the drive entrance. I would usually travel by train, walking with my bag from Aylsham station, or occasionally bicycling, luggage on handlebars, to Rippon Hall.

Miss O'Sullivan's was a most interesting character. Lord Lothian had the highest opinion of her intellect – she had been a graduate of Trinity College, Dublin – and efficiency. After his death Lionel Curtis wrote to G.M. Trevelyan, then Master of Trinity College, Cambridge, and chairman of the Trust's Estates Committee, that she was worth her weight in gold and the Trust would be very unwise to dispense with her services. She adored Lord Lothian's memory and echoed his political sentiments with an added touch of *New Statesman* fanaticism in pursuit of lost causes. She was very much more than an embittered spinster although she would pick a bone or two with life. She was poor and very delicate. She regarded Blickling as a sacred trust. To her it was sanctified territory. She cherished its every content, tradition and even superstition. This seemingly matter-of-fact woman positively believed in the ghost of a black dog which she claimed to have seen scampering down the long gallery to disappear through the floor-boards of the upper ante-room, formerly part of the main staircase, before reaching an exit in the south-east turret. The dragon of the RAF was respected by one and all. Unlike Birkbeck, who, as I have already intimated, did not care to expostulate with our brave boys, she was not afraid to raise Cain with the Wing Commander. Unannounced she would boldly stalk into his office waving her arms in indignation and abusing his subordinates as barbarians. Whom, she would shout, did they presume they were fighting? She identified her Radical brand of politics with an uncompromising Evangelicalism. A regular communicant and church warden she included the church on the edge of the garden within her jealous guardianship. She maintained that 'the English' did not deserve to win the war for it was idle to presume they were fighting for a Christian cause. A pacifist, she reprimanded me for lack of principle and courage in having joined the Army in 1940. If I had had any guts I would have refused and become a stretcher-bearer. In between abusing the RAF Miss O'Sullivan dedicated herself to cataloguing the 12,000 volumes in the library. Because she was an amateur all her hard work was done for nothing. The next generation of National Trust officials scrapped it, engaging a professional to do it all over again. She was extremely forbearing and kind to me, and I grew to be very fond of her.

Miss James the housekeeper also became a friend because I decided to keep her on for the 'duration'. She enjoyed recounting her experiences in previous grand houses – Clandeboye and Blenheim especially – in the last of which she had put on two stone in weight. Far from refraining I fear I egged her on. In fact the best way of calming her when driven to distraction by the delinquencies of the RAF (they even stole her little dog) was to encourage her to let off steam and gossip about the Duke of Marlborough's unnatural feud against dogs which lifted their legs on curtains, and the Duchess's addiction to stimulants. She confirmed what I had read in books about servants' hall precedence up to 1939, that visiting valet and maid adopted the name, without the title, of their employer, becoming say, Mr and Miss Buccleuch or Westminster; and that the valet of the eldest son of the house always sat on the housekeeper's right at meals, no matter whether the valet of the Archbishop of Canterbury or the Prince of Wales were present. Miss James (like Miss O'Sullivan) also thought me grossly disloyal for having tea in the officers' mess, whereby incidentally I managed to retrieve from their quarters furniture that ought never to have been left with them in the first place.

My duties frequently involved meeting officials from government ministries as well as museum experts from London come to inspect or check this and that object of art on their mysterious lists. With two surveyors from the Ministry of Works Birkbeck and I spent an April day – it was not, I fancy, the 1st – crawling on hands and knees under the roof of the west wing looking for, I am glad to say, non-existent death-watch beetle in the rafters the ticking of which the RAF complained had been keeping 'our boys' awake at night. Another evening we spent stamping out a fire in Hercules Wood which had either been started mischievously by whom I would not like to guess, or inefficiently by the Home Guard in constructing, unknown to Birkbeck, a bomb dump under dry bracken. In May of that year Forsyth and I motored Professor Trevelyan from Cambridge to Blickling. He wanted to choose for himself an appropriate colour to paint the cottages on the estate. It was not by rights within his province but he was so distinguished that no one cared to dispute his decision. Yet the truth was that this great historian had no taste whatever and little conception as to whether crimson or Shanghai yellow would be appropriate. On all other counts he was highly respected and indeed venerated by all of us. I noted at the time that he was 'dry as a stick and totally lacking gaiety and humour. He is very uncouth in his dress and person, and has long untrimmed hair down the back of his neck. I was sitting behind him and as we approached Blickling he took out his false teeth and cleaned them with his handkerchief' – a habit I observed on another occasion when arriving at a destination. Clearly a nervous tick. Mr Forsyth was in great awe and rather obsequious. We made a melancholy trio. When we set foot inside the house Miss James threw her arms round and practically embraced me as though I were the prodigal son returned after a decade amid the husks and swine. And when we left for Cambridge, Willey the head gardener handed me a plant to take to London. I was delighted but embarrassed when Professor Trevelyan remarked rather sourly, 'You seem very popular here.'

If there were hazards at Blickling to be reckoned with, those contents which on the outbreak of war had been removed from the house to London were in no less danger. Three important paintings stored at Partridge's shop in King Street – the Holbein copy of Henry VIII, Zucchero's panel of Queen Elizabeth and Samuel Scott's *The Thames* – were badly damaged in an air raid when water flooded a basement safe. In contrast other treasures removed to the country fared very well. By arrangement with Colonel and Mrs Price Wood a consignment had been sent to Henley Hall near Ludlow in Shropshire. The elderly couple lived surrounded by fine but conventional English furniture, mostly Queen Anne walnut and Georgian satinwood, which they had collected under the auspices of Percy MacQuoid, the Edwardian expert. I visited them from time to time to make sure that above all the Mortlake Abraham tapestries were in good order. I had no need to. The Woods had somehow contrived to retain throughout the war eight servants on the understanding (I will not say with any commitment) that they were leaving their collections to the nation. And indeed Henley Hall was one of the houses I had nursed before the war ever since a first visit when Mrs Price Wood almost turned me from the door because I was not the venerable greybeard she supposed every official from London ought to be. Needless to say, her head housemaid kept the tapestries scrupulously sealed against the depredations of moth and corruption, rolled up in wax paper and sprinkled with naphthalene flakes. Nevertheless Mrs Wood insisted that I unroll them in her presence on trestle tables out of doors, brush them with hard bristles, spread them loosely on the shaven lawn, and even drag them face downwards through the early morning dew. Her motives were to make sure we had no cause to take the Blickling things away. She even begged for more National Trust treasures to keep the evacuees at bay, threatening if we did not do so to spread the Blickling treasures more thinly into more rooms. I was rather alarmed by Mrs Wood who after the first encounter and her disappointment treated me indulgently like an undisciplined child who needed ordering about. What happened to the Woods' collection when they eventually died I have no idea.

My friend Marshall Sisson succeeded Forsyth as architect to Blickling. I was very fond of this dour, sardonic, whimsical man and his invalid wife Marjorie, a most intelligent, cultivated and charming woman, with whom I often stayed, once at Sherman's Dedham during a country air raid, and later at Farm Hall, Godmanchester. Incidentally the Sissons gave covenants over both these Georgian houses. Sisson would motor me over to Blickling and it was a joy to elicit his cautious but always sound advice over the partial redecoration of, amongst other apartments, the Peter the Great room which we commissioned from Müntzer's, a firm in Albemarle Street bought at the very end of the war by Lord Jersey. The work consisted chiefly of repairing and tinting the ceiling, repairing and cleaning the immense tapestry panel which depicts the Tsar on horseback, and patching the tattered pink wall hangings in so far as that was possible, in a very rough and ready fashion. It involved stripping whole areas of the rotted silk and replacing it with some temporary plain stuff which more or less matched the old in colour, though not in texture. At the same time festoon curtains and chairs and sofas were also repaired by us in the matching fabric.

Our makeshift hangings and upholstery did not last long. By 1952 the Trust was somehow able to afford to have the four walls completely rehung with silk woven in the same old pattern. In 1987 this again had to be replaced. The Blickling Peter the Great room hangings and upholstery have to the Trust's knowledge been renewed four if not five times since the 1780s when the Ivorys designed the room. In other words walls and furnishings which retain their original silk stuffs even from late Georgian times are more rare than most people imagine. If one hundred years are an unusually long duration, thirty-five years are admittedly an unusually short one. But at the end of the last protracted war the quality of fabrics procurable was abysmally poor.

By 1945 I was so involved with Blickling that I decided to spend my annual fortnight's holiday there in order to begin my first book. This I did from the middle of June to the beginning of July, ensconced at a table on a raised platform within the window embrasure of the south end of the long gallery, surrounded by Miss O'Sullivan's 12,000 calf-bound volumes and overlooking the beautiful but unkempt, unmown, unweeded garden. I never remember being happier although the ultimate fruit of this idyllic visit was the worst book I have yet written.

Snatching an occasional bath from RAF hot water (a further act of disloyalty in Miss James's eyes) in the bathroom attached to the Chinese bedroom, I slept in Miss O'Sullivan's flat and ate all my meals at the Buckinghamshire Arms where the landlady, motherly Mrs O'Donoghue, was another friend and an excellent plain cook. One evening after work was spent with Wyndham Ketton-Cremer who motored over from Felbrigg. He pointed out to me that the Blickling library included the finest collection in England of seventeenth-century political pamphlets, notably Civil War tracts. Another evening he took me to call on old Mrs Bulwer at Heydon where she showed us her hundred teapots, a Queen Anne doll's house and a pair of velvet shoes worn by Charles I; and another to Wolterton Hall, at the far end of the lake, where we were given tea by Lady Walpole whose husband was still away in the Army. She had officers billeted on her throughout the war.

I went on my hired bicycle for excursions in the long evenings. Thus I saw Little Barningham church, Cawston church (with angel faces and outspread wings like huge bats suspended from the hammerbeam vault) and Salle church, more magnificent still, planned on symmetrical lines almost classical, although a Perpendicular structure, its clear windows so vast the mind boggles over the mystery of how the perforated walls can sustain the roof. The contemporary pews and furnishings of this superb church perfect one of the greatest Gothic monuments in all England.

And I would walk: to the 2nd Earl's brick tower in the park, then wire-fenced and growing corn and cabbages, and beyond and round by the lake. I would accompany Birkbeck to his new plantations of young oaks, and talk with Salmon the carpenter and Attew the woodman, and Sidney, the simple and saintly odd-man who had been engaged as hall-boy by Constance Lady Lothian in the last century and never moved away from the parish. And one weekend wandering in the park with John Wilton, who came down for a night, we were driven to shelter in Bonomi's pyramidal mausoleum during the most terrifying storm I have ever been in. Lightning lashed the iron doors and thunder roared and reverberated round the echoing dome while we crouched in an empty niche. I felt like Leporello in the churchyard scene from *Don Giovanni* when the petrified servant is told to invite the statue to supper and the voice of the Commendatore booms above the undisturbed graves. So too the Buckinghamshire coffins remained motionless on their marble shelves.

Polling day for the first general election after the war came and went without my making up my mind how to vote. 'My dislike of Socialism is almost equalled by my dislike of what Mr Churchill stands for,' namely Russian occupation of Eastern Europe, I wrote at the time.

One day the Gainsborough Company filmed a scene, with Margaret Lockwood starring, in the library. This was an interruption but an interesting one. The producer, whose name I forget, was a sensible and historically minded man. When I harshly criticized the lumpish 1870 bookcases and the constipated frieze above, which John Hungerford Pollen had designed and painted for the 8th Marquess of Lothian, he strongly remonstrated. 'You must not remove them,' he said, 'for they have a period interest and show how the house has grown over the centuries.' He was eminently right I now see, though I still find them ugly and inappropriate to their setting. The late Lord Lothian evidently thought the same and made the mistake of taking away Pollen's Florentine fireplace and replacing it with nothing. The blank space left means neither one thing nor another. The Country Houses Committee seriously considered scrapping the bookcases, but was prevented by wise Lord Esher who liked them no more than I did.

On 5 July 1945 Birkbeck, with the staff painter, met me at Aylsham Old Hall, a perfectly preserved red-brick house on the estate. Nearly all the airy rooms are panelled with William and Mary wainscot. It had just been de-requisitioned by the Army and required much attention. Of the £450 compensation given by the Army for dilapidation the Trust was permitted by the government to spend on repairs £100 a year so long as the work was begun in less than four weeks' time. And after the specified date of 1 August the expenditure of £10 a year only was to be permitted. How these absurdly arbitrary figures and dates were calculated is unclear. They merely indicate the difficulties that thwarted owners of historic buildings in those lean days of privation and prohibition.

During my last weekend an American friend, still in army uniform, came for a night. He slept at the inn where we were joined for dinner by the Sissons who happened to be staying. After dinner he and I strolled round the lake, 'pausing at the remote end to take in the view of the house. Across the placid water it looked like a palace in a dream, insubstantial,' such as Inigo Jones might have devised for a masque at the court of Whitehall, 'and as the darkness crept between us, it melted like a palace in a dream.' Returned to the inn we smoked and talked until midnight struck. The front door being barred and bolted, no key anywhere visible and all ground-floor windows barricaded, I was obliged to go upstairs and from an empty bedroom let myself out of the window into a bed of nasturtiums. Luckily Miss O'Sullivan, with whom I was staying, never bothered to lock her front door, and so I got back to bed.

The Trust was in no position to open the staterooms to the curious public until 1 May 1947. First of all every attempt had to be made to fulfil the wishes expressed in Lord Lothian's will regarding use of the house. For he had desired that the house should be let 'as a family residence to persons who will love appreciate and respect Blickling Hall and will use it not only as a private residence but as a place from which', as he quaintly phrased it, 'public or intellectual or artistic activities go forth and in which persons or conferences of persons interested in such things are entertained and who have the means necessary to enable them to live at Blickling and use it for such purposes.' He named those whom he had in mind in order of precedence: namely his successor in the title, Lord Lothian, and the three sons of his great friends Lord and Lady Astor. All were approached by the Trust and all turned down the suggestion.

Secondly, after two years of peace, wartime restrictions had not yet been lifted to make our task of reconditioning satisfactory or complete. However the garden, which had never been allowed by the resourceful Willey to go hopelessly to seed, was soon tidied up. Within a year of peace there were seven working gardeners under him. The problems of the house were less easily resolved. Miss O'Sullivan, looking tired and ill, was nevertheless reluctant to surrender her sacred charge and unwilling to continue under a new regime. Miss James had by now bettered herself. Finally Miss O'Sullivan consented to my installing a couple of caretakers and a housemaid under her authority. With only two months to go there were many preparations to be completed. Furniture stood in stacks under dust-sheets. In April I stayed several days at Bradenham Hall with Alec and Frances Penrose, he having agreed to be the Trust's honorary representative for East Anglia. He was extremely resourceful and encouraging. On 30 April the two of us stayed late at night shifting furniture with the help of the willing Sidney, to motor back to Bradenham just before dawn. Poor Miss O'Sullivan was very opposed to anything being put where Lord Lothian had not had it, and unable to understand that rooms the public went round could not remain exactly as if they didn't. We had a moment of horrible anxiety when the posts and ropes we had ordered turned out to be of the wrong measurements.

May Day was opening day. It poured with rain and was icily cold. Expecting an invasion of thousands we were surprised and disappointed that a mere twenty bedraggled visitors turned up. And the charge for admission was only one shilling.

In November I spent several days at Blickling with Carew Wallace who had recently joined the National Trust staff. We arranged furniture and pictures, as we supposed, for the better. We also gave luncheon at the Buckinghamshire Arms to Somerset and Thelma de Chair who to the general amazement proposed to rent the whole house, and not just part of it. Until 1945 Somerset had been MP for South-West Norfolk and private secretary to Oliver Lyttelton, the Minister of Production. Author of numerous books he was a person with cosmopolitan interests and a lover of country houses. The Trust, in a quandary as to how to use Blickling 'as a private residence and a place from which public intellectual or artistic activities go forth' in accordance with Lord Lothian's rather vaguely expressed wishes, without risking the expenditure of much money, welcomed prospective tenants with such admirable qualifications as the de Chairs, prepared to pay a fairly large rent. Unfortunately their marriage came to an end in 1950 and Mrs de Chair left Blickling. She returned for a time alone and then as the wife of Sir Jocelyn Lucas MP. Yet during his short tenancy Somerset was an enthusiastic resident. He discovered in the house the original building accounts with references to Robert Lyminge and Edward Stanyan the plasterer. How many conferences he actually held at Blickling I am unable to testify.

With drastic post-war reorganization and the very necessary increase of staff, the management of National Trust properties fell to regional agents, representatives and committees. My association with Blickling therefore slackened. One of my last duties was to assist Ben Nicolson, editor of the *Burlington Magazine* and Deputy-Keeper of the King's Pictures, to rehang portraits in the south drawing-room; and another to hand over to the present Lord Lothian, then a young man of 25 who had inherited the bulk of the Scottish properties from his cousin, what personal belongings in the house he might choose to take away. With extraordinary constraint he selected a few engraved wine glasses and one bag of golf clubs.

After Thelma Lucas's lease terminated in the 1960s the east ground floor of the house below the long gallery was let to a succession of tenants, harmless, but not, it is true, qualified or able to observe the donor's intentions. Now there is no tenant and yet the house does, so the National Trust firmly hopes and believes, fulfil more rather than less of the donor's intentions, although Blickling is no longer a private residence. Further rooms have recently been shown to the public, including a newly opened document room for display of papers, drawings and relics pertaining to Blickling, in the north-west corner of the ground floor. Also a series of conference rooms have been equipped for entertainment of large numbers. They are in constant and regular demand. As for the two detached south pavilions, the eastern is used for the visitors' restaurant and the Conservation Workshop, where historic tapestries and needlework from all over the country are repaired by expert hands; and the western, where Miss O'Sullivan and the gardener Willey lived, is occupied by the National Trust's East Anglia regional office. Today Blickling is very much alive and very flourishing. And the number of its visitors is prodigious.

CHAPTER THREE

VERNON OF HANBURY
Worcestershire

JOHN Betjeman called Worcestershire the dimmest of all the English counties.. Dimness used to be its most endearing quality. Apart from the Malverns on the western and the Cotswolds on the eastern periphery (each properly belonging to Herefordshire and Gloucestershire respectively) it had little to offer the tripper. With few outstanding features it could be dismissed as a sort of undulating pancake burnt at the northern edge by the threatening Black Country. On the other hand until the iconoclastic twentieth century got into its stride Worcestershire was remarkable for hop-, cherry-, apple- and plum-laden orchards, and soporific meadows heavy with oak and elm. The elms have of course all gone, the oaks are stag-headed and the fruit orchards have been uprooted for bungalows. Worcestershire has become an unsightly overspill for small commuters from Birmingham and the Five Towns. Very little of the old Worcestershire I remember and love is left. But the immediate environment of Hanbury, though under threat, still survives, a dream island of the past, on the brink of absorption into subtopia.

Worcestershire was never rich in great country houses. To that category belong Croome Court (the Coventrys), Westwood Park (the Pakingtons), Hagley Hall (the Lytteltons) and Madresfield Court (the Lygons). Ombersley Court (the Sandys) and Hanbury Hall are runners-up. The last two are not perhaps great in size, but certainly large squires' large houses. No further evidence of a county family's antiquity is needed beyond the number of monuments to its members in the local parish church. In the Vernon Chapel of Hanbury church is contained a veritable pantheon of English statuary in effigies by Edward Stanton, Christopher Horsnaile, Roubiliac, Chantrey and other sculptors.

The Vernons, of whom there are several branches, can certainly boast descent from a Norman baron who accompanied William the

Conqueror to Hastings. The first Vernon to be associated with Hanbury was the Revd Richard whom Queen Elizabeth presented to the rectory in 1580. He remained in office for forty-seven years. But he was not the squire. His son Edward bought the manor and advowson of Hanbury in 1631 from the Leighton family. Edward's grandson Thomas was the builder of the present house. After several vicissitudes his marble bust still presides in a niche of honour over the hall fireplace to frown upon his successors in fee-simple. As a leading Counsellor in Chancery he amassed a great reputation at the bar and a great fortune.

Hanbury Hall is the ideal of a William and Mary country house, or, to be correct, William alone – for Mary was dead when it was finished in 1701. Of glowing red brick and absolute symmetry it sits primly on the ground wearing a jaunty central cupola and dormer windows under surprised eyebrows. What distinguishes it from other contemporary textbook houses of the period is the remarkable Baroque staircase and hall, covered on ceiling and wall with mythological frescoes by the famous Sir James Thornhill who painted the dome of St Paul's and the great hall of Greenwich Palace. Although signed for all to see these paintings were attributed by the Revd Treadway Nash's classic *Worcestershire* of 1781 and subsequent history books on the county until very recently, to Sir Godfrey Kneller.

On Counsellor Vernon's death without issue he was succeeded by a number of alternatively spendthrift and impecunious owners. The Counsellor's cousin and heir, Bowater Vernon, belonged to the former category. As his epitaph quaintly puts it, 'he regulated his expenses with a wise economy if you except his charities in which, if it were possible, he was liberal even to profusion.' And not only his charities: his style of living. Bowater's son and successor, another Thomas, belonged to the latter category. He was of 'unblemished honour and integrity . . . tender and affectionate', and very parsimonious. And so the pendulum swung throughout the generations. To these extremes the beautiful house may largely owe its architectural survival throughout the centuries with so few alterations in spite of two catastrophic dispersals of the contents. Both were brought about by unconventional love affairs which caused much local scandal in the county and ostracism of the chief participants.

The first happened like this. In 1771 Emma Vernon inherited the property as a young girl from her virtuous but parsimonious father Thomas. Her mother was ambitious and foolish. She immediately embarked upon a hectic search for suitors for her teenage daughter. Soon the advances of young Henry Cecil, nephew and heir to the 9th Earl of Exeter, were eagerly accepted. The marriage proved a disaster.

The pair rapidly dissipated Emma's fortune. They spent little on the house beyond redecoration of the drawing-room and small library in a feeble adaptation of the Adam style then in vogue; and they demolished the old stable block which stood to the north of the entrance front. Then, in the words of Emma's guardian, the Revd Treadway Nash, 'they ran themselves aground and were obliged to break up house-keeping, but what was worse, they both entreagued'. In other words they took lovers. Reduced by Henry's unkindness 'to Norris's drops and Madeira', Emma eloped with the Hanbury curate, Will Sneyd, first to Birmingham and then to Lisbon. Cecil, under the assumed name of John Jones and masquerading as a Shropshire yokel, soon courted and married, at first bigamously and later, after a costly divorce, legitimately in church Sarah Hoggins, a small farmer's daughter who ultimately, when Henry succeeded as 10th Earl of Exeter, became Tennyson's famous *Cottage Countess*, bride of the Lord of Burghley. In disentangling himself from Emma by Act of Parliament Henry became Hanbury's owner for his lifetime. Until his death in 1804 Emma had no legal rights to her inheritance. In the meantime Hanbury fell into serious disrepair and Cecil sold all the contents of the house and even the Counsellor's magnificent iron gates from the forecourt.

On Henry's demise (he had been elevated for some reason unknown to Marquess of Exeter in 1801) Emma returned to Hanbury, not with Sneyd whom she married and who died of consumption in Portugal, but with a third husband, John Phillips. She found the house an empty shell. In considerable financial straits the Phillipses lived there till Emma's death in 1818. She was buried 'by her particular desire' in Hanbury churchyard, 'near the coppice'. Why? Was this spot the scene of her original trysts with the curate? And she was shrouded by her maid in the sheet which had covered the corpse of her beloved Will Sneyd. A handful of earth which she had gathered from his grave in Lisbon twenty-five years before was cast upon her coffin.

During the remainder of the nineteenth and well into the twentieth century Hanbury was in the possession of sound and God-fearing squires who lived there comfortably but unostentatiously. Again little was spent on the house and few alterations were made. In fact the building was allowed gently to stagnate if not crumble. Sir Harry Foley Vernon (he was made a baronet in 1885) reigned for over sixty years at Hanbury.

A pillar of conservative rectitude Sir Harry did everything that was right in the county, the eastern half of which he represented in Parliament. He married Lady Georgina Baillie-Hamilton, a daughter of the 10th Earl of Haddington. He was Master of the Worcestershire Fox-Hounds, and Honorary Colonel of the Worcestershire Hussars. He listed his recreations in *Who's Who* as hunting, shooting, cycling, skating. He did not make any improvements to the house. Rather the reverse. He constructed a forecourt to the entrance front of clumsy Moorish-style pavilions and retaining walls of the wrong sort of brick. He festooned the outside walls of the house with magnolias and creepers, and the staircase and hall with tiger skins, the horns of buffalo and bison, and the antlers of deer. Beyond these ephemeral adornments he did not venture. Sir Harry and Lady Georgina were revered and loved by all.

Sir Harry and Lady Georgina had two sons and one daughter Auda who married a neighbour and lived in Hanbury village. The younger son was killed in the Boer War in 1902. The elder George was unfortunately not a chip off the old block. He became a Captain in the Worcestershire Yeomanry, having served in the South African war as a trooper with Rimington's Guides. And that is as far as he distinguished himself. In 1905 he married Doris, the daughter of James Allan of the Allan shipping line, and rented from the Vernon estate a charming but lugubrious Regency Gothick dower-house on the far side of Ombersley village, called Shrawley Wood. Sir Harry and Lady Georgina were always fond of and good to Doris who warmly reciprocated their affection. It is doubtful how fond of and good to Doris George ever was.

In 1920 Sir Harry died at the age of 86. Foreseeing likely trouble ahead he had arranged that Hanbury Hall and garden were settled upon Doris for her lifetime in the event of her surviving her husband. No doubt he thought that thereby his daughter-in-law's interests would be fully protected. In fact they were protected only partially.

Sir George and Lady Vernon led an uneasy sort of life at Hanbury until Doris could bear it no longer. I do not know exactly which year they broke up but Lady Vernon told me – she was very outspoken about her marital troubles – how one day she went to her husband's room to find the parlourmaid sitting on his knee. She heard him saying to her, 'Repeat after me, "Hang your hat high up in the hall, Harry", and after a pause, "No, no, dear, that's not quite right yet. Try once more."' Lady Vernon immediately packed her bags and was driven to her mother's at Shrawley Wood where she lived until Sir George's death.

The first time I went to Hanbury was in August 1938 after Sir George had called on me one day in the London office. He explained that he was childless and the last of his line. He thought that the National Trust might as well on his death take over the house and garden which were not then his to dispose of, whereas the park and the rest of the estate were his to do what he liked with. I feel sure that he was fond of Hanbury in a way, and vaguely liked the idea of it being preserved in the future so long as he did not have to provide an additional acre of land for its upkeep. I am not absolutely sure how much he thought that thereby he might be disobliging his wife.

When I got to Hanbury the park looked like a battlefield, overgrown with nettles, the elm trees diseased and those that had blown down lying rotting on the ground. After exercising some persuasion at the lodge I was allowed up the front drive which was fairly choked with weeds. Presumably there was a back entrance somewhere for the tradesmen. It was as though no one had passed by the front drive for several lustres. And this I think was more or less the case. For the neighbours would not go near the baronet. The county systematically cut him. Afterwards one or two people expressed incredulity that I had actually seen him in the flesh and been given tea. They asked what he was like, expecting me to say he walked on all fours and had a forked tail. Rob Holland-Martin of Overbury Court, a member of the Country Houses Committee, described him to me charitably as 'mad as a hatter'. But I recall him as a sane, fairly handsome, tall, lean man with a saturnine face and as down-at-heel in his clothes as the place looked. His adopted daughter Ruth, a plain, simple and shy young woman, was living with him. She was to be, he told me, his heir to everything he was able to leave her.

I paid another visit exactly a year later to explain to Sir George how the Trust, proud though it would be to hold this lovely house, could not see its way to doing so unless some endowment in either land or cash were forthcoming. After a certain amount of correspondence I persuaded him to include the offer of two farms. He then insisted that the secretary of the National Trust should be nominated a trustee of his father's testament because he feared that, were his wife to survive him, she would sell her life interest in the house. At that time I had not met Lady Vernon, who as it turned out never entertained the idea for a single instant.

In 1940 Sir George died and was buried among his ancestors in Hanbury church. His tablet bears the words, 'Then shall I know, even as I am known' – which I fear he has never been either kindly or respectfully. Indeed Sir George left the whole Hanbury estate (other than the house and garden) including Shrawley Wood, and all the contents of Hanbury Hall down to the family archives, to his adopted daughter. She subsequently married and prefixed the name of Vernon to that of her husband, Horton. As the years went by, Mrs Vernon Horton behaved handsomely to the Trust whose staff always kept on good terms with her. She and her husband, Frederick, returned the bust of Counsellor Vernon to its niche in the hall and gave back, or bequeathed most of the family portraits and much of the furniture from Hanbury which she had inherited. Furthermore the park reverted on her death to the rest of the Trust's Hanbury property.

The situation of Sir George's widow was not so enviable. She and her old mother were obliged to leave Shrawley Wood for the benefit of whom she termed 'the female'. She was left a large, completely empty house in terrible disrepair and a large garden, without even the park which was in view from every window. Like the rest of the estate it was managed by 'the female's' brother who had formerly been the Vernons' chauffeur. To add to a bitter pill nearly every tree in the park was soon marked for felling. But the National Trust managed to get this disaster averted on the grounds that it had a future interest which would otherwise be adversely affected. There was scarcely a soul, where once there had been dozens of servants, to help Lady Vernon in a remote place redolent of unhappy memories; and the war was raging. But she had loved her parents-in-law, was touchingly proud of the Vernon name and determined to live in the Hall by hook or by crook; and moreover determined that the National Trust should ultimately come into possession of it. She admitted that when she drove through a wasteland to the derelict, empty house with her aged mother her heart nearly failed her.

When the war was over I saw a good deal of Lady Vernon. She was extremely gallant and tough beneath an apathetic and rather hopeless manner. She always looked bewildered and vulnerable and was no doubt a prey to predators and a victim of other people's guile. Never a word in overt criticism of her husband passed her lips but she maintained a hatred for 'the female', so gentle and harmless a woman, whom she held responsible for all her wrongs and misfortunes. 'Do you not think, Lady Vernon,' I might venture when I had got to know her well, 'that the orangery roof needs a little attention?' or, 'Would it not be a good idea if someone came from Droitwich to make the front door lock work?' to receive the inevitable sigh and response, 'I fear the female has the wherewithal', or 'I haven't a penny to bless myself with, what with the female taking all the money.' Blame was never imputed to the errant Sir George, but to the innocuous object of his last infatuation. Lady Vernon had of course been wretchedly treated by – well, fate – but I fancy she was one of those people who invited, if they did not positively relish, disaster. She could not open a bazaar without twisting her ankle on the way to the platform. She could not go shopping in Droitwich without having her handbag rifled. I discussed her character once with my mother who remembered her from old days of Worcestershire archery meetings and croquet matches. 'Yes,' said my mother, 'Doris was very gullible. It was child's play to cheat her at croquet even when her back was not turned. She never detected an opponent covering her ball under a long skirt and shuffling it off the lawn to Jericho.'

During the widow's regime Hanbury was at first very sparsely furnished. I suppose what there was came with her mother from Shrawley Wood. There were, and are, two Buhl cabinets filled with some good Worcester porcelain and Chinese export plates, and a full-length portrait of Doris herself in a lavender dress holding a basket of delphiniums by the Hon. John Collier. Gradually more things accumulated. But she lived only in two rooms downstairs, the library on the left of the front door and the tea room, where she ate, behind it. This was a gloomy apartment heated in winter by the single filament of a small electric fire. One rectangular pane of sash window was kept permanently open for her cats, enormous creatures of some strange breed, 'with seven toes (not six) and rabbit's fur', to jump through. This egress and ingress afforded the only ventilation in hot weather to a room with a foetid atmosphere. She was looked after by one elderly maid, called Lilian, a mysterious figure, very thin with enormous eager black eyes who vividly suggested Mrs Steerforth's companion Rosa Dartle in *David Copperfield*. Lilian indulged in mysterious innuendoes and enlisted one as a party to hushed secrets. She would hover over Lady Vernon like a protective shadow, reaffirming with nod and wink what her mistress had been saying. Once while we were in a bedroom with a large four-poster and Lady Vernon was walking out of the door Lilian grabbed my arm and hissed, 'Look! This is where 'e did himself in. See the bullet holes on the wallpaper! And a good job too!'

Although Lady Vernon lived in apparent dingy penury and exclusion she always seemed glad to see me and after me my successors on the National Trust staff. Many a time I had luncheon – Irish stew or Lancashire hot pot, and cheese, good simple fare cooked and served by Lilian. Once there was a sweet. Lady Vernon sighed and asked, 'Is there no other puddin' than this?' 'I only cook queen's pudding,' came the reply from Lilian, 'and I cook it *very* well.' Conversation was usually about the good old days (which were really bad old days) and the bad new ones (which were better). 'Droitwich is gettin' very queer,' my hostess would say. 'Oh dear! How's that, Lady Vernon?' 'All the buildin's' are topplin' over because of the brine.' It was only too true; the salt extraction was causing mischief. But it always had done. As she got older and shakier so her conviction that she was penniless increased. When the Bishop of Worcester, who was a kind, attentive friend, asked himself to luncheon, 'just for a bite', as he put and meant it, she said she would be glad to entertain him provided he brought his own sand- wiches. But when she died in 1962 she left a large private fortune of Allan money – surely a serious indictment of her lawyers who ought to have assured her that she was perfectly well off and in no need of stinting herself or her guests.

In 1952 one of those almost unbelievable miracles happened. The whole house was crying out for repairs and the famous Thornhill ceilings were threatening collapse. At the time an anonymous benefac- tor approached the Trust. He or she offered a very large sum of money to recondition and endow a really fine William and Mary house. The benefactor was conducted to Hanbury, saw it, fell in love and decided there and then that it was to be the recipient of the bounty available. Repairs were instantly put in hand and Michael Gibbon, a professional expert who lived nearby, dedicated himself to a first-rate salvage of the staircase walls illustrating the exploits of Achilles in colour and monochrome, and the staircase ceiling depicting an assembly of classical deities. He also attended to the *trompe-l'œil* ceiling of the hall and the two ceiling paintings in brown and blue of the long room.

The work was a perfectly satisfactory example of conservative repara- tion. Before it was completed Lady Vernon persuaded the National Trust to take over the property in 1953 although she still enjoyed a life interest in the house and garden. This necessitated consent being obtained from the next heir, Mrs Vernon Horton. Mrs Horton gener- ously gave it. Some skilful diplomacy was demanded from the National Trust whose solicitors had to get simultaneous signatures by Lady Vernon and 'the female' without them meeting. Neither lady trusted the other an inch. As it happened Lady Vernon, wearing a huge hat for the occasion, gave her signature from Hanbury after receipt of a telephone message that the other's had already been appended in the solicitor's Droitwich office.

After Lady Vernon's death the National Trust, in accordance with its professed policy, endeavoured to let the house as a family home. Mr and Mrs Edmund Bayliss rented it. Unfortunately it proved too large for them and after a few years they left. Another tenant was forthcom- ing but did not stay long. So the Trust decided to convert the upper floors and some premises to the rear into self-contained flats for hand-picked tenants while keeping the ground-floor rooms, the Thornhill staircase and one bedroom for the public to see.

The bulk of Lady Vernon's furniture was in accord with her wishes very kindly given to Hanbury by her nephew Mr A.H. Allan. Even so this was not enough to fill the rooms on show. The Trust has done its best to supplement it with appropriate furniture, particularly paintings, portraits and objects associated with the Vernons or other Worcestershire families. A fine set of Queen Anne walnut chairs are on permanent loan from the Lady Lever Art Gallery. Hanbury has been extraordinarily fortunate in attracting benefactors. Apart from the anonymous one of 1952 several donors have helped support the house. During 1976–8 the Merrill Trust in the United States paid for further restoration of the show rooms and the acquisition of more contents. In 1977 Mr R.S. Watney presented a collection of eighteenth-century English furniture, porcelain and flower paintings, and in 1981 bequeathed the residue of his fortune. In the Blue Bedroom the splendid angel bed with hangings of worsted damask dating from the 1730s, surprisingly fresh in colour, came from Zeals House near Mere in Wiltshire.

Because this unsophisticated and most homely of English houses is not to be reckoned for size among the great country seats, because its immediate surroundings are still unspoilt, and because it is fairly close to Birmingham, one might suppose it to be eminently desirable as a residence. But this has not proved to be the case. Inadequately endowed, Hanbury has always been a problem to the Trust which now feels obliged to use it for rather unsympathetic purposes. It is hired out day by day and evening by evening for conferences of businessmen, assemblies, weddings and what is termed 'corporate entertainment' of all sorts. To equip it with the luxury standard of heating and air-conditioning deemed essential for these purposes, the entire interior, save for the Thornhill ceilings and walls, was in 1990 stripped from ground to rafters, walls to the bare brick and floor-boards to bare earth or air, in spite of the major restoration of 1952 and several minor restorations since that date. These additional basic 'improvements' have been carried out on an immense scale. Now all is put back, much redecoration has been done in the process, and the contents have been rearranged. The rooms have been submitted to that suave good-taste expertise which it may be difficult to criticize and yet is easy to lament. The flavour, the ethos of the old Hanbury Hall, the Sir Roger de Coverley, the Squire Western house, has somehow subtly gone. I ask myself why and how. The contents are unexceptionable. Many were at Hanbury in the old shabby days and have been commendably retrieved, smartened up and reassembled where they properly belong by that most historiological of National Trust representatives, Jeffrey Hawarth. Yet somehow the new curtains seem too sumptuous, the pelmets too swankily draped, the wall hangings too vivid, the William and Adelaide Gothick wallpaper in the upstairs corridor (although copied from a fragment found under layers of later paper) almost too imperial, the whole air of well-being too exquisite for Counsellor Vernon in his old wig and bands, even for coquettish Emma and her adolescent Lord of Burghley, and certainly for homely Sir Harry and his reprobate heir, to have felt comfortable amongst such pretension. God knows Hanbury was shockingly neglected by Sir George and has with sweat and tears been retrieved from perdition. So why not be intensely grateful and shut up? It is cavalier to complain. And yet . . . and yet . . . Is Hanbury wholly real inside? Can an ancient squirearchical house be quite the same after such tremendously drastic treatment? Is it not bound to look glossy and almost new? And just very faintly suburban?

CHAPTER FOUR

BERWICK OF ATTINGHAM
Shropshire

UNTIL the 8th Lord Berwick's death in 1947 the Atcham estate south of Shrewsbury had passed by descent over nearly 250 years. It had been bought and presented in 1705 by Richard Hill, a Shropshire squire of Hawkstone, as a marriage portion to Margaret, the younger of his two sisters. In due course the Hawkstone estate went to a brother's son who became Sir Rowland Hill, 1st Baronet, ancestor of the Viscounts Hill, and no apparent relation to his namesake the inventor of penny postage.

Richard Hill of Hawkstone, an immensely rich bachelor, was as well as landowner a prominent statesman, diplomatist and foreign envoy under William of Orange, Anne and George I. He also belonged to some mysterious religious order when it suited him and is said to have refused a bishopric. The name of his sister Margaret's husband was Thomas Harwood, a respectable Shrewsbury merchant of modest means whom he decided should be raised to the status of a landed gentleman. The couple had a son, likewise Thomas, who in gratitude for the uncle's benefaction dropped the Harwood name and took for himself and his descendants that of Hill in perpetuity. This Thomas Hill married well, produced a son christened Noel after his mother's surname – she was likewise an heiress – and by the middle of the eighteenth century was already established among the leading Shropshire families. When his father died at the age of 89 Noel Hill set about aggrandizing himself to some tune. He partly encased the modest seat called Tern Hall which his grandparents had built, engaging a little known Gaelic-speaking Scot, George Steuart of Harley Street, to raise for him a far grander seat which he fancifully called Attingham, thus reviving a defunct medieval rendering of Atcham. It must somehow have been made clear to the Crown that the possessor of so splendid a palace deserved ennoblement. At all events before Attingham was even

53

completed in 1785 Noel was duly created Lord Berwick, the title deriving from an inconspicuous hamlet on the estate. The attained Duke of Berwick-upon-Tweed, James II's great-grandson, may not have been best pleased by the coincidence, if he ever came to hear of it.

The 1st Lord Berwick of Attingham survived a bare four years to enjoy his new splendour, dying suddenly in 1789 aged 44. The eldest of his three sons, who succeeded in turn, namely the 2nd Lord, was a zealous traveller in Italy and lavish spender on works of art. On his return home he commissioned John Nash, the Prince Regent's architect, to construct in 1807 a picture gallery to contain his treasures, and Humphry Repton to landscape his park. Unfortunately he so overspent himself that in 1827 most of the treasures had to be sold. However the next brother, the 3rd Lord, who as William Noel-Hill had been British Minister to the court of Sardinia in Genoa where he several times entertained Lord Byron, and at the court of the Two Sicilies in Naples, where he rented a palace of the ex-Queen Caroline Murat, was able to replenish Attingham with much of the fine furniture and pictures which remain in the house.

Until we get to the 8th Lord and donor of Attingham to the National Trust there is little to relate of the intermediate holders of the title, except possibly the 5th who had an aptitude for gadgets and invented an improvement to the military rifle.

My first visit to Attingham on behalf of the National Trust was in August 1936. Having put my bicycle in the guard's van at Paddington I pedalled the four miles from Shrewsbury station. After pushing the machine over the old hump-backed bridge at Atcham and freewheeling down the other side, I turned smartly left under an imposing archway off the main Wellington road. I had time to take in the family motto carved overhead, *Qui Uti Scit Ei Bona* which I interpreted as 'May he who knows how to enjoy the good things of life have the means to do so', before speeding airily along a shortish drive with tall trees on the left and a flat terrain on the right. In the far distance an irregular range of hills, Caradoc, Wenlock Edge and the Wrekin hove into sight. But when the great house hoved a moment of apprehension assailed me. Would Lord and Lady Berwick be very formidable? What would they think of an official from London arriving on a two-wheeler? Then I consoled myself with the reflection that the National Trust rather prided itself on its charitable status and deserving poverty. Extravagant means of travel was frowned upon. In those days there was not even a communal motor-car for the male staff of four, and when one was bought it was second-hand. Instead we regarded ourselves as dedicated like the clergy, and if not superior, then slightly special. I dismounted and in case there might not be a later opportunity took some oblique snapshots of the great pile staring south across an empty park towards Caradoc. A curved colonnade from the main block to an attached pavilion spread towards me. I concluded correctly that a duplicate one stretched in the hidden direction. I did not yet know that to the north and also out of sight was a vast enclosed office court approached by an entrance under a temple-like cupola, and beyond that a separate quadrangle of stables for sixty horses.

I had no need to feel in awe. From the moment that a chatty parlourmaid, not even in uniform, opened the front door under an extremely high portico I was at ease. Until she showed me into the drawing-room and withdrew I wondered if she were not a member of the family. In the ravishingly beautiful yet slightly distressed apartment Lord and Lady Berwick were sitting bolt upright talking to each other. The true condition of things at Attingham was soon borne upon me. Lady Berwick rose from a stiff settee in a rather stately manner, it is true. She was young middle-aged, very handsome with wavy hair parted in the middle so as to make her naturally oval face look almost rotund. There was a severity in her demeanour mitigated by a kindness about her generous eyes and mouth. Lord Berwick seemed about sixty, painfully shy but smiling, hesitant, a shadow. First of all, would I like to see round before talking, she asked. Lord Berwick echoed the inter-rogation in an indistinct mumble. I replied that I would.

They were surprisingly unreserved in explaining that in spite of a large estate the house was a cruel burden to them. But it had to be preserved at all costs, however onerous, and the marvellous contents kept intact. The estate was what they called 'embarrassed', even then in the inter-war period. Nevertheless not an acre should be sold. Perhaps fortunately, they had no children and no heir with claims on them. Childlessness was not unusual in the family for indeed out of the nine holders of the Berwick title six died without issue. Now would and could the National Trust help them, and if so, how? I said I was absolutely sure they somehow would and could, although it was not for me to unravel the means. When I left at the end of the day, my pockets stuffed with delicious sandwiches for the return journey to London, my kind host and hostess stood above the portico steps watching me take to the saddle and pedal, he still fluttering a nervous smile, she a royal but affable wave. While I bicycled back to the station I was so intoxicated by Attingham and a determination to save it that I nearly missed the train by taking a wrong turning in the Shrewsbury suburbs.

I certainly went back to Attingham once if not twice during the remaining years of peace, staying one December night in 1937. Meanwhile reports were being prepared by a qualified local estate agency (the Trust had no professional agent on its staff) on the property as a basis for estimating income and expenditure. The Berwicks' own agent Gordon Miller, whose office was in the library wing, was exceedingly co-operative and helpful. He fully understood the predicament of the Berwicks whom he protected in an engaging paternal manner.

Subject to the estimates proving favourable (and the great advantage of ownership by the Trust was that it paid no income tax) the Country Houses Committee readily agreed to accept this property on the understanding that Lord and Lady Berwick would continue to inhabit the house for the remainder of their lives. As things turned out the Attingham estate did not come to the Trust until 1947, and then by bequest. Even so, during the lapse of eleven years the Trust as heir apparent was closely concerned with Attingham. Moreover I was constantly meeting Lady Berwick on her visits to London to discuss matters, she being the operative partner in the transactions just as she was the inspiration behind her husband. Had it not been for her, and had Lord Berwick been solely in charge, Attingham would not have been saved. The Trust owes immense debts to several positive wives and widows for taking matters into their own hands. Other examples in the chatelaines of Hanbury Hall, Coughton Court, Oxburgh Hall and Berrington Hall come to mind.

There was something almost clandestine about my meetings with Lady Berwick, at the Ladies Carlton Club and the houses and flats of the friends with whom she stayed – the fabulous Edwardian beauty Lady D'Abernon to whom she introduced me at Stoke D'Abernon Manor was one, and Christabel Aberconway another. She was always at pains to make me believe she was acting solely on her husband's instructions. Of course the better I got to know them both the sooner I learned that this was nonsense, for Lord Berwick was incapable of attending to any issue or making up his mind on any business which he found awkward or disagreeable.

My confidences, if I should use such a word, with Lady Berwick became in these early years of negotiation considerable though never intimate. We were never on Christian name terms and I knew from the start we should not be. She was just not that sort of person. Besides in those days it was unthinkable for a young man to address a woman older than himself by her first name unless asked to do so. I heard her called Teresa by her women friends and wondered if any man, other than her husband, would take that liberty. To me she remained a sort of Grecian goddess whom I held in respectful homage. I dined with her occasionally in London and once gallanted her to somebody's Mayfair ball – I forget whose – where we danced the Lambeth Walk and Palais Glide fervently yet distantly. It was a most enjoyable evening. Neither of us danced with anyone else. Another evening I took her to supper at the Café Royal which in spite of her comparatively bohemian upbringing she found novel. For the first and only time we discussed things not associated with Attingham, yet without becoming the least personal. After more than half a century's reflection I conclude that ours was a strange relationship. What I am certain of is that she was an intensely sad and even lonely woman. And come to think of it her lot was passing strange.

Lady Berwick was more Continental than English. She spoke with a seductive and slight Italian accent. Born in Asolo and brought up in Venice she was a daughter of William Hulton, a rather underestimated English painter of small Venetian scenes, palace interiors and the landscape of the Veneto. Hulton was a close friend of Sickert, who became a kind of adopted uncle to Teresa and her elder sister Gioconda. There is at Attingham a full-length portrait by Sickert of Teresa, entitled *Lady in Blue*, which the subject never admitted to be a good likeness and was for some unaccountable reason a little ashamed of. Perhaps she did not wish to be identified as an ordinary model; and I think she objected to the staring whites of the eyes as being unseemly. Her portrait by Gerald Kelly shows her as she wished to be shown and became, a stately, middle-aged, English peeress. Hulton's wife Costanza was half English, half Italian by her mother, and herself brought up in Italy. Her circle of friends included Robert Browning, Henry James, Sir William Eden, John Sargent and, later, Berenson and Iris Origo. Teresa was devoted to her family and her home in the little Palazzo Dona which faces across a narrow canal the Campo dominated by the famous SS Giovanni e Paulo church and the Colleoni equestrian statue by Verrocchio. It was to this enchanted corner of Venice that Lady Berwick's childhood affections were tethered.

She was clever rather than intellectual. Logan Pearsall Smith who knew her well in her youth assured me that of his two categories of women she was distinctly a dove as opposed to a serpent. He called her beautiful, gentle and guileless, inclined just a little to silliness. He once introduced her to two serpents which turned out a mistake for she felt abashed and awkward in their company.

One can imagine the confusion of a 29-year-old Venetian-bred beauty, admired and courted by the cosmopolitan intelligentsia, a talented piano player who once contemplated becoming a professional, on being transported to a remote English county abounding in fox-hunting and pheasant-shooting squires just after the European war in 1919. Merlin Waterson in a fascinating and discerning memoir entitled *Lady Berwick, Attingham and Italy* has paid tribute to the knowledge and taste she brought to her future home which already owed the greater part of its adornment to the influence and spoils of her native land. What he does not tell – indeed he could not even if he knew – is why she married the nervous, shy, unsocial and assuredly even then unglamorous English peer, thirteen years her senior. He merely hints discreetly that when little more than a girl she suffered deeply from an unfulfilled love affair. On the outbreak of the First World War she submerged her unhappiness in work for the British Red Cross at Carvignano close behind the front lines, and narrowly avoided capture by the enemy. She received the *Croce di Guerra* from the King of Italy. One thing the Berwicks certainly shared – a love of the arts. He was a connoisseur with a very sure eye. He added several treasures to the 3rd Lord's collection, including an oil portrait of Caroline Murat by Gérard, a contemporary copy of the head of Canova's dancer and a full-length replica statue of that sculptor's Italian Venus, both in marble. Other purchases by him were two panels of Dufour's coloured wallpaper series of *Vues de l'Inde*.

Lord Berwick was in his way an extraordinary man. People who mistook him for an amiable fool could make fools of themselves. It is true he made little stir in the wide world. Son of a parson of a family living and a parson's daughter he inherited from an uncle his title and large estate while still an Oxford undergraduate at Trinity College. Off and on between 1903 and 1916 he was honorary attaché at the Paris embassy, becoming a captain in the Shropshire Yeomanry. I was told by one who knew him in his early years that if not a senior wrangler he was an advanced mathematician, which may perhaps account for his seeming absences of thought while one was talking to him. Throughout his bachelordom Attingham was left empty and neglected. On his own he seemed unable to cope. Then came Teresa who after a year or two decided they must make a go of the big house.

The Berwicks were always hard up. At one time Teresa set up a dress-making shop in London in an endeavour to earn pin money. They loved entertaining but could not afford to do so on a grand scale. Nevertheless the house was beautiful in its down-at-heel fashion, comfortable and the food always excellent. Until 1939 the Berwicks had house parties of friends. The visitors' book discloses that writers like

Rudyard Kipling, Charles Morgan, L.P. Hartley, David Cecil and Iris Origo, artists like John Nash and Gerald Kelly, and English and Italian intellectuals generally outnumbered the merely smart and certainly the sport-loving.

With the outbreak of the Second World War negotiations with the National Trust were at a standstill. I did not see the Berwicks again or go to Attingham until invited to stay for two nights in July 1943. By then they had withdrawn into a few rooms and the WAAFs were in occupation of the greater part of the house. I had previously persuaded the Ministry of Works to protect the principal rooms by boarding up the fine marble fireplaces of statuary marble and even the dadoes. The first evening we drank champagne to celebrate our and Attingham's survival to date. In spite of prevailing conditions Lord and Lady Berwick were pleased with the WAAFs and seemed happier than I remember them before or since.

Nevertheless his shyness seemed worse than ever. She was always at pains to make believe that he took the initiative in our negotiations. After expressing her views at some length she would say in a peremptory tone, 'Now then, Tom, you talk to Mr Lees-Milne.' This occasioned considerable nervousness in both him and me. So when obliged to speak to me in the presence of his wife he would turn away from me to cast a furtive eye at her, and instead of turning back would continue shuffling clockwise on his own axis. I therefore had to follow him like a satellite moon through interstellar space, for I should explain that during these serious discussions the three of us were always standing up.

The following day Lady Berwick took me round the estate and then to tea with their tenants at Cronkhill where she and her husband had first lived for a short time after their marriage. This house, built in 1802 by John Nash in a romantic irregular style, with one round tower and a colonnade of overhanging eaves, looks down upon the baby river Severn and water-meadows a mile to the west of Atcham. It is thought to be the first Italianate villa built in England. I noticed how Lady Berwick behaved towards her neighbours with a studied affability and queenly graciousness that must have seemed a trifle patronizing.

And here I cannot do better than quote verbatim from a passage of my diary for 8 July of this year:

After tea I walked with Lord Berwick in the deer park, having been enjoined by her to talk seriously about Attingham's future, and press him for a decision on various points. I did not make much progress in this respect. On the other hand he expanded in an endearing way. When alone he loosens up and is quite communicative. All the seeming silliness and nervousness vanish. He talked to me earnestly, in his shy, diffident manner it is true, of the ghosts that have been seen at Attingham by the WAAFs. Lady Berwick would not, I know (and he also knew full well), have tolerated this nonsense, if she had been present. He kept stopping and anxiously looking over his shoulder lest she might be over-hearing him, but he did not stand stock still and then revolve, which he does in the drawing-room whenever she starts talking business. He told me that Lady Sybil Grant, his neighbour at Pitchford, constantly writes to him on the forbidden subject, passing on advice as to his health which she has been given by her spiritual guides. She no longer dares telephone this information for fear, so Lord Berwick asserted, of the spirits overhearing and taking offence, but I suspect it is more likely for fear of Lady Berwick overhearing and strongly disapproving. He is not the least boring about his psychical beliefs but is perplexed by the strange habits of ghosts. He asked me, did I think it possible that one could have been locked in the house-maid's cupboard? And why should another want to disguise itself as a vacuum cleaner? Really he is a delicious man.

At this time the Trust was having negotiations with the Grants which ultimately came to nothing. Lady Sybil Grant was even more eccentric than Lord Berwick, whose superstitions and spiritual experiences she worked upon much to his wife's annoyance. Lady Sybil lived with her husband Sir Charles Grant, a retired general and owner of Pitchford Hall, which is the most splendid half-timbered country house in Shropshire. But 'lived with' is not entirely accurate because Lady Sybil, owing to the house being haunted, so she admitted, actually lived alone in the orangery by day, and in a Georgian black-and-white tree-house, with a very pretty rococo plaster ceiling, by night. The couple would meet for coffee in fine weather on the lawn without impinging on each other's territory.

By March of the following year I was shuttlecocking between Pitch-ford and Attingham. At the former place I would veer from the house, where I discussed problems of his ancestry, his friends and other irrelevancies with the charming general, to the orangery where his wife, wearing a tall, pointed Welshwoman's hat and long orange veil down to the ground and suffering from a sprained ankle, obliged me to souse it with a solution of Pond's Extract from an extremely heavy eighteenth-century watering-can of lead. Conversation with her was equally difficult to steer on to the future of Pitchford. She digressed upon her maid's madness and thievery, and Lady Sybil's recovery of stolen objects from the Abbess of the convent where the maid went to confession; upon the low-flying aeroplanes which drove her to seek sanctuary in a caravan, and Lord Berwick's supranatural acquaintances. 'Poor Tom,' she sighed, 'he should not have lived in this age. He cannot drive a car, ride a bicycle, fish or shoot. He would have stepped in and out of a sedan chair so beautifully.'

From Pitchford I moved to Attingham for a night. In the deer park I found Lord Berwick walking his little fluffy dog Muffet. 'I think he is one of the most endearing men I have ever met in my life – feckless, helpless and courteous,' I wrote at the time. He seemed really pleased to see me, smiled and giggled, and plunged into confidences about the spooks' latest escapades. We had an exquisite four-course dinner and a bottle of Burgundy. The next morning Mr Forsyth called and Lord Berwick took us round the inside of the house. I never saw him more relaxed or more spry. Once the shyness wore off he elaborated at fascinating length on each room with extraordinary knowledge, understanding and pride. Through the hall with its grey mottled walls and scagliola columns, the magnificent dining-room with its walls painted Pompeian red enlivened with gold, the octagon room on the west front, fitted with Regency bookcases and original pink silk linings behind grille doors, and a domed ceiling of flowing stucco foliage, and all deprived of their contents for 'the duration', we were followed by a gaggle of open-mouthed and speechless WAAFs. Then to the 2nd Lord's great picture gallery, windowless and top-lit, not used by the forces and with, thank goodness, the 3rd Lord's picture collections intact, the severely handsome Sheraton-style organ still in place, having been retrieved after the 2nd Lord's sale of 1827, the catalogue of which – the sale lasted sixteen days – I had been perusing in bed the night before. Then to the rooms in the east range, which are feminine in contrast to the marked masculinity of the west range. That in the north corner, balancing the octagon room of the west front, is the exquisite little boudoir. Its dome, stuccoed in flaming lamps within wreathes, is raised on fluted columns between which doors and over-doors are painted with arabesques by Cipriani or Rebecca. And finally, by way of the Sultana Room, to the lovely blue drawing-room with the 3rd Lord's white and gilt Neapolitan furniture, the mirrors, pictures and polished statuary.

In October I called at Attingham, having bicycled from Wenlock Abbey where I was staying ten miles away. Lady Berwick who was alone gave me tea. She was pleased because the Shropshire Education Committee, after several engagements and cancellations, were seriously reconsidering the use of Attingham when the war was over for an adult education college. This indeed came to pass.

In May 1945 I was there again with Mr Forsyth going round the house, examining and criticizing the county council's proposed alterations to suit their college requirements. I stayed the night in the house without Mr Forsyth. I wonder now how and where the poor man was disposed of. Next morning Lady Berwick motored me to Shrewsbury station. She stood on the platform in the bitter weather, talking through the carriage window. When I begged her not to linger and catch cold she said it was such a pleasure to talk to somebody. I thereby deduced that Lord Berwick was not always companionable. But when a few weeks later I had a drink with them both in London they were sparring. She was intensely irritated by his slowness, endless prevarications and inability to confirm her wishes about something. In embarrassment I found myself desperately humming a tune of my own invention until Lady Berwick exclaimed, 'Where is that noise coming from?'

Eighteen months later Lord Berwick was seriously ill. In January 1947 I stayed at the Mytton and Mermaid Inn opposite the drive entrance, and after tea walked to the house. Lady Berwick was wretched and worried. He was laid low with a tired heart and two nurses in attendance. I went to see him in the boudoir where his Empire bed had been moved, and was allowed to stay five minutes. He was even slower of speech than usual but still able to smile in his sweet way. I spent the following morning with Lady Berwick jig-sawing the pictures about, and deciding to keep the two Angelica Kauffmann mythology paintings in the drawing-room while leaving the pompous family portraits in the dining-room which the college insisted on using as a classroom. The rich blue carpet, patterned in fan sections round a circular panel had, I presume, been removed and stored. The magnificent dining-room chairs she had lent us were at Lyme Park in Cheshire temporarily. It was sad that this splendid room, so complete and so contemporary, had to be sacrificed to middle-aged academics, their desks and blackboards.

In her utter dejection and confusion Lady Berwick barely knew what she was doing, and for once was anxious for advice. In the basement we looked at stacks of Capodimonte porcelain which she felt sure had been made, like so much of the Attingham furniture, for Queen Caroline

Murat and acquired by the attractive William Noel-Hill, in Naples, as perks, loot, gifts or honourable purchase from the residue of the banished Murats. During this visit more shifting of contents had to be done than when the WAAFs took over in 1939. In April I returned bringing with me a valuation of those things Lady Berwick was sending to Sotheby's for sale. For a second time she offered me a Victorian nursery scrap screen which I was overjoyed to have, provided I paid for it. Our haggling became a wry joke and finally ten shillings was all she would take, saying, 'So nobody can now accuse you of accepting gifts and bribes from your friends.'

At the end of May I went to Attingham with Charles Brocklehurst who had become the Trust's honorary representative for Cheshire and Shropshire and who, through sharing a number of friends, was much favoured by Lady Berwick. As one of Christies' silver experts at the time he was able to give very useful advice. The scene we came upon was like that of a Russian tragedy. Lady Berwick was hollow-eyed, edgy and on the verge of tears. Since the staterooms were to be on public view the burden of withdrawing irrevocably into the east wing, which meant selling almost everything which would not be wanted by the Trust, was entirely hers. As for poor Lord Berwick he was on the verge of death. A shrunken bundle, incapable of moving hand or foot, and entirely at the mercy of two stalwart nurses costing the earth, was wheeled up to us in a chair. He could barely utter and no longer even force a smile. Charlie spent the day sorting through silver, china and small *objets d'art*, all of which he thought highly of, selecting some for Lyme Park, for which National Trust house he was then responsible, and packing them in his car. They would be earmarked as belonging to Attingham, to which they have now returned. We persuaded Lady Berwick to lunch with us at the Mytton and Mermaid. In the evening Charlie and I parted, I driving off with the posts of Caroline Murat's bed, which the Berwicks were to sell at Sotheby's, sticking precariously out of the dickey of my car.

Within a fortnight Lord Berwick was dead, and his widow faced with probate, death duties, the final clearance of the huge centre block, sales, settling into the east wing with one maid of all work, the incomparable Mrs Durward, adapting to the demands and often alien manners of the adult educational college on her very doorstep, and loneliness. It had always been an understanding that her beloved sister Gioconda would eventually live with her at Attingham, but she had been killed in a motor accident just as Lady Berwick was to meet the same fate twenty-five years later in 1972.

The Berwick title devolved upon a cousin on whose death in 1953 it became extinct. Michael Noel-Hill, the 9th Baron, was left no interests in and had no claims to the estate beyond a reversionary annuity although heir presumptive to the title. His life epitomized the tragedy of a man of decent disposition but weak character, knocked endways by appalling experiences during the First World War and its aftermath. He was perennially out of pocket. Not that his cousin Tom did not at times come to his rescue and occasionally settle his debts. Nevertheless grinding poverty tends to make a black sheep blacker, and other troubles multiplied.

With commendable fortitude and forbearance Lady Berwick was obliged to witness some whimsy goings-on in the college which, not unexpectedly, put the attainment of its ideals and purposes before conservation of the historic rooms of the house. Not by nature complacent or a glad tolerator of fools, but one accustomed to having her own way and rightly confident of her own impeccable taste in the arrangement and treatment of works of art, she undoubtedly suffered, not always in silence, from the behaviour of both the college and the National Trust officials. The latter however, even when not always able to meet with her views, greatly respected her judgement; and those few who saw much of her positively loved her. What her true feelings about them were she kept to herself. But she treated them all with infinite courtesy. As Merlin Waterson has written, she would sometimes refer to individuals as ' "poor dear Mr . . ." and so manage to convey both genuine affection as well as awareness of painful inadequacies'. If Merlin was under few illusions as to his inadequacies, I am under none as to those of poor dear Mr L-M. Yet I like to hope that she reciprocated some of the affection I had for her. And I shall always treasure the little Georgian glass and silver inkstand she gave me (with absolutely no ten shilling quid pro quo) for a wedding present.

I continued to visit Attingham at intervals. In June I spent a day with Keeble the decorator, estimating the work required to be done to the staterooms. We found that the WAAFs had not treated the beautiful mahogany doors and exquisite gilt bronze handles and locks too badly. Women are usually more house-proud and protective of furniture than men. In August I lunched with Lady Berwick, one of whose eyes was giving her considerable trouble. Afterwards Keeble and I settled with George Trevelyan (the son of Sir Charles and nephew of G.M.), the college principal, a tricky matter of colours for the ante-library which was in college use, and persuaded him that the original hall walls, which he found gloomy, could on no account be 'cheered up'. In the autumn

Keeble's work needed frequent supervision. When cleaned the picture gallery looked splendid, and after Lady Berwick's arrangement of the furniture the blue drawing-room was sparkling. One morning she took me to the site she had chosen for her husband's cenotaph. He had directed that his ashes were to be placed in a tomb above ground in the deer park. The romantic site was suggested to her by Constable's well-known painting in the National Gallery of a pedestalled urn in a forest clearing with the deer grazing around it. I agreed that, once the army camp and the unsightly wire fence were removed, it would make the most perfect and fitting memorial. And so it has proved. Both her and her husband's ashes were in fact scattered on the spot. On one of the four faces of the classical cenotaph designed by W. Curtis Green a lapidary inscription, composed by the Berwicks' friend L.P. Hartley, testifies to his virtues. I hope that one day an appropriate inscription will somewhere at Attingham testify to hers in spite of her modesty in discouraging any such remembrance.

For the opening of the staterooms to the public in August 1949 I took my chairman Lord Esher, and Lady Esher, to Attingham. We stayed at the Mytton and Mermaid. The evening before the ceremony Lady Berwick invited them to dinner. I regret that Oliver Esher, so entertaining and attentive to women, did not take to her. He had little sympathy for other people's self-pity and was bored by her sighs and tragedy-queen manner. She certainly took a long time to recover from her bereavement. Irritated though she undoubtedly had been at times by her husband in his lifetime she could not for years after his death hear his name mentioned without the tears welling to her eyes.

At the opening ceremony Lord Esher delivered the speech I had drafted for him, but so improved and embellished by his customary witticisms that I could not recognize my hand in it, and found myself applauding loudly.

In the years to come I had little to do with Attingham which I visited seldom. But occasionally I met Lady Berwick, usually at luncheon parties in London. The last thing I did for her as a member of the staff seems on recollection almost incredibly impertinent, if not mean; and I recount it merely to show how far this proud *grande dame* and former chatelaine of one of England's great country houses was reduced. I managed to persuade the National Trust to pay her £5.10s. a week towards the wages of her maid in order to cover work which Mrs Durward did indirectly for the National Trust. Such charity is painful to record. It brings to my mind the condition of Matilda Talbot after she had given to the Trust the abbey, the village and the entire estate of

Lacock Abbey which was the house's endowment. She was left to live on – I think the figure is about accurate – £400 a year for her own needs. The generosity of many donors, especially women, to the Trust has been beyond words noble.

In 1986 a second education college, having fulfilled its purpose, closed down and the Shropshire County Council's lease of Attingham came to an end. The National Trust moved its regional office to the north side of the house where it now occupies rooms originally intended for the indoor servants and the usual backdoor premises, brew-house, wash-house, still-room, steward's room and carpentry shop. These offices abut on the large courtyard dominated by the cupola'ed entrance. All unsightly outbuildings and lean-tos which accrued over two centuries have been swept away and the expansive oval lawn shown in a contemporary sketch by Repton has been re-instated. The courtyard is one of the most satisfactory architectural units of Attingham. During weekdays some thirty or forty cars assembled on the surrounding gravel indicate the number of the National Trust staff today in only one regional area. Steuart's detached stable block for sixty horses now contains the headquarters of the regional Nature Conservancy offices as well as providing two estate cottages. Some of the stalls in a series of curved and urn-capped partitions have been preserved.

Within the last few years the Trust has carried out many improvements to the house. The parcel gilding of the iron balustrade under the entrance portico is the first to impress the visitor. It makes a welcome relief to the starkness of a too overpowering architectural protuberance. The library pavilion has been reinstated; the shelves have been filled with books and the grisaille paintings above them cleaned. Further restorations are contemplated, such as rehanging of the protective draperies shown in George Steuart's design, between the tall Corinthian pilasters that enclose the shelves. Some statuary has been lent by the Walker Art Gallery to replace what was lost from this grand apartment after the sale of 1827.

In the dining-room with its blood-red walls, highlit with gold, heavy curtains of drab cloth bordered with purple velvet have been copied from remnants of the originals. This has been a bold but successful venture because of the palatial proportions of the room. The great picture gallery has had an additional glazed roof imposed upon John Nash's curved iron ribs and glass panes. The glass of the new outer roof has an ultra-violet filter to moderate the fading effect of the midday sun upon the paintings and the delicate parquetry margins of the floor.

The upstairs rooms formerly used by the college and students have now been freed. Archives and dresses are being stored in some. To let the remainder as separate flats (in theory a nice idea), particularly those over the staterooms, presents in practice problems: first, the great expense of conversion and, second, the danger to the stucco and painted ceilings, not to mention the works of art below, from leaking or burst pipes and the perpetual menace of bath-water overflow. A very hand-picked tenant has already been permitted to rent the floor over the east wing staterooms.

The splendidly robust basement of the old servants' hall and wine cellar on the south front, with stone vaulted ceilings, has lately been arranged to display in specially designed glass cases some of the superb Attingham porcelain and silver of which there are specimens by Paul Storr and George IV's favourite firm of silversmiths, Rundell Bridge & Rundell. Most of the porcelain was acquired by William Noel-Hill in the course of his diplomatic duties in Italy.

There is still more to be done to this elegant late Georgian house as money becomes available. Those responsible for it are advancing with sure tread. Their expertise and taste are beyond criticism. Nevertheless and doubtless, they will bear in mind that Attingham has always been a home as well as a repository of works of art; that on the gilt Neapolitan chairs people sat, and on the inlaid marble table-tops left their books and knitting. Clocks ticked on the mosaic-encrusted chimney-pieces and little dogs frisked, when they did not relieve themselves, upon the Axminster carpets. Attingham was not built as a museum and the Lords Berwick did not inhabit it primarily as curators, but as managers of a large agricultural acreage. Members of Parliament, ministers of the Crown and State, entertainers of large parties and fathers of large families presided in proud, albeit often casual autocracy.

The 8th Lord would certainly be gratified were he to know that within less than half a century after his demise the Attingham estate was flourishing and the house was reinstated to a condition far better than it ever enjoyed during his reign. He never stipulated in precise terms what he hoped would be Attingham's eventual user. But in his will he repeatedly referred to his gift as 'for the public benefit'. And in a final clause he merely expressed a 'desire that the principal reception rooms of the said Mansion House may be so decoratively complete that it may remain a good example of eighteenth century architecture with such contents in the principal reception rooms as a nobleman's house of that period would have had'.

CHAPTER FIVE

HOARE OF STOURHEAD
Wiltshire

O N an April morning of 1936 the sort of letter which we on the infant National Trust staff got tremendously excited about lay on the secretary's in-tray. From Messrs Longbourne Steven & Powell, solicitors, it began, 'Our client Sir Henry Hoare has asked us to communicate with you on the following matter', and disclosed that the baronet owned an eighteenth-century house in Wiltshire with historic contents and 6,000 acres of which about 2,000 were woodland. There was no mention of the garden, one of the most famous in the south of England, which on its own merits without the rest would have been very acceptable. Sir Henry had in mind leaving by will the whole estate to the National Trust with investments at an approximate value of £150,000. How was he to set about it? The property had been strictly settled by Sir Henry upon certain male relations and their male issue. Ah, that was the rub: those entails which presented every sort of obstacle, and expense, to disentangle and re-entangle, which all lawyers delighted in. On the letter MacLeod Matheson scribbled in pencil, 'I think no likelihood of Trust refusing.' I should think not indeed. The secretary was very busy. I had not been on the staff a month and was considered too new, inexperienced and altogether ineligible to visit. So Christopher Gibbs, my senior by one year on the staff with a land agent's training to boot, was sent to inspect.

Stourhead house was understandably not on the sacred 'definitive' list of the 230 most important country houses of England and Wales because the centre block had been gutted by fire in 1902 and rebuilt first by a local architect Doran Webb, and after his dismissal by Sir Aston Webb (no relation), fabricator-to-be of the façade of Buckingham Palace. Although nearly all the contents had been miraculously saved from the furnace and the two flanking wings were intact, perhaps it would not qualify. Christopher Gibbs however was bowled over. The contents were superb, not only the furniture specially made by Thomas Chippendale the younger for the surviving library and picture gallery, but also the books which filled the library from floor to ceiling, and the paintings and family portraits which crammed the picture gallery, and spilt into passages and other rooms of the house. There was also the superlative landscape garden of lakes, temples, grottoes and follies, contrived by Henry Hoare, styled the Magnificent, between 1741 and 1785. This paradise, enclosed by wonderfully tended trees composing those 2,000 acres of woodland, and beyond them the splendidly well-ordered agricultural land, appealed to him more than the rest. Christopher, who had been invited to luncheon, was understandably impressed. 'Exceptionally beautiful' was his verdict upon the whole.

Stourhead was the first property offered to the National Trust under its country houses scheme. Sir Henry Hoare had read the brochure, lent him by a neighbouring owner of an historic house which was on the list of 230, and was interested. As it happened Stourhead was not to be the first country house estate actually taken over. Eleven years were to elapse before it was vested in the National Trust.

The usual correspondence was set in motion (if motion be the right word) between Sir Henry Hoare's and the National Trust's solicitors. The usual family trusts had to be dissolved, not without a plethora of supposititious complications first being envisaged by the respective attorneys. The most pressing quandary was how to convey by will the revenue-producing agricultural land without involving Sir Henry's heir in a high rate of death duties. For a moment Sir Henry even considered making over the property immediately, subject to life interests to himself and his wife only. To this end the Trust had a detailed report prepared by Messrs Whatley Hill & Co., estate agents and surveyors. Then Sir Henry changed his mind. Like most gentlemen landowners in emergencies he believed in always going to the top. He took the matter up with Sir John Simon, Chancellor of the Exchequer. Simon confirmed by letter, a copy of which Sir Henry sent me, that as the law stood, any farmland, no matter whether of natural beauty or not, conveyed by will with an historic house, would be liable for death duties. Sir Henry wrote in a covering letter that even to avoid possible future taxes he could not after all bring himself to part with Stourhead by gift. Fortunately the obstacle was eventually overcome by the passage of the National Trust Act of 1937 whereby devised endowment land, provided it was classifiable as being of natural beauty and declared by the Trust inalienable, would not be taxable.

In fact the Hoare negotiations did not present as many problems as some others. Sir Henry and Lady Hoare had had but one child, a son Harry who was the apple of their eye. He was a casualty of the first war. His loss dimmed the whole of their subsequent existence which was devoted to making Stourhead into his enduring monument. Although his spirit was everywhere present at Stourhead his name was never mentioned. Once only Lady Hoare let fall before me that the then heir to the baronetcy, a distant cousin, or maybe his parents since he too had served in the Kaiser's war, had been disinherited by Sir Henry, because he or they omitted to write a condolence letter on Harry's death. Instead another more distant cousin Rennie Hoare was made Sir Henry's residuary legatee (there was a large property outside the acreage designated for the National Trust), and it was he whom Sir Henry decided should enjoy the option to reside at Stourhead.

So happily did negotiations proceed that the following year Sir Henry contributed handsomely to the Trust's appeal for funds to save Glastonbury Tor. Sir Henry made no secret of his intentions with regard to the Trust and many people assumed that the place already belonged to it. The Bristol Museum even pressed us to return to the city the Edward III stone cross which the citizens had removed from the High Street in 1762 and which Henry Hoare the Magnificent salvaged and re-erected near the entrance to the gardens at Stourhead. They now wanted the cross back. Sir Henry instructed me to issue a stern refusal. Indeed he expected the Trust, in anticipation of its inheritance, to be supportive. They have continued to be. Twice within recent years Bristol City have asked for the cross back again; and twice two stern refusals have been issued in the spirit of Sir Henry.

Until the outbreak of the last war I saw a good deal of the Hoares. In May 1939 I took a distinguished party of the French *Les Demeures Historiques* to Stourhead for the day. The Hoares gave a princely reception and were extremely gracious and hospitable. The members, nearly all country house owners themselves, were fascinated by their hosts. They said they had never met any people quite so archaic. It is true that Sir Henry was a bluff John Bullish figure in his unvarying pepper-and-salt knickerbockers winter and summer, and a fawn billy-cock (he is the only man I ever saw wearing a hat at luncheon). He was impatient and a little alarming, but astute and wise, and absolutely dedicated to Stourhead. Set in his ways he was singularly old-fashioned, which was not altogether surprising for his father had been born in 1804 and his grandfather (who was also his wife Alda's great-grandfather) in 1762. When he succeeded to the baronetcy from an improvident cousin in 1894 the estate was in a deplorable condition –

he described it as practically derelict. He spent his life resurrecting and improving it.

Lady Hoare was enchanting. Tall, upright and tightly corseted, she had not altered her style of dress since the day their son Harry died. She wore a long trailing skirt, and a net blouse with whalebone collar gripping the neck. Her greying, wire-like hair was puffed out like a ring of Saturn round the head. She had jet-black eyebrows over spectacles with extremely thick lenses. A tremendous reader and annotator of books she was unsparing of praise and denunciation. She adored and hated people in public life and worshipped the memory of Thomas Hardy whom and his two successive wives she knew intimately. The great writer would submit drafts of poems to her; and his *Song of the Soldiers*, published in *The Times* in September 1914, was inspired by young Harry's enlistment to fight. She was no less devoted to Stourhead than her husband and until old age thought nothing of walking ten miles a day round the estate. She positively encouraged the public to visit the gardens. 'I love the trippers,' she wrote to the Hardys in 1911, '& love to see them enjoying themselves. Besides, I think one's no right to, always, shut a thing up, that others want to see.' The fact that she spoke fluent French endeared her to the members of *Les Demeures Historiques*.

In May 1939 Sir Henry was much upset in coming upon a person from the Air Ministry making a survey for an aerodrome just south of Stourton village and less than half a mile from the house. He wrote to the National Trust. Would they please at once take steps to stop it? Matheson wrote to Professor Patrick Abercrombie, chairman of the Council for the Preservation of Rural England, who pronounced the scheme an 'absolute calamity'. The Trust's chairman Lord Zetland wrote to the Secretary of State for Air, Sir Kingsley Wood. Sir Henry rallied the Duke of Somerset, hinting that he might rescind his will.

The Air Ministry denied that it wanted 500 acres in the middle of the Stourhead estate, but was cagey about how much it did want. So the National Trust wrote a letter to *The Times*, published on 6 June. There was much sympathetic response from readers; and several friendly estate agencies suggested acceptable alternative sites for the aerodrome. Sir Henry told Air Commodore Donald, who paid him a reassuring call, that if the Ministry went ahead, he would not merely scrap his will but break up and sell the whole estate piecemeal. He could not 'stand the worry and racket of it'. He too sent a letter to *The Times*, reiterating this decision. The Trust had 1,000 copies of it printed for circulation by dozens of amenity societies like the Georgian Group and suitably responsive individuals in the locality like the Duke of Somerset and Lord Cranborne. A body of protesting Members formed in the House of Commons.

On 28 June Sir Kingsley Wood, faced by this battery of opposition, decided not to proceed with the aerodrome, 'in consideration of all the factors'. He regretted the oversight in not having warned the National Trust of his intentions, now nullified. Sir Henry was overjoyed, thanked the Trust warmly for its pains and offered to defray the expense of sending out the leaflets. Gratefully the secretary sent Sir Henry the total bill, amounting to £4.18s.10d.

The rejoicing was not long lasting. Nine weeks later came the war and the land was requisitioned for much-needed training flights and a camp, to be ready for service by the spring of 1941 at the latest. Abercrombie, who was then adviser to the Air Ministry on planning, told them that the Stourhead site must be held only for the duration of the war and all buildings be of a temporary sort. The Ministry accepted these conditions and undertook not to lay down hard runways, and to make do with grass. The buildings would be restricted to wooden huts. Of course few of these terms were adhered to. Finally the Ministry begged Sir Henry and the National Trust to appreciate that the war had reached a critical stage.

Matheson thanked the Under-Secretary of State for Air, Captain Harold Balfour, for his courteous way with Sir Henry who was naturally upset by the reversal of affairs but was prepared to accept it in the distressing bellicose circumstances. 'I am in great difficulties at present', Sir Henry wrote to Matheson, 'in trying to find a butler. We have got a good old man in the pantry but want a really active, reliable working butler.'

Communion with Sir Henry and Lady Hoare during the war was on the whole calm and intermittent. In 1942 Sir Henry appealed to us to prevent the Mere and Tisbury Rural District Council from taking the late-Georgian drive gates for scrap. I successfully enlisted the help of F.J.E. Raby, permanent head of the ancient monuments section of the Ministry of Works, on the legitimate grounds of the gates' historic interest. Raby, roused from his scholar's lethargy, duly averted this particular threat of vandalism from the overzealous local authorities. My furtherance of the good news to Sir Henry provoked another piteous plea, 'We are in terrible difficulties in carrying on here ... We now want a cook *and* a butler. We have only got a boy of 17 and he will shortly be called up.' As it was they kept five indoor servants in place of the pre-war ten.

It is easy enough today to be shocked and disapproving of the Hoares' attitude. But for people in their position who had been born in mid-Victorian times and owned enormous houses, lack of adequate staff was a hideous deprivation. The husbands hadn't a clue how to set about the most superficial housework, not to mention how to turn on and off the heating system. The wives often couldn't boil an egg. They were too old to adapt to their adversity. They could not move into the lodge with one servitor as ancient as themselves and leave the great house either to rot or to fall to the mercy of troops, lunatics or Borstal boys. Their plight was often insoluble, and in many cases brought their grey hairs in sorrow to premature graves.

In spite of their domestic woes the Hoares insisted on my staying a night in October in order to discuss at leisure a variety of problems concerning furniture and pictures and Sir Henry's offer to leave with the home farm the live and dead stock of great value. He impressed on me that I must get the Executive Committee to agree to carry on the farm and his pedigree herd of cattle.

The committee did agree and so I wrote to tell him, adding that they hoped to be able to maintain the pedigree herd. I received a disgruntled letter beginning: 'At the end of a very long life I have found *hope* a lean diet . . . this is not what I expected.' In reply I thought fit to quote the exact words of the committee's minute which, while gratefully accepting the offer, would 'endeavour to carry out Sir Henry's wishes'. He wrote asking for a more definite assurance. At their next meeting the committee reworded the minute thus: 'The Trust would gratefully accept the dairy herd . . . and carry on the farm through Countryside Trust [a device to satisfy the Inland Revenue that the National Trust did not engage in trade] or some similar means and maintain the pedigree herd in accordance with his wishes to the best of their ability, though without any legal obligation to do so.' On 18 December Sir Henry wrote that he was more or less satisfied. And there the matter rested.

Meanwhile he wrote to Matheson, 'We are up against it now, as our only housemaid is leaving. Only a char left.' They were living in practically two downstairs rooms and an upstairs bed- and dressing-room, and seldom had visitors. The greater part of the house was 'shut up or occupied by a squadron of the liaison regiment free of charge, 6 to 7 officers and about fifty men' who were no trouble. Indeed I was present when the squadron said their goodbyes, and I don't know whether Lady Hoare or the officers were nearer to tears. 'Please find me a housemaid,' Sir Henry reiterated. To which sad petition Matheson responded, 'I have been looking for one for my mother.'

Now the trouble was that although the squadron and I found Lady Hoare infinitely charming, entertaining and sympathetic, servants found her impossibly exacting. Notwithstanding her and Sir Henry's withdrawal into reduced quarters the remaining bedrooms and reception rooms were not put under dust-sheets. They were left to gather both dust and moth. Moreover they were cluttered with knick-knacks to an extent hardly credible by a housewife of today. There are on view in the house photographs of the staterooms before the fire when the Hoares were a young married couple. Except for the lack of potted plants, ferns, aspidistras and palms, owing to the greenhouses no longer functioning, the rooms in the 1940s were no less inspissated. There were occasional-tables bursting with bric-à-brac, miniatures, beads, buttons, rings and trinkets of every description. On every shelf and piano lid were forests of silver trowels, silver vases containing decayed peacocks' feathers and silver photograph frames of relations, maharajas and royalty. And the housemaids were expected to keep these things polished and cleaned even when the rooms were ostensibly not in use. One palsied glance at the picture gallery by an untrained, still un-called-up village girl during the war was enough to send her fleeing the premises before listening to Lady Hoare's severe injunctions to treat every object as tenderly as she would her little sister.

Poor Sir Henry's epistolary plaints became as regular as the moon's phases. I used to dread the familiar headed writing paper, beginning 'Dear Lees-Milne' and ending, 'Please do *something*.' They were invariably signed with the old-fashioned, even eighteenth-century abbreviation of the Christian name, 'Hy Hoare'. In March 1943 a repetition of the *cri de coeur* reached me, 'We are in great difficulty here being reduced to only three servants, all of them old,' to be followed by another in September, 'We are up against it again. Our cook has given notice as she can get on with none of the servants here.' They needed another cook and a kitchen maid. In October: 'We have only got two permanent servants . . . The strain is breaking us both.' Lady Hoare was then 83, he 78. Would the National Trust please apply to the Ministry of Labour? This was always an unwelcome task for me. The Ministry were surprisingly tolerant and tried to be helpful. They would investigate a case once, if not twice, but they were seldom of use. I rang them up. They could supply two part-timers. A month went by. 'We are up against it again,' wrote Sir Henry. 'The married couple are hopeless.' I have no doubt they were. They came from Brixton, and would doubtless have gone anywhere to get away from the bombing. 'The

National Trust really ought to help.' The Ministry gave up. By June 1944 I received a further plea. 'We are desperate now.'

I began to feel as I do at the time of writing on hearing over the radio that a hundred thousand people in Bangladesh have been drowned by a tidal wave. It is very dreadful, but what can I do? At least I can send £10 to Chittagong, but the equivalent (?10 shillings) in 1944 would not have been well received at Stourhead. Poor Sir Henry's plight was momentarily distracted by a dreadful disaster. In August of that year he wrote that an American aircraft had crashed into Alfred's Tower, one of the Magnificent's most conspicuous landscape features built in 1772 on the edge of the estate, and knocked off 30 foot of the top. The airmen were killed. John MacGregor, doyen of the SPAB restorers of ancient buildings, went to assess the damage. A fortnight later Sir Henry wrote to me, 'The Ministry is most unbusinesslike. What we need is a housemaid. Surely with so many people evacuated from London, etc., etc.' Well, few people evacuated from London were qualified to polish silver vases with peacocks' feathers and none was forthcoming. Sir Henry, tormented by his desperate condition, decided to make a deed of gift of Stourhead without delay, as though that might induce the Trust to conjure up a housemaid. He soon changed his mind. When he learned in 1945 that Matheson was leaving the Trust he wrote him a very sweet letter for so seemingly unemotional a man, ending up with the news that although they still needed a housemaid they fortunately had a chef. By September he told me, 'I engaged a man as pantryman. He only stopped three weeks.'

When the war ended the poor old people managed somehow to rally a makeshift indoor staff, albeit the most obliging, untrained dailies were for them small compensation for professional, residential servants, although most owners of large houses today probably feel the opposite. At first Sir Henry was very put out that the Air Ministry did not within a week of the war's end clear the airfield and remove every vestige of the huts. However within a year the last vestiges were happily gathered, surely a record achievement. It was a great relief to both of them in their declining months. They did not survive the war long. They died on the same day, 25 March 1947, without either realizing how seriously ill the other was. On that day the Stourhead estate, garden, house and contents became the Trust's property absolutely. That is to say all but those outlying farms which were left to Mr Rennie Hoare. Some complications were caused by the fact that Sir Henry died a few hours before his wife. Thus some Hoare silver which, had Lady Hoare had time she would doubtless have passed on to the Trust with the other family possessions, went with her personalty to the Italian children of her sister Countess Visconti di Massimo, and was with difficulty bought back.

Whereas the farms and woodlands of Stourhead became the responsibility of the chief agent in London and the regional agent established in Stourton village, the house and works of art were the responsibility of me in London and Eardley Knollys who lived in Dorset.

I had found Eardley, whom previously I barely knew, on my return to the National Trust staff in 1942. He had lately been taken on as assistant to Matheson, who was left entirely on his own in 1939. During the remaining war years Eardley and I worked very closely together. Whereas the secretary was usually kept at head office we two spent a great deal of our time travelling, looking after existing Trust properties and inspecting prospective ones. Eardley was already a recognized authority on Post-Impressionist and early twentieth-century painters such as Modigliani, Utrillo and the Euston Road School. Until the war he owned the Storran Gallery in Knightsbridge. He was a close friend of Graham Sutherland, Edward Le Bas, Vanessa Bell, Duncan Grant and Clive Bell. In fact he moved on the fringes of Bloomsbury. But his interests in the arts were wide; and he dearly loved and understood architecture. He was extremely well qualified to become after the war south-west regional manager for the National Trust. His achievements on behalf of the National Trust were very considerable. He acquired amongst other properties the Stone Circle at Avebury and the Sandham Memorial chapel (with its Stanley Spencer murals), and turned Arlington Court in Devon, with its motley collection of birds' eggs, sea-shells, glass paperweights and model ships, into one of the most popular museums of the West Country.

Eardley shared a house at Long Crichel between Salisbury and Blandford with Edward Sackville-West, Desmond Shawe-Taylor and Raymond Mortimer. It became a notable centre of musical and literary criticism. Eardley's urge to become a painter himself led him in 1957 to give up the National Trust work and devote himself entirely to his obsession.

After Sir Henry and Lady Hoare quitted the scene together, the brunt of day-to-day care and maintenance of Stourhead was borne by Eardley. Since Rennie Hoare very properly exercised his moral right, laid down by Sir Henry and agreed by the Trust, to live in the house, Eardley and I quickly realized that a dichotomy of management between Rennie and the Trust's officials must at all costs be avoided. It was still very much the Trust's policy to encourage donors' descendants to regard the houses as their homes. At first Rennie Hoare was anxious to adopt the role of glorified caretaker. Not only was he very clever (he was a managing partner of Hoare's Bank and a member amongst other things of the Forestry Commission's regional advisory committee for south-west England), but also very fond of Stourhead with which his ties were strong. In 1947 he was impatient to move into the house as soon as certain structural alterations were done to façades and roofs. He had no intention of living on the pre-war scale of his old cousins. Although he would have unrestricted access to the staterooms and even use them whenever he wanted to, normally he and his family were to inhabit private quarters. The whole thing must have been a daunting prospect for his newly married young bride. While bringing her to England from Montego Bay, Jamaica, which she had never before left in her life, he received a cable on the liner announcing Sir Henry and Lady Hoare's deaths. Instead of the modest house to which she had expected to be introduced Margaret Hoare soon found herself plunged into an immense country seat with all the duties, and not all the liberties, of a squire's lady that were totally alien to her carefree upbringing.

Eardley and I foresaw from the start that the arrangement would be a tricky one. Rennie might not unnaturally regard the contents of Stourhead, inherited by generation after generation of Hoares, as his, and resent the interference of a bunch of alien officials. On the other hand the Trust were the owners on behalf of the nation, and responsibility for the works of art was solely theirs.

Rennie, accustomed to authority, was soon irked and felt bogged down by all of us with whom he had to deal. He could not resist taking matters into his own hands. After all he lived on the spot and knew before anyone else did what needed doing. It became insufferable to have to ask permission by telephone or letter before shifting a table or stool in the staterooms. So he would do it himself and be maddened when Eardley, with natural tact, or I who often lacked it, felt obliged to remonstrate, for we were endeavouring to arrange the rooms for the public to see. This necessitated some drastic elimination of the old Hoares' surplus clutter. If left where it was there literally would not have been space for the druggets, ropes and posts which were then deemed essential. To have a warden in every room, as the Trust does today, was then out of the question. Funds simply did not permit it.

The breath was barely out of Sir Henry's body before Anthony Blunt, Surveyor of the King's Pictures and director of the Courtauld Institute of Art, asked for the loan of Poussin's *Choice of Hercules* hanging in the picture gallery for an important exhibition. With Professor Water-house, reader in history of art at Manchester University, he promptly descended upon Stourhead. The two experts not only examined and approved the Poussin, which the Trust consented to lend, but made recommendations on how to rehang all the paintings in the house. Rennie was so taken by Waterhouse and impressed by his knowledge that he begged him to stay, and together they concocted all sorts of alterations without consulting Eardley. A further misunderstanding was caused by Rennie sacking Geddes Hyslop who had been employed as the Trust's architect for the interior conversions, repair of the garden temples and for the design and construction of a gazebo at the entrance to the garden for the sale of tickets.

I mention these teething troubles between a donor's heir (albeit in this case not a son but a fairly distant cousin) and the Trust as an example of differences bound to recur whenever an amicable as opposed to a strictly defined arrangement enforceable by rule and regulation, was drifted into. All the while Rennie Hoare was consist-ently polite, often extremely generous and always most hospitable to the National Trust staff.

To forestall similar differences over the garden Eardley and I advocated that all planting, which concerned species, grouping, colour and even texture of the delicate landscape tapestry, over which Rennie had no vested control, ought to be dictated by an individual, for apart from horticultural knowledge taste was a paramount consideration. We had in mind Vita Sackville-West or Lord Rosse, both highly respected garden owners serving on National Trust committees, or G.A. Jellicoe, the well-known president of the Institute of Landscape Architects, had one of these busy people been willing. It would have been a time-consuming commitment which unfortunately did not come about. Instead the task was entrusted to a handful of individuals, the Trust's gardens adviser Graham Stuart Thomas (who alone gave instructions to the head gardener) and two or three others, horticulturists and landscape historians. They formed a small, unofficial committee which met infrequently. What they chiefly accomplished was to madden and frustrate Graham Thomas who felt he would have got more work done on his own. For, what often happens with committees, questions of historic exactitude and taste were not always answered in chorus.

In 1978 these ambiguities and anomalies were finally resolved in a printed formula, which laid down conservation principles and rules of management particular to the outstanding Stourhead garden. The

Trust's regional director was to be in charge and give orders to the head gardener in consultation, whenever necessary, with the gardens adviser, the regional representative and one landscape historian (to be a member of the Trust's Garden Panel). This plan holds today.

The number of experts Eardley and I called upon for advice about the works of art seems almost legion. Mrs Arundell Esdaile came down to tell us how the plaster casts of the statues in the Pantheon, which were splitting, should be repaired. She was the leading authority on post-Reformation sculpture in England. Numerous names of Stuart and Georgian sculptors now familiar to historians were her discoveries. But Katharine Esdaile was very elusive. Once her attention was enlisted her knowledge was freely given and highly valued. But it was not easily won. I recall writing to Eardley (we always wrote to each other absolutely without inhibition) who felt obliged to cancel a date for her visit to Stourhead in 1948, 'You are an intolerable nuisance! To pin down Mrs Esdaile to a date is like spearing an eel and now you say I have got to start all over again. This will mean a spate of lunatic letters, making no sense whatever.' Her letters were seldom decipherable. But in the end we got her down. Calling at Wilton where she had been staying, I found her clutching a large sack, chewing cigarette ends as though they were rather tough beef and sitting on a public bench by the roadside. She made me drive off at a tangent to an obscure village, called Silton, to look at a standing monument in High Baroque style to a Wyndham judge, his two wives mourning at his feet, by John Nost. 'A stunner' she called it, and she was not far wrong. She wrote afterwards that she enjoyed herself at Stourhead enormously and her charges for the day were £2.10s. They were worth every penny. I gained the impression that apart from church monuments, of which her knowledge was inexhaustible, this erudite lady was totally oblivious of everyday things like clothes, food, trains, timetables and pounds, shillings and pence.

Stourhead proved a treasure house for the experts few of whom had been inside it when the old people lived there, or if they had, now felt free to pick their own way through the clutter and see the wood for the trees. Graham Reynolds, a gentle person with the manner of a mouse, and seemingly bent by care, came to examine the miniatures, Leigh Ashton the porcelain and Margaret Jourdain the furniture. Mrs M.I. Webb came twice to see the Rysbrack sculpture – any coincidence with Mrs Esdaile, the authority on Rysbrack's rival Roubiliac, having been carefully avoided. I found her pedantic and her niggling 'discoveries' very boring. Nevertheless I was grateful to her for correcting what I had to say about Rysbrack, Cheere and Flitcroft, the architect of Alfred's Tower, in my guidebook to Stourhead.

An expert of a very specialized sort had to be, and was found, in Mr Reece-Pemberton, to repair the large lunette south window of the library. The subject is a Gospel scene in painted glass by Francis Eginton, matching in size and shape three canvas panels of scenes from Raphael's *Parnassus* painted by Samuel Woodforde in the opposite lunette of the apartment. Reece-Pemberton revealed that the colours of Eginton's window were applied to clear glass on two sheets, the rear one painted in replica. When he finished his repairs it was impossible to see where the cracks in the glass had been.

The books at Stourhead presented their own problem. Apart from those in the library they were everywhere. It did not at the time seem to us that Lady Hoare had been discerning, although she was a selective reader. She was certainly a voracious one. There were hundreds of second-rate novels annotated by her extremely thick nib on the page margins and endpapers. Explosive interjections of indignation, 'Pshaw!' 'Rot!' and 'What next?' nestled against less frequent notes of approval, 'Splendid', 'Genius' and 'I agree!!' At a local sale we got £50 for what we described as 'Alda's books ruined by her scribbles'. Now that learned articles are written about her literary friendships our action may provoke comment. But I have minimal retrospective regret. I feel sure we let little go that had any intellectual significance.

In fact at an early stage we got the bibliophile Robert Gathorne-Hardy to sort through all the books in the library. Bob reported that it was, though large, not an outstandingly important country house library, mostly of eighteenth- and nineteenth-century books, of which the chief section was archaeological, the dominating collector having been Sir Richard Colt Hoare, the Regency traveller and historian of *Modern Wiltshire*. The next member of the Hoare family to leave a notable imprint was undoubtedly Alda. Bob described her as 'a striking personality [who] should not be extinguished, handsome, witty, widely read with a large knowledge of French literature'. For some reason much of her childhood had been spent in France and she remembered the privations undergone in Paris during the Commune. In addition to Hardy another of her intellectual contacts was Charles Whibley, scholar, critic and High Tory journalist. For years Whibley contributed to *Blackwood's Magazine*. He had been the friend of Marcel Schwob, Stéphane Mallarmé and Paul Valéry and from him Alda in her Wiltshire fastness delighted in listening to tales of *la vie bohème* on the Left Bank. Whibley was also a passionate Francophil. There were in the library many estate papers and accounts which with Rennie Hoare's and the Historic Buildings Committee's consent we deposited in the Wiltshire county record office.

A far greater problem than books was furniture. This simply had to be weeded out for practical reasons, as I have already indicated, first to enable the public to pass through the staterooms, and secondly to allow Rennie to bring his own to the rooms he was to occupy. Besides there was an immense amount in upstairs bedrooms, which was never likely to be used. Much of it had been brought to Stourhead by Sir Henry from Wavendon, the house in Buckinghamshire inherited from his father, and then saved from the 1902 fire. Some of this surplus furniture came in handy for other National Trust houses which were sparsely furnished, like Montacute and Lyme. Eardley and I were adamant that every stick that came from Stourhead must be listed as belonging to Stourhead, so that in years to come our successors should be in no doubts as to its provenance. Also we stipulated that those properties to which Stourhead furniture went should pay into the Stourhead account the expense of its removal. No doubt we made some mistakes, but they were not irrevocable. For instance we rather took against, and so either removed to or left in an upstairs store-room, several astonishing paintings by an Irish friend of the Hoares, called St George Hare. His idiosyncratic portraits with their period flavour of Sir Henry and Lady Hoare we of course left in the hall where they had hung them. But we did not think some of his allegorical and suggestively erotic paintings, like the semi-nude captive slave chained to a rock by the wrists with a butterfly hovering over her, either good art (how smug we were) or even then wholly suitable because of the slave's extraordinary likeness to Alda. Today there is a move among the National Trust staff, which I wholly commend, to bring into prominence these discarded paintings, so eloquent of their time and indicative of the late Victorians' and Edwardians' suppressed and almost kinky artistic tastes, and let visitors judge them for themselves. There may yet be revealed a more curious relationship between St George Hare and the fox-hunting Sir Henry and literary Lady Hoare than we are yet aware of.

I do not suppose that Eardley's and my choice of fabrics pleased everybody. It was always our tendency, whenever possible, to leave well alone, unless old stuffs were hopelessly threadbare. Certainly some chairs and sofas had to be recovered and curtains replaced.

There was much ado over the disposal of twelve out of a suite of twenty-four so-called *Marie Antoinette* chairs in the saloon. Handsome they were, and are, but have nothing to do with the French Queen, being solid English make of about 1740. Twenty-four were too many to show. Besides half of them were later reproductions. We thought fit to allow the reproductions to go on loan to Lyme Park, Cheshire, where Charlie Brocklehurst was anxious to have them. Lyme, a splendid Elizabethan and Georgian palace, was then practically empty. Lord Methuen, a member of the Historic Buildings Committee and owner of another great seat, Corsham Court, in Wiltshire, got to hear from Rennie what was afoot and was scandalized. He strongly objected to the set of *Marie Antoinette* chairs being split up and told Eardley so in no uncertain terms. Methuen complained to Lord Esher; Rennie complained to Lord Crawford, the Trust's chairman. Brocklehurst, when he supposed he was not going to get his dozen, announced that he would take no furniture from Stourhead at all. Eardley, hurt and piqued, complained to the then secretary, Admiral Bevir, that unless he and I were allowed a free hand he for one would decline to have any further truck with the Stourhead arrangements. Let us, he pleaded, get on with the job, and when it is finished then by all means let members of committees and anyone else interested visit, criticize and approve or veto. The Admiral, whose role at the Trust was short-lived, shunned all kinds of unpleasantness and calls upon his authority. Totally untarred by the quarterdeck, he must have been the best-intentioned and least assertive sailor whom the Royal Navy had ever raised to high rank. He wished his subordinates health and happiness and begged them not to squabble amongst themselves. At this particular juncture he handed over the reins to Lord Esher. Esher was, as usual, sympathetic towards us, and wise. He decreed that we should be given a free hand in the arrangements and in the meanwhile not get rid of any Stourhead furniture that was not clearly junk until his committee saw the finish of our labours. In other words Paul Methuen, whom I liked very much, admired as an artist and respected when he was not truculent (he was addicted to bees in the bonnet), was asked to pipe down.

I know that Eardley's and my painful choice of a red damask-type wallpaper of rather mean design on a gold background for the lamentable saloon positively shocked a number of good-taste connoisseurs. John Fowler observed in his straight-faced, would-be impartial, ironical manner, which I dearly relished, 'Laddie, it is what you would expect to find in the Bewlay-House pipe shop.' To which I retorted that the saloon, reconstructed after the fire of 1902, with the fine original coved and plaster-panelled ceiling obliterated, and all the proportions reinterpreted just wrong, looked from the hands of the Edwardian

Webbs exactly like a Bewlay-House tobacconist's and to just such a shop we deliberately intended the walls to conform. This may have been a slightly tendentious evasion of a merited rebuke. At all events our successors have cleverly and at little cost moderated the wallpaper's offensiveness by spraying out the gold background.

Eardley and I spent many a day sorting, eliminating, arranging and shifting the furniture at Stourhead. There can be few if any pieces, save Pope Sixtus V's solid marble cabinet in the alcove of the room called after it, that we did not move and carry with our own hands or upon our own backs. There seldom was any manual help at Stourhead. As for Le Sueur's bronze bust of Charles I, for a long time I could hardly bring myself to look at it. On one occasion its weight caused the worst attack of sciatica I have ever suffered from. Since that near collapse of my spine its matt brown surface has been partially gilded as apparently it was meant to be. Whenever I now inadvertently meet the monarch's eyes they have a slightly less menacing glint than they had forty-three years ago. Nevertheless I say to him reproachfully, 'You may be called the Martyr King, but what about me?'

Rennie Hoare's son Henry (now chairman of Hoare's Bank) no longer lives in the house, but on the estate, the greater part of which was left by Sir Henry to his father. But he takes a lively interest in the property. Furthermore he and his son Timothy have the option, as understood by Sir Henry's memorandum of wishes, to reoccupy a part of the house, an option which one or the other may well one day exercise.

The administrator has a flat on the premises and a member of the Trust's headquarter's staff rents another.

The spectacular landscape garden laid out by Henry the Magnificent is open to the public every day of the year, and the house every day of the summer except Thursdays and Fridays. In the spring and autumn access to the house is limited according to the estimated demands made by the public and the dictates of good husbandry.

CHAPTER SIX

ABRAHAM OF LITTLE MORETON
Cheshire

THROUGHOUT our childhood our parents went annually to
Scotland, not for the 'Glorious Twelfth', but towards the middle
of September when for them the end of the school summer
holidays was blissfully looming. They would drive in an open touring
car, my sister, brother and I on the back seat, the luggage strapped
behind under tarpaulins which loosened and flapped. At breakfast soon
after dawn my father, who kept to a very strict timetable, announced
that we might stop to look at his favourite building *en route*. We would,
allowing for punctures, arrive at 11.35 prompt, to resume at midday. So
from a tender age I became familiar with Little Moreton Hall. As we
approached some familiar landmark on the road my father, consulting
his watch to check the time, would announce, 'You wouldn't think it.
But it belongs to a bishop with a biblical name who was an Old Etonian.'
This never-failing statement became a family joke. How my father
became aware of the astonishing information I never discovered.
Someone must once have told him and there lurked in his mind the
curious discrepancy of a man called Abraham being a Christian
ecclesiastic, owning an historic country house and having been educated at *our* school. Sure enough, as I subsequently discovered, my
father was right. But he did not know that Mrs Abraham was the niece
of William Cory (Johnson), eccentric paedophiliac usher at Eton (who
left under a cloud) and author of the poem, 'They told me Heraclitus,
they told me you were dead'. Had he known I doubt if he would have
been pleased.

Aware of my father's intense reverence for Little Moreton Hall,
according to his taste the most beautiful house in the British Isles, which
implied the world, I would tease him every time we approached a
modern county council cottage with the suspicion of a half-timbered
gable, of which in the 1920s there were many, by calling out, 'There's

Little Moreton Hall!' This joke, unlike the other, would pall after the first few miles of the hundred and more to be covered before we reached the sacred shrine. By the time I reached the tiresome age of sophisticated 17 I absolutely hated the building and despised it as the nadir of architectural style. This was foolish of me and a prejudice long since reversed. For now I admire and even love Little Moreton Hall. I love it for its autochthonous sincerity, its absolutely unpretentious happy-go-luckiness, its having sprung like some portentous growth from Midlands soil, and its undeniable picturesque jollity. The close oblique view from the Newcastle–Congleton road of the absurd half-timbered structure, crowned by an unbroken length of gallery window like some fantastic, elongated Chinese lantern, and toppling, if not positively bending over the tranquil water of a moat, the whole an ancient pack of cards about to meet from the first puff of wind its own reflection, is something which once seen can never be forgotten.

Little did I then suppose that in ten years time I would be instrumental in preserving it for ever. I hope the small part I played has gone some way to redeem my priggish pretension that the classical was the only acceptable style of building, and my beastliness to my father.

I can see now the reverent, almost hushed manner in which my father, extending both arms, would walk across the narrow bridge over the moat to the gatehouse door, half medieval, half Tudor Renaissance, and wholly English and cosy, and declaim the house's beauties. Then he would fumble in his pocket for the sixpenny pieces demanded for adult admission and protest that surely his lanky offspring qualified for the half price of infants.

Until the present century the ownership of Little Moreton Hall had passed, certainly since King John's reign, and maybe earlier by descent. In the mid-thirteenth century one Geoffrey, a younger son of Sir Graham de Lostock, inherited the property from his father and changed his name to de Moreton. After Geoffrey it went from father to son without a break down to the mid-eighteenth century. The long line of Moretons were prosperous but fairly undistinguished squires and squarsons. William Moreton supported Charles I in the Civil War, was imprisoned and with his son Edward suffered forfeiture of land and benefices by Parliament. Edward's son, another William, sympathized with James II, and became Bishop of Kildare and Meath. Then in 1763 a niece of the Bishop transferred the property to her son Richard Taylor who assumed the Moreton surname. In 1884 Richard's grand-daughter Annabella Moreton (Mrs Craigie) became heiress. She lived at Pau, seldom came to England and was embarrassed by her inheritance.

When she died in 1892 the Hall, which had not been regularly inhabited by the family since the seventeenth century, and had been only partly lived in by tenant farmers, was in a state of dreadful disrepair. Indeed the structure had plumbed the depth of its long decline. Even in 1797 a tenant reported that she was obliged to use 'every endeavour to prevent the rain from doing damage to the sealings below'.

Nevertheless from late Georgian to early Victorian times Little Moreton was beloved by antiquarians who came from near and far in pilgrimage. It featured in textbooks like Britton's *Architectural Antiquities of Great Britain* (1808), Habershon's *Ancient Half-Timbered Houses of England* (1836) and Nash's famous *Mansions of the Olden Time* (1839–49). The Norfolk painter John Sell Cotman did a series of drawings in 1806, one of which showed the great hall with long table (in place today) and bench, and hens pecking at the earthen floor. The painter James West visiting in 1847 depicted the chapel in use as a coal cellar and the main rooms piled with junk. He was free to wander all round the building at will. 'I had groped and stumbled into every available corner disturbing much ancient dust and alarming many venerable spiders,' he wrote.

Gradually however the condition of Little Moreton Hall was to improve. Mrs Craigie left the property to an unmarried sister Elizabeth, the last of the Moretons by descent. She was a Sister of the Clewer Society of St John the Baptist, given leave to visit the house only from time to time when she stayed nearby with her agent. She was immensely proud of and devoted to the old place. Its preservation amounted to all that her loving hands and limited funds allowed. She prevented a total collapse of the long gallery by insertion of iron struts under the ceiling and brick buttresses against the substructure. She restored and re-furnished the chapel. Little Moreton's survival is chiefly due to the Sister of Mercy.

In 1892 Sister Elizabeth wrote to a second cousin on her mother's side, who was not of Moreton blood, offering to leave him the property on the strict condition that he did not sell it. Charles Thomas Abraham was a young curate with little money and son of a Bishop of Wellington in New Zealand, whose missionary zeal Sister Elizabeth admired. The Revd Charles Thomas recalled in later years how one fine day he took a train from Lichfield to Kidsgrove station to inspect the old house of which he had never before heard. On walking across fields he saw from a rise by Scholar Green a shaft of sunlight strike the chequered mass of lath and timber in the distance, and instantly fell in love with it. It became his dream house and he determined to live there on his retirement, which in fact he was never able to do. This was the first of many visits to Little Moreton during his cousin's lifetime. To Abraham too posterity owes a deep debt of gratitude. Twenty years later he inherited Little Moreton which for the remainder of his days was the object of ceaseless care, expense, worry and joy. By 1912 he was appointed Vicar of Bakewell and Suffragan Bishop of Derby.

He instantly sought the advice of his friend the eminent architect Sir Reginald Blomfield. Blomfield put him in touch with A.R. Powys, a sibling of the well-known brotherhood of writers and for many years secretary to the Society for the Protection of Ancient Buildings and author of the great textbook, *Repair of Ancient Buildings*. The society's leading architect-craftsman William Weir, who had once been William Morris's secretary and Philip Webb's favourite pupil, took charge of Little Moreton Hall for the rest of his working life. The dour little Scot, with his prim manner, sandy moustache, twinkling eyes under an everlasting pork-pie hat seldom taken off, was the first of several SPAB experts to 'repair' – for 'restore' is a word banned by the society – this important Tudor building throughout the ensuing decades. The first thing Weir did was to clear away the ivy smothering the south-east corner of the house.

In years to come I gleaned much from Weir about the treatment of old buildings for he was a direct link with the Pre-Raphaelite and Arts and Crafts founders of the SPAB in 1877. I sometimes accompanied him to various National Trust properties, and it was wonderful to watch him actively scrambling over roof-tops and under floor-boards, and to hear him explain in his soft Scots accent the mysteries of medieval craftsmanship. Never can a man have been more dedicated to his calling. He led a nomadic existence, having no office, and seemingly no real home. But there was always an address which found him. He was his own master, with a handful of peripatetic craftsmen whom he called upon at will. He was methodical, scrupulous and reliable; in fact businesslike. Totally without airs and graces he did not direct his pupils so much as convey by example, and the work of his own hands, how things should be done. He treated old buildings with the reverence of a priest towards the vessels on his altar. His principle was to preserve every vestige of old stonework, brickwork, woodwork or plasterwork so far as that were possible. I hold his memory in profound veneration and regret that circumstances did not allow me to become one of his pupils, if indeed he would have countenanced the idea. However, his great experience and methods were passed on to other worthy disciples, the chief of whom was probably John MacGregor, until a few years ago technical adviser to the SPAB and himself a master craftsman and architect in the undeviating Weir tradition.

In a cellar of the old house the Bishop resurrected all the pewter plate used by the Tudor and Stuart Moretons, and from the kitchen retrieved the great hall table and splendid oak spice chest mentioned in an inventory of 1601, and from beneath layers of plaster refuse the octagonal oak table and the original Moreton armorial glass belonging to the great hall windows.

In 1936 Joan Royden, honorary secretary of the Cheshire branch of the Council for the Preservation of Rural England, alerted the National Trust to the condition of Little Moreton Hall which she said alarmed her. This admirable lady who in spinsterhood totally and, even after marriage, partially kept a weather eye on every old building and every square mile of unspoilt landscape within her region, may not then have been aware that the Hall's somewhat seedy and distressed state was perennial and always had been, longer than anybody could remember; that bits and pieces fell off year by year and had to be stuck back again as best as could be afforded; that suspended decay was its natural state and that, although it should not be trumpeted abroad, constituted its ineffable charm. Some reasons for her anxiety might have been attributed, had I but thought the matter out at the time, to the highly contrasting condition of her father's amazing composite house in which she kept her office. For Hill Bark at Frankby in the Wirral was G.E. Grayson and Edward Ould's half-timbered masterpiece, if not wholly modelled on then certainly copied as regards window grouping from Little Moreton Hall. It was built for Robert Hudson the soap king in 1891, and was taken down and miraculously re-erected at Frankby between 1929 and 1931. Hill Bark was exceedingly spruce and meticulously maintained, as it was meant to be, with not an exposed beam out of the true, a terracotta finial missing a spike, a door latch a thong or a carved motto the stroke of a letter. I stayed there once or twice for Joan Royden was extremely hospitable to the National Trust staff and the most generous and appreciative helper of any enterprise we might be engaged in near Liverpool or Birkenhead and in her part of the world.

I suppose that Bishop Abraham somehow got to hear of our shared anxieties through the Trust's unwonted visits to Little Moreton Hall and enquiries of the caretaker, for the house was regularly open to the public. He wrote a rather aggrieved letter to the secretary of the National Trust asking to see a member of the staff in London. I was deputed to meet the Bishop at his club, the Oxford and Cambridge in Pall Mall, one July day of 1936. I was ushered by a footman up the spacious staircase of that imposing neo-classical institution and shown into the library. The Bishop was a delightful old man with white hair, a soft mouth and slanting lids over eyes that radiated benignity and kindliness. He immediately ordered tea and talked for nearly two hours. He told me the whole story of his inheritance from Sister Elizabeth and his endeavours to keep the Hall going on his own slender means throughout the war until 1931 when he handed it over to his son Rupert, then living abroad. Even so he still had to look after it on the absent son's behalf. It distressed him that Cheshire people and the preservation societies should be criticizing him for not spending more on the house than he could afford. At least structurally the house was then sound. The gist of this conversation was confirmed in a long letter in which he thanked the National Trust for its interest and concern. 'Your enquiry of late', he told the secretary, 'was too good a chance for me to get the truth about the old hall, as far as known to me, into your hands for preservation if you choose, or at any rate for perusal, and I hope to increase the assurance that in my hands care has been taken for 25 years. I can promise that the care will not be relaxed.' Such was the courtesy of a diffident, unassuming and distinguished cleric of the old school. Most country house owners of his day might have strongly resented what they would term the rank interference of a public body.

It was not long before Bishop Abraham and his son decided that it was in everyone's interest for Little Moreton Hall to be taken over by the National Trust. After all it was a black-and-white elephant which never could become a family residence. It had absolutely no mod. cons. They could never be provided without ruining the building and destroying the ethos of an unaltered Tudor relic. Its rooms were devoid of all decoration and furniture dating after the sixteenth century, its walls, ceilings and floors being bare to the bone, basic, in a sense void. Father and son Abraham offered the property provided the Bishop could be reimbursed the £4,000 he had spent on it over the years. The old man was extremely reluctant to appear to be making money out of Little Moreton. The Trust undertook to raise the funds plus £2,000 still needed for urgent repairs. It estimated that no endowment was needed, and that sufficient money would be forthcoming from the gate. It had not a penny of its own to contribute to the total sum to be raised.

How on earth was the Trust to raise it? Matheson the secretary began begging from the rich in Manchester and Liverpool, and the county palatine of Cheshire. He got £1,000 from Lord Leverhulme, £250 from the Duke of Westminster and a promise of £500 from the county council. The Bishop himself contributed rather quixotically another

£500; and later generously agreed to accept less than the £4,000 originally asked for. His agent, Mr J.H. Pardoe of Cawthorne, who loved Little Moreton no less fervently than his employer, offered to manage the property, when acquired, for the National Trust free of charge, save out-of-pocket expenses. Then we got stuck.

The Bishop consented to the issue of a public appeal. Joan Royden was active in preparing and printing leaflets and having me to stay. The appeal dragged on. Response was minimal. Contributions came in driblets. Finally the National Trust in a sort of desperation agreed to take over the property without having reached the target because of the building's importance and the anxiety, age and frailty of the Bishop.

He was mightily relieved and lived well into the Second World War. He gave the Trust his blessing in all we did, confident in our continued employment of William Weir as architect. Once only he was moved to unwonted ire, fortunately not directed against the Trust. It came to his ears that the vicar, a 'so-called Canon Alcock' of Odd Rode in which parish Little Moreton was situated, in league with a certain Bishop Vibert Jackson, contemplated 'improvements' to the chapel and its use for services according to rites which Bishop Abraham strongly disapproved of. 'Both of them are members', he fulminated in a letter to the secretary, 'of a small, self-complacent and ignorant clique of Anglo-Catholics who despise English Catholicism and ape everything Italian, just when many Roman Catholics, learned Liturgiologists are denouncing Italian and honouring the old Eastern and Western uses (other than Roman) and especially the old English uses.' Moreover Alcock was not a canon at all. I remember being amazed by the vituperation of this mild and saintly man over a sacerdotal issue of seemingly minor importance.

I am glad that for several years the Trust managed to preserve the farmyard flavour of Little Moreton Hall which I had remembered since childhood. The tenants were kept on. I rejoiced that their name was Dale, for they claimed to be descendants of the Elizabethan craftsman who built and carved the fabulous canted bay windows of the courtyard for William Moreton in 1559, leaving the date and inscription, 'Richard Dale Carpeder Made Thies Windows By the Grac of God.' Mrs (Louisa) Dale, the farmer's mother, was still allowed to take the entrance money while visitors were left to roam wherever they wished unaccompanied. This latitude and the fire hazard in so inflammable a building is now dreadful to think back on. And sometimes unauthorized hooligans penetrated while the gatehouse was left unattended. In February 1941 Lady Annabel Crewe, a daughter of Lord Crewe, a founder committee member of the National Trust, wrote to the secretary complaining that she had been to Little Moreton, found no bell to ring, saw no one in charge, and walked all round the house at leisure, without being confronted by a soul even when she went out. Nevertheless until she became infirm Mrs Dale provided delicious scrambled eggs, home-made scones and tea from a huge pot encased in a woollen cosy resembling a fat brown hen, while chickens scampered across the courtyard cobbles (without actually invading the great hall), and cows ambled up to the moat (and only occasionally beyond).

But with increasing numbers of visitors this delightful and lack-adaisical manner of running an historic monument was soon consi-dered unprofessional and out-of-date. Mrs Dale's daughters proved less picturesque and less efficient than the mother. After the old lady was asked to sell the official guidebook in lieu of her own rather fanciful effusion and to remove her brand-new suite of furniture from the show rooms, and told that 'nails must not be driven into the panelling' for the hanging of watercolours of dogs dressed as acrobats, the Dale family retired into limbo. I was sorry about their departure but it was inevitable.

Today the overall picture of Little Moreton Hall is somewhat different. Gone are the dog kennels and the nettles within the moat. Gone are the chickens and cows – and the eggs and the cream. Instead a fancy knot garden, exactly reproducing what the Tudor Moretons may possibly have had, or if they didn't, ought to have had, graces the east front, hitherto obscured by rubbish. The greenest of dwarf box borders form polyhedrons filled with grey gravel or grass. A yew tunnel and neatly kept borders of consciously period plants, even standard gooseberries, enliven the surroundings. Mown lawn now slopes into the moat, no longer stagnant and weed-choked, but clean and clear and swarming with fat carp. The west garden has been left more or less an orchard though far sprucer than of yore.

Visually the structure is much the same as when I first knew it although when decayed old beams have to be replaced the Trust now leaves their substitutes in the natural grey. This has given rise to criticism from those who maintain that the Little Moreton Hall beams were always tarred black. How then are we to explain a water-colour of *circa* 1886, hanging in the house? It shows the beams of the house definitely untarred, even ochre-coloured, as are the fillings. This surface may have been some temporary aberration of a lime-washer because there is evidence from early nineteenth-century sketches that the exterior beams were tarred like so many Cheshire and Lancashire houses of the time. Had this tarring been done to protect the timbers from the weather? Or in accordance with a fashionable belief that black and white, which coincided with the Gothick novels of Horace Walpole, Mrs Radcliffe and Sir Walter Scott, had been the authentic treatment of old half-timber work ever since the Middle Ages? At any rate, to judge from Regency sketches and engravings, black or natural grey for exposed timbers seemed optional; but to judge from early Georgian and Stuart drawings and woodcuts the natural grey was the more usual.

Immense sums have recently been spent by the Trust on the gatehouse and the long gallery. The principal rooms are still kept pretty empty of furniture as they have been these three hundred years past. Some very interesting late Tudor decorative painting has been revealed in the upstairs parlour. It consists of simulated panels, each with a diamond centre, painted alternately red and green over the plaster fillings and the upright and horizontal timbers alike. Above are an elaborate painted frieze and scenes from Scripture, summarized in black-letter texts. The temptation to over-improve, re-edify in the light of archaeological research and generally 'beautify' a building as un-sophisticated as Little Moreton Hall is one which the National Trust will be wise to resist.

CHAPTER SEVEN

FAIRFAX-LUCY OF CHARLECOTE

Warwickshire

UNTIL 1946 Charlecote Park had belonged since Richard I's reign to the Lucy family albeit twice the name passed through the female line, first in 1786 and again in 1890. 'Warwickshire', Henry James declared after lunching at Charlecote in 1877, 'is the core and centre of the English world; midmost England, unmitigated England.' And Charlecote Park, 'whose venerable verdure seems a survival from an earlier England, and whose innumerable acres, stretching away, in the early evening, to vaguely seen Tudor walls, lies there like the backward years receding to the age of Elizabeth,' being itself, if not midmost, then certainly unmitigated Warwickshire. Henry James went on to ruminate upon the antiquity of the house, 'rambling, low-gabled, many staired, brown wainscotted chambers ... deep window seats to sit in, with a play in your lap [doubtless a first folio of Shakespeare]', where you 'might find a very congruous asylum.' In fact he was taken in by his hostess Mrs Lucy's very recent alterations to the place. What his compatriot Washington Irving saw on a visit in 1818 and Sir Walter Scott ten years later was nearer the genuine article for then the Elizabethan house had merely survived a light Georgianization of a few rooms, whereas Mrs Lucy and her late husband George Hammond's drastic treatment in the interval had amounted to positive demolition and re-edification in a style purporting to be more Tudor than the original structure.

At the time of Henry James's visit Charlecote was, financially speaking, at a high. The then owner, fox-hunting squire Henry Spencer Lucy and his widowed mother (née Mary Elizabeth Williams) were enjoying the fruits of the dead father's massive expenditure on the house and contents. The prosperity did not last long. A steady decline was caused by the late Victorian agricultural depression, accelerated by heavy death duties and two world wars.

A few years before the outbreak of the second, namely in 1935, the National Trust secretary MacLeod Matheson was in correspondence with the husband of the tenant-for-life of Charlecote Ada Christina, the fox-hunter's daughter and heir. Colonel Sir Henry Cameron-Ramsay-Fairfax, 3rd Baronet, had married Ada Christina in 1892 and tacked on Lucy to his three surnames, making a fourth mouthful in that English landed way. He took over the management of Charlecote in addition to his own Scottish estates for Lady Fairfax-Lucy soon became an invalid. Sir Henry, very active in county work of Roxburgh and Warwickshire, was chairman of the Warwick Territorial Army and a committee member of the Council for the Preservation of Rural England. He was also a qualified barrister-at-law of the Middle Temple and, like others I have come by versed in the law, developed a tortuous mentality which revelled in ambiguities, misinterpretations and confusions. For nine years until his sudden death Sir Henry indulged in a spate of letters with the National Trust over the prospective transfer of Charlecote, haggling over obscure details, making last-minute propositions and contradicting them, and displaying such manifestations of penny wisdom and pound folly as practically to drive his correspondents to lunacy. The chief butt of his pen was Matheson who to his credit retained not only his sanity throughout but also his patience and courtesy.

Sir Henry was anxious to learn whether the National Trust's about-to-be launched country houses scheme would be of benefit to Charlecote. He made it plain that the opening of the house to the public would be valueless and fruitless. Charlecote was not as he put it 'on the Cook's Tour route' which, since it was a mere four miles from Stratford-upon-Avon and bristling with Shakespeare associations, is just about what it was. What was needed by owners he said was retention of their houses, remission from death duties and no opening to the public. If however an owner was obliged to hand over his property to the Trust then he should be allowed to reserve a life interest to himself, whereas his son and even grandson should be allowed to pay only a nominal rent 'without impeachment of waste'.

In July 1936 I was sent to Charlecote. It was the first of many visits. I confess I did not much like Sir Henry. He was pernickety, contrary, fussy, consequential, very pleased with himself and displeased with everyone else. He strutted like a bantam cock. He spoke with a peevish lisp. He was so convinced that Charlecote was the most important house in Great Britain that at first he would not let me see more than the outside. 'There was absolutely no need.' On my second visit I was presented to Lady Lucy, an enormous bundle of docility, sweetness and taciturnity, spreading over an invisible armchair in the library. I was assured that Charlecote was a settled estate of which Sir Henry, by virtue of his wife, was the tenant for life, and after him Montgomerie their eldest son. With the latter's consent, which could be taken for granted, there was no need to apply to the Court of Chancery. Sir Henry in a very explosive manner reiterated that he must retain full rights over the property, 'without impeachment of waste', of which I was not at all sure of the meaning, beyond understanding that he must be exempt from all taxation and interference. Rather feebly I daresay I kept mumbling that 'without impeachment' was almost bound to attract taxes and suggested that he would do better to express certain wishes and rely upon the Trust honouring the acceptable ones. This somewhat ineffectual confrontation was followed up by a letter from Matheson quoting Sir Charles Trevelyan's example, his circumstances at Wallington Hall near Cambo in Northumberland being similar. The very mention of the name Trevelyan sent Sir Henry into a fury. In no circumstances would he consent to mere wishes. He must have binding conditions and no taxes. Besides Sir Charles Trevelyan was 'an extreme Socialist . . . I am not aware that Cambo – where we both stayed in the present owner's father's time – would come into category A of your scheme.' It was a curious quirk of Sir Henry when cross to get the names of unfavoured people and their properties just slightly wrong. 'Your representative Mr. Milne [that was me] to whom my wishes were made clear', had surely passed them on lucidly? As for endowment, he wrote, 'I really do not quite understand the reason of your letter received this morning when you say that the Trust have no funds to maintain properties that are not self-supporting. If properties were self-supporting I presume there would be no need for a National Trust, nor do I think that it would necessarily make a property self-supporting to have agricultural land included – at the present time, probably just the reverse.'

Matheson suggested that perhaps Sir Henry would allow the Trust's solicitor to explain to his the niceties of the transaction since he found it so involved. 'I do not think solicitors getting together would be the slightest use,' came the answer. On Matheson informing him that the National Trust Bill of 1937, in granting the Trust an extension of its powers for the preservation of historic buildings, had passed unopposed through the House of Lords, Sir Henry wrote that a close perusal of the Bill showed him that it fell far short of what he had hoped. Matheson propounded that an anonymous benefactor might consider the purchase of Charlecote for the Trust while permitting the Lucy family and their heirs to remain in residence. Sir Henry turned down the idea as preposterous and impertinent. A year later he wrote that it was a pity the Trust 'did not get hold of some rich men who have been distributing their money with such *lasciviousness* [my italics] in other directions.' In April Sir Henry, eating humble pie, enquired whether the benefactor mentioned by Matheson was still interested in the purchase of Charlecote. Regretfully Matheson replied that it was now too late; he had bought another house.

After a year and a half of war, in March 1941, Sir Henry announced that he was ready to re-negotiate seriously. But dead secrecy must be enjoined. 'I think we have met before – or at any rate corresponded,' he wrote ambiguously. Would Matheson see him at his house Maxton, St Boswell's N.B.? Matheson was sorry he could not go to Scotland for the day. On 5 April Sir Henry no longer wished to reserve interest for himself and Lady Lucy, but for his eldest son who was unlikely to live at Charlecote. He was quite ready to rely upon a gentleman's agreement.

In June they met in London. Sir Henry complained of a leakage of the secrecy 'somewhere in Warwickshire'. Through me perhaps, whose home was just over the border in Worcestershire? In a letter to Benjamin W. Horne, the Trust's old solicitor, Matheson let fly: 'He thinks he knows everything, and is extremely difficult, tiresome and stupid.'

By July Sir Henry naturally assumes that Charlecote is listed Grade A by Ministry of Works standards and therefore there is no need to consult the Ministry. Matheson knows there is need and does consult Dr Raby, asking for a certificate as is customary under the country houses scheme. George Chettle, the chief inspector, whom nobody dislikes, is the representative sent by Raby to Charlecote. By a mercy Sir Henry approves of Chettle. After five months' cogitation the Ministry gives a rather grudging consent, because 'the alterations that were made to this house in the 19th century make it impossible to be placed in the first rank', but it may just be placed in the second rank of three. A certificate would be forthcoming.

Matheson instructs Mr Clive Powell of Messrs Chesshire Gibson & Co., land agents and surveyors of Birmingham, to prepare a financial report for the Trust on the house, flower garden and 60 acres of the park provisionally offered. Meanwhile Matheson points out to Sir Henry that the Trust must have in writing the consent of the next heir in tail, his son Montgomerie. Sir Henry doesn't like this idea at all and remembers that he has omitted the mention of some other members of his family with interests in the estate, like annuitants. 'As for the Office of Works man Mr. Chettle was very pleasant. I think there is no doubt the house has been passed Class A. As regards Mr Powell, I am afraid we did not get on very well. He struck me as being much more accustomed to look at properties amidst urban surroundings such as Baron Ash's place [Packwood House, given in 1941] – in other words "rus in urbe".' The family must now approach the Charlecote problem in an entirely different way. They must leave out farms (not indeed offered) and simply hand over the mansion, park and two meadows. The Lucys should not be asked for an endowment.

Mr Powell's preliminary advice to the secretary was that, although the land at Charlecote was not bad, the cottages were not up to standard and might even be condemned to demolition by the local authorities. He maintained that the minimum endowment required was £27,000 for a thoroughly dicey property. Had not the whole deal better be called off? If it were he guessed that the family would sell the entire estate, which might be the best solution for everybody. Matheson inwardly agreed and begged Powell, who had nothing to lose from Sir Henry's bad books, to carry the can as it were, and in his written report advise the Trust to ask for such an endowment as Sir Henry was bound to reject. This Powell did. But before he did Matheson warned Sir Henry that 'some endowment is essential'. This timorous letter was followed by a later one quoting the substantial sum suggested by Powell. Sir Henry was dumbfounded and inflexible.

On 9 October the Country Houses Committee recommended that on financial grounds the Charlecote offer be turned down. Sir Henry was very indignant, accusing Powell of suggesting the same endowment for Sir Henry's latest offer which was of less acreage. Mr Lees-Milne was delegated to visit Sir Henry as an emollient. This was a delicate commission indeed. I went one bleak November afternoon. Sir Henry greeted me with a look of ineffable hurt and disappointment. The Trust's latest demands were 'absolutely fantastic'. While expressing friendliness towards me he spoke of Mr Chesshire (i.e. Powell of Messrs Chesshire Gibson) with deep loathing. As for the National Trust it misled owners by enticing their properties from them whereas in fact it was 'fleecing' them of their capital. I interpreted this remark as a threat. Sir Henry demanded to appear before the committee. Anyway wild horses would not drag from him one farthing over £10,000. This sum he would magnanimously offer. The secretary wrote to thank him gratefully as though Sir Henry were conferring on him personally a most generous present.

While declining politely to receive him at their boardroom table, which was contrary to National Trust etiquette, the committee invited Lord Esher to see Sir Henry and explain the Trust's problem. This Lord Esher did. Whereupon the committee somewhat faintheartedly consented to re-negotiate for the property provided that over and above the rents from the two fields securities to yield £450 per annum were assured. The secretary reminded Sir Henry that Montgomerie who lived in Kenya must bar the entail before a transfer could be affected. Sir Henry ignored this reminder. There then ensued some appalling haggling over the kitchen garden expenses. Who was to meet them? Sir Henry who would reap their produce? Or the National Trust who would not? On 31 March 1942 Clive Powell wrote to me that he was completely mystified. Arguments by post ensued. In June I wrote to Lord Esher, 'It is really extremely difficult to understand how Sir Henry's mind works.' In return for the Trust paying for labour in the kitchen garden Sir Henry offered to pay the Trust a rent for feeding his deer. Then Sir Henry wrote that Lady Lucy was seriously ill and there was need for haste. In July Lord Esher to me: 'This makes confusion worse confounded.' Sir Henry endeavoured to press the deed of transfer through without obtaining his eldest son's consent.

In October Sir Henry in a letter to Lord Esher evinced irritation: 'Mr. Milne writes me that there would be death duties on the leasehold interest only, but I should be glad to have further guidance . . . One is absolutely in the dark.' Mr Milne supposed that this particular obscurity had already been illuminated time and time again, but kept the reflection to himself. In demurring over Matheson's point about the necessity for his son's consent Sir Henry demanded to see Lord Esher again. Lord Esher to me: 'I must have some idea what it is all about, if, that is to say, either you or Mr. Horne [the Trust's solicitor] have any idea yourselves.' Some unremembered distraction prevented Sir Henry from keeping the engagement. 'There seems a fate against our meeting,' he wrote to Lord Esher who to me wrote: 'That was my lucky day.'

Poor Lady Lucy, we were told, was now under heroin. Sir Henry wished to impose a condition that the house be open to the public only during three months of the year (and presumably December to February). Horne opined that such a condition in the lease would undoubtedly attract tax. In January 1943 the Finance Committee refused Sir Henry's new request that his legal and other expenses should be borne by the National Trust no matter whether negotiations proved successful or not. But the committee agreed that if successful, his expenses might be met out of the income from the property. It took the opportunity of restating the latest agreed endowment figures, viz.: £750 p.a. in toto, namely £300 from the rents and £450 from securities. Sir Henry's reaction was to throw in with the land the kitchen garden (a doubtful asset), thus reducing the endowment figure by £14 p.a. He added the ambiguous postscript, 'I have not the authority of Mr. Matheson.'

While contracts were being deviously drafted by the solicitors to both parties, an amicable arrangement was reached by the parties themselves that of the historic contents of Charlecote only the 'gifts' from Queen Elizabeth to the Lucys were to be handed over to the Trust, everything else to be on loan. It transpired that the 'gifts' from the great Queen Elizabeth did not seem to have survived and those relics so piously treasured turned out on subsequent expert investigation to be frauds. For instance, the famous napkin, far from having touched the royal lips during her progress to Charlecote, was made in the early eighteenth century. But those historic contents, several of which certainly are of considerable interest, were to be retained by the family who would give the Trust first option to purchase were they ever to put them on the market.

In October Montgomerie Fairfax-Lucy duly signed in Kenya the document barring the entail.

In November Hubert Smith, recently appointed the Trust's first chief agent, in looking through the figures relative to the Charlecote endowment, calculated that the net income anticipated from the land by Sir Henry as £438 amounted to no more than £378, thus reducing the total income from £750 to £690. This discovery, admittedly tiresome and annoying, by a new Trust official, vexed Sir Henry very much. He resolutely refused to readjust the endowment sum by an increase of land. Furthermore he demanded a condition that five persons, namely his resident agent and wife, his gamekeeper and wife acting as caretakers, and his daughter Alianore, acting as gardener, should live in the house without rates becoming liable. The refusal of more endowment and the new condition put the Finance Committee on their mettle. 'If we are not to be diddled by the tortuous mentality of this man we must not alter the ground upon which we base our £750,' Lord Esher declared. And the committee decided not to proceed with the Charlecote negotiations any further. Sadly the long-suffering Matheson wrote to Esher in December, 'He is already weaving a complicated web of getting his own way in some strange manner.' On 15 December he wrote to Sir Henry that the National Trust regretted it was unable to accept Charlecote on Sir Henry's financial terms.

On 20th of the month Matheson received a letter from Sir Henry announcing that Lady Lucy 'passed away on Friday night'. Unabashed, he supposed that it was then too late to avoid death duties on *his* life interest. On receipt of this news Lord Esher wrote to Matheson: 'So Lady Fairfax-Lucy is dead and the old man has not been so clever as he thought he was.'

During the first six months of 1944 in Matheson's absence through ill health I was acting secretary and in receipt of the usual circuitous rigmaroles from Sir Henry, who paid no heed to the Trust's intended closure of further negotiations. In vain I endeavoured to assure him that he could not be relieved of death duties on that part of the estate which he once again proposed the Trust should take over, for it was still his property and not the Trust's, no contract having yet been agreed. A further involved scheme was advanced by Sir Henry consequent upon Lady Lucy's death which involved raising a mortgage on one of his farms. Delays ensued over further consultations with the absent Montgomerie. Then out of the blue we learned that Sir Henry, rising 74, had on 5 August taken to himself a second wife. And on 20th of the same month he as suddenly died. It is dreadful to say so but nobody seemed to regret his demise very much.

Just before it happened I was beginning to think that perhaps Sir Henry's preposterous self-importance was rather pitiable. After all the best of us had our little faults of which we were blissfully unaware. I even supposed that within that tight, opinionated, swaggering frame a kindly old gentleman was desperately struggling to get out. But after reading Brian Fairfax-Lucy's *The Children of the House* (Brian being Sir Henry's second son), I am afraid I reverted to my original estimate of Sir Henry. For in this touching autobiography of childhood the father is revealed as a monster of severity, meanness and unkindness, a Victorian household tyrant of whom his children were mortally afraid and whom they intensely disliked. And then I remembered Brian once telling me how as children his brothers and sisters were often so hungry that they would walk into Stratford-upon-Avon and press their faces against the windows of pastrycooks in the hope that some indulgent passer-by might buy them a halfpenny bun. To similar conditions of unhappiness and deprivation were the offspring of large country houses occasionally reduced by neglectful Edwardian parents; but in the case of Charlecote by a father who was a positive sadistic bully.

So came about the end of the first phase of negotiations between the Fairfax-Lucy family and the National Trust after nearly a decade. It had been marked by a sort of stagnant costiveness induced, if not by ill-will, then by the innate obfuscation of Sir Henry's inquisitorial mind. His make-up was a mixture of quite a lot of learning and much stupidity. If ever Shakespeare's Justice Shallow in *The Merry Wives of Windsor* was to be incarnated, surely Sir Henry Fairfax-Lucy of the twentieth century was a far more substantial candidate than poor Sir Thomas Lucy of the sixteenth. For Sir Thomas according to written accounts did not resemble Shallow in all respects whereas Sir Henry, who was not actually a Lucy by blood, most certainly did, as well as evincing several disagreeable qualities which both the Elizabethan knight and the Shakespeare Justice apparently lacked. Goodness knows for how much longer, had Sir Henry not departed this life, the idle discussions and arguments would have lingered on. The National Trust was far too polite, or subservient, to break them off on the grounds of the owner's obstructiveness, to put it mildly, and clearly Sir Henry had no intention of bringing them to a close.

With the advent of Sir Montgomerie the new baronet, and his brother and deputy Brian, the Charlecote atmosphere changed over-night. Montgomerie, who on leaving Eton had been banished by his parents to Africa for some innocuous boyish peccadillo, remained painfully shy, reclusive and gentle. He was now 48 years old and had scarcely been back to England since his teens. He delegated the ensuing negotiations to Brian and his wife, Alice Buchan. Occasionally he felt obliged to come over to attend to indispensable business. He would stay in the Victorian wing, seemingly hating every moment of his visit and longing to return to Kenya. He barely saw a soul except his unmarried sister Alianore who lived in a small house on the estate, wore knee-breeches and worked all day long in the garden and the tack-room by her own choice. She was a picturesque and enduring figure on the Charlecote landscape, adhering to very old-fashioned views which she expressed in an old-fashioned voice, and clipping her Gs in the way of Victorian county ladies. Even towards Alianore Montgomerie behaved oddly. The moment six o'clock struck of an evening he declined to address a word to her or anyone who might cross his path until dawn the next morning. Instead he had a habit, which Alianore took amiss, of loudly clapping his hands whenever he wanted anything. Alianore attributed this habit to the number of black servants her rich brother must have had at home. Whether this was the case I never discovered. At any rate Alianore, who was the most obliging woman in the world, resented the attribution of herself to the status of an African domestic.

Although Montgomerie had not the slightest intention of residing at Charlecote he held his patrimony in deep veneration and was determined that it must be preserved at whatever cost and trouble. Through Brian a proposition immediately came that the National Trust might purchase the house, the chief contents and 250 acres of the park for £30,000, and an additional 750 (the number seemed to be a Lucy fixation) acres of agricultural land for £20,000, if only some benefactor were forthcoming. And assuredly the very same anonymous benefactor whose advances Sir Henry had turned down with contumely in 1937, was sounded.

Mystery surrounded the Trust's important anonymous benefactor as far as the public were concerned – or so we liked to believe, although the staff were well privy to him. Ernest Cook was a millionaire member of Thomas Cook & Sons travel agency, painfully shy and a collector of old master paintings and purchaser of large estates with historic buildings. He had already bought and given to the Trust through the SPAB Montacute House and the Bath Assembly Rooms, both in Somerset, and was to bequeath amongst others the Coleshill estate with its ill-fated Inigo Jones-style house in Berkshire. His agent and confidential adviser Captain John Burrow Hill, who was on the Estates Management Committee, enjoyed the manipulative role of intermediary.

Professor G.M. Trevelyan, chairman of the Estates Committee, was very keen for the Trust to issue a public appeal. But since a public appeal for Little Moreton Hall, a genuine Elizabethan house, did not raise £4,000 in 1938, would there be much response to one for £30,000 for a Victorianized Charlecote Park in 1945 before the Second World War was even ended?

Time dawdled on. Sir Montgomerie, whose financial situation, contrary to Alianore's surmise, was parlous, grew fretful and anxious. The Trust approached bodies like the Pilgrim Trust and fingered pockets of the rich and 'lascivious' to no effect. In March Mr Cook made a straight offer of £80,000 for the whole estate. This seemed a godsend, but with anxiety Sir Montgomerie's appetite had grown prodigiously. He brushed the offer aside. Mr Cook, who had really intended to confer on the National Trust yet another blessing, was indignant. Captain Hill, who had conducted the negotiations, was furious. The estate, he reported, was in a deplorable condition, the house in his opinion anyway a beastly fake, and the Lucys too pleased with themselves for words. Montgomerie then gave Brian power of attorney and sloped home to Africa.

An extraordinary volte-face by both the Lucys and the National Trust then took place. In April 1945 the family offered Charlecote with certain chattels as a gift subject to agreement that they might live in the Victorian wing. After so many long and tedious years of battling with Sir Henry over trivia the National Trust then and there accepted the vague proposition. On the Trust's part it may have been a case of hopeless despair and submission to brow-beating, first by aggressive and then by pathetic means. At all events the Trust's staff surrendered to Brian's invincible charm. They recommended acceptance to the Executive Committee, without even reconsidering how it could afford the upkeep.

I was present at the meeting of the Executive Committee which reached the quixotic decision. There was a good deal of initial opposition to Charlecote not merely on financial grounds. Several members shared John Hill's opinion of the house. It was G.M. Trevelyan, that highly revered figure, who swayed them. Naturally unemotional and reticent he rose from his seat (a thing members never did) at the boardroom table and delivered a passionate speech in favour of Charlecote, based on the Shakespeare association, namely that the poet had stolen deer from Charlecote park and been arraigned by the first Sir Thomas Lucy, Justice of the Peace, in the great hall. I was to hear his evidence of the legend's authenticity on a second very moving occasion, the handing-over ceremony. The dissenting minority was silenced, the majority were swayed and from 2 June Charlecote, for better or for worse, was theirs to maintain for ever.

Once more an appeal to the public for endowment seemed the only solution. It is always difficult to raise money in order to pay for something already acquired. The wise course is to announce to would-be contributors that unless they stump up, such and such a property cannot be saved. Salvation is up to them. In this case it was too late to pretend that Charlecote was not already theirs. £25,000 was deemed an adequate sum to raise. Matheson who had resigned the secretaryship because of recurrent ill health offered to go on a begging tour to the United States. Americans were considered suckers for any sort of Shakespeare venture.

The Lucys were overjoyed, the National Trust less so. The former had shed the appalling burden of upkeep. They saw their beloved ancestral home secure for all time. The latter were pretty desperate as to how to pay for another white elephant; and apprehensive about the appeal outcome. Indeed in September I was obliged to tell Brian that the new Labour government had vetoed appeals to America; that Matheson's tour was therefore off, doubtless for the greater benefit of his health; and that Lord Esher recommended letting the house to an institution and removing the principal contents into the gatehouse for show. Brian was deeply shocked, and his brother Montgomerie threatened, from his black homeland if it was not too late, to call the whole deal off. The committee was extremely embarrassed about how to make both ends meet. By the end of the year the appeal had brought in only £1,210, mere chicken-feed.

A lesser but still an awkward problem was the historic contents and their value for insurance. I asked Clifford Smith, who was always ready to earn an honest penny, to make a list for submission to the family. He agreed for a sum of 15 guineas a day. To his delight and everyone else's he discovered a Tudor silver wine-cup with a hallmark of 1524. Surely the Virgin Queen must have drunk from it in 1572? Leigh Ashton, now director of the V & A, valued it at £10,000, 'hideous though it be', he told me. Charles Oman, the great silver expert, was enthusiastic. On behalf of the family I was asked to sell it through the National Art Collections Fund, which turned it down. Lord Crawford, the Fund's chairman, also thought it ugly. Notwithstanding its demerits in the pundits' eyes the cup, the fourth earliest wine-cup in existence, reposes today on the dining-room sideboard of Charlecote on loan from the family, and is widely admired. A second folio copy of the works of Shakespeare of 1632 proved to be all right. So did the quarto copy of *The Merry Wives of Windsor* of 1619. Unfortunately neither had been presented to the Lucys by the Bard, each being bought in the nineteenth century. But the miniature by Isaac Oliver (authenticated by Leigh Ashton) and purporting to be of the third Sir Thomas Lucy (bibliophile grandson of 'Justice Shallow') proved to be of a Tudor admiral, called Sir Richard Leveson. Evidently George Hammond and Mary Elizabeth Lucy had confused the pronunciation (Lewson) of the name with their own. The ebony bed which the Virgin Queen was said to have slept in turned out to have been made from a seventeenth-century settee by William Beckford of Fonthill, where indeed it may have been slept in by the un-virginal Lord Nelson and Lady Hamilton. The Holbein portrait of the Queen was debunked by Ben Nicolson, distinguished editor of *The Burlington Magazine*, and the Gainsborough of the eighteenth-century George Lucy deemed indifferent.

Professor Ellis Waterhouse who spent a brief afternoon at Charlecote was scarcely more enthusiastic about the pictures. While I shifted and shunted a long ladder against the walls of the great hall he rushed up and down like a squirrel, flashing a torch across the faces of portrait after portrait, never pausing an instant to admire or comment. At the end of this hectic performance I could not refrain from observing,

'Professor, I have never met a man who so much disliked pictures as you.' 'What do you mean?' he barked. 'Why!' I said, 'You haven't even looked at a single one.' On the other hand S.C. Kaines Smith, late Keeper of the Birmingham Art Gallery, was enthusiastic in that the Lucy portraits provided an unbroken chronology from the sixteenth century of an old county family. Katharine Esdaile, the pioneering expert on post-Reformation sculpture, explained that the busts of Queen Elizabeth, Sir Thomas Lucy I and his grandson Sir Thomas Lucy III were casts from the Queen's effigy in Westminster Abbey and the two Lucy monuments in Charlecote church. At times my blood runs cold when I recall the seemingly casual way in which I carted some of the treasures – the busts, cups, miniatures, folios and the Erasmus book, possibly illuminated by Holbein – up to London for inspection and back, often on a circuit of other visits round the country, in the boot of my old motor. But car thefts and robberies in general were far less common before the decades of prosperity and permissiveness.

An Historic Buildings Committee minute of September 1945 agreed to the exhibition in the house of the Charlecote treasures whether they were the Trust's or the Lucys' – mere details of ownership to be settled in due course – 'so long as the public were not led into supposing that the nineteenth-century exhibits purported to be of historic interest or artistic merit'.

The minute sounds rather a shocking ring today by implying that the Historic Buildings Committee considered all Victorian objects of virtu and artefacts to be trash, and all Victorian buildings unworthy of preservation. This was not, strictly speaking, the case, although there is a distinct element of truth in the imputation.

I have to admit that the prevailing opinion about Charlecote among the *cognoscenti* who sat on the National Trust committees in the 1940s was that, whereas the park through which ran the river Avon and the unaltered Tudor gatehouse were worth preserving, the house had been grievously spoilt in the previous century by George Hammond Lucy and Mary Elizabeth Williams his wife. It is certain this couple between their marriage in 1823 and his death in 1845 laboured under the illusion that they were rendering the house, in which minimal changes had been made in the eighteenth century, more Elizabethan by sheer aggrandizement than it was when finished by Sir Thomas Lucy in 1558. In brief, they added a large dining-room and library to the west, 're-edified' the great hall from top to bottom, and re-decorated the rooms of the north-east wing out of all recognition. They intended to 'restore' the gatehouse, but mercifully desisted. The widow Mary Elizabeth later added the massive service wing to the south. None of this work was creative architecture. It was intended to copy the Elizabethan style exactly.

In three articles on Charlecote in *Country Life* of 1952 Christopher Hussey wrote that, 'behind the nineteenth century's revivals of fantasy we are always conscious of the lifeless machine that killed each idea in execution'. In this reference to George Hammond and Mary Elizabeth's contribution to the house which they adored Hussey's words were an understatement of what the majority on the Historic Buildings Committee felt. The Duke of Wellington, who was an architect and considered a man of sound judgement, voted against the Trust accepting Charlecote in the first place. Lord Esher the chairman, aware of the Duke being a too exclusive Regency fancier, thought he was going too far, yet himself deemed the house horribly over-restored. I who was the committee's secretary thought along the same lines. I fancy that Brian and Alice Lucy may secretly have agreed with us.

Although now unreservedly in favour of preserving the William IV work and decoration, since it is there and because it constitutes a large proportion of the house's history, I still maintain that what was done to the house by the early nineteenth-century owners was no aesthetic improvement on what went before. And when it came to arranging the house immediately after the war for public show Brian and Alice and I did our best to resurrect what ancient pieces of oak furniture of an earlier age survived in the attics and outbuildings where they had been discarded as junk by George Hammond and Mary Elizabeth. With much labour we brought into the hall the long oak table from the servants' hall. We gave what prominence we could to the sixteenth century while deliberately underemphasizing the nineteenth, in so far as we were able. We did not, I am glad to say, actually banish any of the unsightlier made-up furniture bought from Fonthill Abbey or, to give examples of a slightly later date, the Burmese tête-à-tête, and the highly carved buffet of 1858 in the dining-room. At least we respected these monsters of inelegance as ghastly curiosities of mid-Victorian joinery to be cherished, if not admired.

If the tastes of ordinary connoisseurs change, the expertise of art historians certainly becomes more rarefied as research advances with the years. In *The National Trust Year Book of 1976–7* an article under the heading 'Elizabethan Revival Charlecote Revived', by those eminent scholars John Harris and Clive Wainwright, contained this paragraph:

In recent years, nineteenth-century architecture and interior decoration have returned to favour and in 1974 Sir Brian and Lady Fairfax-Lucy and the National Trust, with the assistance of the Department of Furniture and Woodwork at the Victoria and Albert Museum, attempted to revive, as far as possible, the character of the house as it appeared one hundred years ago. The furnishings have been re-arranged with the aid of Mary Elizabeth Lucy's diary, written in 1861, a nineteenth-century inventory and various documents and old photographs. Some items have been brought back to the main rooms from attics, corridors, servants' rooms and outhouses, and portraits and busts have been returned to their places of honour.

In other words the genuine old oak was in its turn once again banished and the mid-Victorian fakes, if this is not too partisan a word, retrieved. The authors concluded:

> We feel the new arrangement of the furniture does improve the appearance of the house but perhaps the lesson to be drawn from this is that a more coherent effect can result from an authentic re-arrangement of furnishing than from an empirical approach based on modern principles of good taste.

These views may well be right. But they are open to dispute. The lesson to be learned from this reversal of taste within nearly thirty years seems to me to be that no one generation's judgement is infallible, not even that of John Harris and Clive Wainwright. Who today has a right to judge whether a Victorian or an Elizabethan rearrangement of Charlecote has the more coherent effect or indeed can even be authentic? The truth is country houses do not stand still; and even when belonging to the National Trust will not stand still. The arrangement and decoration of their rooms will change. It is necessary and desirable that they should. Their custodians, whether descendants of the donors, whether amateurs or art historians, are inevitably moved by 'empirical notions based on modern principles of good taste'. Who can say in what direction so-called good taste will move in another generation's time: towards an adaptation of the Norman, Plantagenet, Tudor, the William and Mary, the Georgian and the William and Adelaide or the Victorian adaptations? What is certain is that every revival and re-revival of style is in the eyes of posterity that of its time. Those society ladies who went to immense lengths to dress themselves for the Devonshire House Ball in 1897 as Mary Queen of Scots or Madame du Barry look to our eyes nothing of the sort. They look like society ladies of 1897. In other words the indelible stamp of the *Zeitgeist* can never be erased.

On 1 June 1946 took place the opening ceremony at Charlecote. I was in a frenzy of preparation. As usual essential adjuncts like posts and ropes, guidebooks and guides turned up only at the last minute. The lavatories for the public were not even installed in the old game larder, as had been enjoined. Chaos reigned and anxiety clutched at my heart. Alice Lucy had got Sir Barry Jackson, the popular Shakespeare Theatre director to declare the actual opening. This genial man with a commanding presence was the rich son of Maypole Dairies' founder, fearless and bold. He introduced Shakespeare in modern dress. His *Hamlet in Plus-Fours* had made a great sensation in the 1920s. Professor G.M. Trevelyan motored from Cambridge to receive on behalf of the National Trust the deeds of Charlecote from Brian Lucy. He had been a friend and admirer of Alice Lucy's father John Buchan. Trevelyan delivered another impassioned speech. He said that ever since he was a small boy living at Welcombe House, his mother's home, on the other side of the Avon Charlecote had seemed the essence of romance. For over 800 centuries ('Think what it means!') the Lucys had lived there. 'The very name Charlecote means much to every educated Englishman and to every lover of Shakespeare the world over.' The Shakespeare connection was as familiar as the legend of Alfred and the cakes to every schoolboy, 'and is very much more true'. He was thoroughly convinced that the Bard had poached Sir Thomas Lucy's deer, had been arraigned by the knight who was a Justice of the Peace, had been obliged to leave Stratford for London in consequence and had reaped an amused revenge by identifying Justice Shallow with the pompous knight, besotted with his lineage and 'the dozen white luces' in his coat of arms. True the legend had been scouted by some scholars like Sir Sidney Lee. Yet two late seventeenth-century sources, Nicholas Rowe, Poet Laureate, and Archdeacon Francis Davies, confirmed it independently. Rather touchingly and indeed very generously Trevelyan concluded that, 'As I am largely responsible for the acceptance [of Charlecote] I feel I ought to fork out' to the tune of £5,000 – in those days a large sum. At the same time he announced that Chancellor of the Exchequer Hugh Dalton was to launch the following month the Charlecote endowment appeal which he, Trevelyan, had so urgently advocated the previous year. Dr Dalton had promised from the government a pound for every pound subscribed by the public. Trevelyan also announced on this occasion that the Chancellor intended henceforth to accept land in lieu of death duties as a means of endowing historic houses which might be made over to the nation.

I think it was Clifford Smith who first remarked on the survival practically intact of the brew-house at Charlecote. Nearly every great country seat had one but few survived beyond the Victorian age. Formerly the staple beverage of a large household, the servants and visiting tradesmen had been home-brewed ale. Dr H. Shaw, director of the Science Museum, put me in touch with a Mr J.D. Bexon of Bromyard who pronounced the Charlecote brew-house a rare and important specimen. As the greatest living authority on the subject Mr Bexon was an incalculable help in restoring where necessary and putting to rights the primitive machinery and the wooden conduits, vats and tuns. Likewise we persuaded Colonel Mackintosh, late director of the Science Museum, to visit and report on the carriages at Charlecote. The result was the display in the coach-houses of the family travelling coach, handsomely upholstered inside with heraldic luces and cross-crosslets, the barouche, the wagonette omnibus, the victoria, the spider phaeton and the buggy. The adjoining tack-room was in mint condition at the date of transfer, the saddlery and harness having been meticulously burnished and polished by Alianore who spent hours of every day there. It has proved extremely popular.

My subsequent visits to Charlecote were made a delight whenever they coincided with those of Brian (who inherited the baronetcy on Montgomerie's death in 1965) and Alice. Unfortunately they did not reside at Charlecote, merely spending an odd night or two in the Victorian wing. Their kindness and hospitality were truly wonderful. Together we rehung pictures and rearranged furniture according to our inexpert lights. I sometimes slept in a cosy Victorian bedroom with flowered wallpaper, flowered washstand and china jug, and maplewood four-poster with flowered chintz hangings. In winter a cheerful fire fluttered in the blackened grate. And it was great fun when thirty years later we watched – I cannot claim that we were much help – our successors undo our painful work.

Charlecote was about the first country house of which I supervised the showing after the war. Working on a shoe-string for an underendowed property I doubtless made some lamentable mistakes. Informed visitors and correspondents left me in no doubts. Like St Sebastian I was the target of opprobrious arrows. Critics complained of our untutored guides assuring visitors that Shakespeare was brought before Sir Thomas Lucy in the 1829–34 library; that the Henry VIII portrait supposedly by Holbein was by Romney; and that Charles II was

Charles I. Since so many of Charlecote's swans of the past had turned out to be geese these erratic slips of attribution did not strike me as so dreadfully reprehensible. The ethos of Charlecote in its ancient park set on the meandering Avon's brim was little affected by a few solecisms from over-enthusiastic helpers, who were after all volunteers. It was worse when a clergyman guide, no doubt a godly man with the best intentions, pronounced the dining-room and library to be so ugly that they ought to be demolished, and made 'an ill-placed remark, not repeatable' (how I wish I had recorded it) about the portrait of George Hammond Lucy who had been responsible for these interesting apartments.

Until the National Trust set up regional committees with staff to cope with the needs created by its stupendous growth I remained responsible for the welfare of house, outbuildings and contents, caretakers and cleaners. I seem always to have been on the road – taking the Stuart casket to a V & A expert for mending (at the cost of one shilling), Shakespeare's portrait to the National Portrait Gallery for identification (another goose) – when not at the top of ladders sticking labels on skied pictures or endeavouring to make mended sections of the forecourt balustrading look, with the aid of cow dung, genuine stone instead of the artificial sort, for we had no money for the real thing. And Charlecote was only one of dozens of the Trust's historic buildings crying out for attention and love. I may have been behindhand with the former, but not with the latter.

Sir Brian died in 1974 to be succeeded by his son as 6th Baronet. Sir Edmund Fairfax-Lucy is one of Britain's leading painters of landscape and the interiors of country houses. While I write he has an exhibition at Mompesson House in Salisbury Close. He lives in the 1860 south block at Charlecote where he has his studio, surrounded by the beguiling treasures of his Victorian forebears. His presence prolongs the Lucy continuity since Thurstane de Cherlecote was granted the land by Henry de Montfort in the twelfth century before the family had even adopted the Lucy surname. The greater part of the house is not occupied, apart from the administrator's floor, but is regularly opened to the public. So too is the park containing the descendants of the 'Shakespeare' deer and the flock of Jacob sheep, and, overlooking the river Avon, the garden laid out by Mary Elizabeth Lucy.

CHAPTER EIGHT

ELLEN TERRY AND EDITH CRAIG OF SMALLHYTHE

Kent

THE picture often comes to my mind of two middle-aged friends, closely united, not by passion but by a partnership which brought them both worldwide renown, leisurely jolting one warm autumn afternoon of the late 1890s in an old hackney carriage across the Level between the Isle of Oxney and the Tenterden heights. Where are they coming from and where are they making for? The old coachman – I like to think of him as old, and benign – flicks the whip gently across the withers of the dear old horse as they clatter through Appledore. After a few miles down a sleepy lane between hedgerows festooned with travellers' joy the dear old horse clipper-cloppers to a halt in a tiny hamlet consisting of a cluster of half-timbered buildings and a crow-stepped church of red brick. 'Where have you got to now, coachman?' calls the beautiful lady in her sweet, crystal-clear voice. 'This be Smallhythe, lady.' 'Well, then,' she says, turning to her lean, dark companion, 'this is where I should like to live and die.' 'Well then, buy it!' retorts the companion. Two years later she did.

In 1899 Ellen Terry was in her early fifties, with only a few more years to run before she ceased, on account of advancing age, to be Henry Irving's leading lady. She was the greatest actress of the day as he was the greatest actor. Her domestic life had not been uneventful. At 17 she had married G.F. Watts, the allegorical history and portrait painter, thirty years her senior. The marriage proved a failure. Two further marriages to little-known actors were barely more successful. But on leaving Watts in 1869 for the arms of Edward Godwin, architect, stage designer and outrageous aesthete, she enjoyed the greatest romance of her life. After six years of bliss, abated only by the couple's grinding poverty, for Ellen had temporarily left the stage, he bolted with a young pupil, leaving her with two illegitimate children and an abiding legacy of love for all things beautiful, including the English countryside which coloured the rest of her long life.

The house which Ellen Terry had made her home and to which she retreated whenever the stage allowed her, was always called by her The Farm. With its dappled russet roof, walls of packed timber beams, an upper storey overhanging the lower, the house had been a yeoman's dwelling for centuries. Actually it was built, probably early in Henry VIII's reign, as the headquarters of the harbour-master, being then called the Port House of the hythe, meaning small landing-place or harbour. For until the sixteenth century the river Rother, now a trickle, was navigable as far inland as Smallhythe where a large warship was once built for the Tudor monarch. A strip of water known as the Dock still lies to the south of the house. With the years Ellen Terry managed to accumulate adjacent buildings, namely the Priest's House beside the church, Yew Tree Cottage, both coeval with The Farm and likewise built of half timber, and Toll Cottage (alas, burnt down just after the last war). She was immensely proud of her property and to the doctor who wheeled her up the path on returning home for the last time, said: 'This is my own house, doctor, bought with my own money.'

Ellen Terry's life may have been dedicated to the stage but her first loyalty was to her and Godwin's two children, a boy and a girl. Rather curiously, for Ellen was religious, they were baptized several years after their births. The boy was christened Edward (or Teddy) after his father, Henry after Irving whom both children regarded as their surrogate father, and Gordon after a godmother. Ellen quixotically chose for both children the surname of Craig while sailing round the island of Ailsa Craig off the coast of Ayrshire. Bred to the stage Gordon became one of the most brilliant theatrical designers and producers of his time. The girl, Edith or Edy, never married but lived with her mother at Smallhythe where she remained until her death. She was a highly imaginative stage costumier and a notable suffragette. Her devotion to Ellen was singularly close, ambivalent, yet intensely protective. She was a formidable and rather rebarbative person. Her mother once said to a suitor of Edy, 'Two or three benighted youths have come to me praying to be allowed to pay attention to Ailsa [as she called her], but I have warned them of the fearful fate waiting anybody bold enough to ask her. She won't have any of them . . .' Apart from the stage brother and sister had little in common and met seldom in later life.

Edy attached herself to two women friends, the writer Christopher St John, known as Chris, and the artist Clare Atwood, known as Tony. Whereas Chris was frankly ugly and massive with a huge posterior kept together by very tight corduroy trousers straining at the seams, Tony was pretty and slight. These three lived in the Priest's House. Yet another companion, a Mrs Seal, known as Bruce, a rather terrifying individual, joined the colony in later years. I remember her wearing on her big head a minute beret Basque and leaning over the lower section of the stable-like door of Toll Cottage, brawny arms akimbo, in a very defiant attitude, to all the world resembling a bull ruminating whether to emerge and charge the spectator. She had Toll Cottage rent free in return for certain services in the Priest's House and since she referred to Miss St John as Mr Chris and Miss Atwood as Mr Tony I deduced that her status in the colony was relatively subordinate.

On 31 May 1913 the honorary secretary of the Kent Archaeological Society wrote a letter to S.H. Hamer, the secretary of the National Trust, beginning: 'My dear Sir,' and enclosing a copy of a report on Yew Tree Cottage immediately facing The Farm at Smallhythe on the other side of the road. The letter was evidently in reply to enquiries made by Mr Hamer who had learned that the owner, a Major Neene, was about to demolish it and erect two cottages on the site. In confirming the rumour the report stated that the housebreakers were about to launch their attack on the building the following Monday, unless someone was prepared to offer the owner £400. This the local secretary considered 'an exorbitant price; £150 would be 19 years purchase on the cottage's present rental', and anyway archaeologically speaking it was of no value. Nevertheless Miss Craig's mother, living opposite, was fearfully upset, could not afford to purchase and yet was loath to leave The Farm, which two new cottages would certainly force her to do. 'If Miss Craig's friends', the local secretary wrote again, 'cared to give £200 to £300 for it, the lessees would be foolish not to build two new cottages [elsewhere] instead of altering this. I should not care to buy it myself.' It would seem that the National Trust was as usual unable to raise the cash but that friends of Ellen and Edy must have stepped in and bought it, for Yew Tree Cottage became part of the Smallhythe conglomerate.

After Ellen Terry's death at The Farm in 1928 Edy Craig rather rashly launched a hastily conceived appeal for £15,000 with which to form a Smallhythe Memorial Trust, which in fact never came into existence. She was determined that The Farm should become her mother's shrine, in other words a museum in which her theatrical treasures and relics would be displayed for all time, her bedroom to be kept exactly as it was at the great actress's death. Many of Ellen's admirers thought it a bad idea, and there was a good deal of criticism.

At all events little more than £1,000 was raised. Nevertheless Edy defiantly persisted in trying to form the trust. Piously and beautifully she created the museum and arranged the exhibits. Smallhythe Place, as The Farm became, was shown to the public by Miss Craig, Miss St John and Miss Atwood at a charge of 6d. per head which subsisted until well after the war. It was strictly in accordance with Ellen Terry's wish. She had always welcomed strangers who called in her lifetime and gave instructions that no matter who they were they must be addressed as Sir and Madam.

In March 1938 a letter reached the National Trust from Miss Craig's legal adviser and honorary secretary of the 'Ellen Terry Memorial Trust'. Irene Cooper-Willis was a brilliant solicitor and friend and protector of Edy Craig who was hopelessly improvident, unbusinesslike and impecunious. The ten-year option given to the phantom Memorial Trust to purchase Smallhythe from Miss Craig had four more years to run; and the trustees had no money with which to purchase. Would the National Trust take over Smallhythe from the phantom Memorial Trust? On 23rd of the month I replied that the National Trust had no money either, but in any case I would like to see the property. Incidentally, what, I asked, did the funds of the Memorial Trust amount to? My letter prompted one from Miss Craig informing me that the suggestion to hand over to the National Trust had come from Vita Sackville-West who lived near them at Sissinghurst. 'She told me that Mr. Lees-Milne who deals with houses might be interested.' My request to be allowed to come down to Smallhythe was answered by Miss St John who I soon learned was the normal intermediary between Miss Craig and the outside world.

In May I visited Smallhythe for the first time. I was wholly captivated by the seclusion of the place, the picturesqueness of the buildings and setting, the fascination of the shrine, the charm of the elderly ladies, and the casual happy-go-lucky spirit that prevailed. I have seldom walked through rooms more nostalgic of a particular owner. After one of many visits there I wrote that, 'in Ellen Terry's little house one feels that she might walk past one at any minute, and in her bedroom that she might appear before her dressing-table brushing her hair'. It was a very cold spring morning and I was generously supplied with rather milky coffee from an enormous pottery jug. I spent hours being shown everything and then chatting. On parting I was in love with the three; and possibly made the mistake of considering them dear old souls.

The Executive Committee to which I reported agreed to take Smallhythe Place subject to Miss Craig's retention of a life interest, but could give no undertaking to keep every exhibit in precisely its actual setting for ever. Miss Cooper-Willis wrote to me that Miss Craig would in no way accept the committee's proviso. On the other hand, while graciously waving it aside as though it had never been made, she was prepared to convey there and then the museum, contents, the Priest's House, and Yew Tree and Toll Cottages and in addition to bequeath to the Trust all her own fortune which yielded approximately £300 a year. At that time the annual income from visitors was £130, and the outgoings were £160. It surprises me now that the Trust, usually so grasping of money, consented to accept the property with absolutely no endowment beyond the expectation of Miss Craig's pitiful investments on her death, and to renege on the provision about the exhibits. At any rate the gift of Smallhythe to the National Trust from Miss Craig went ahead in 1939.

While I was away on some ploy or other a slight ruction ensued. It served as a warning that there was another side to the smiling medal and all that glittered was not invariably gold. My colleague Christopher Gibbs, the most conscientious, reliable and punctilious member of staff the National Trust was ever to be blessed with and, unlike me, a stickler for figures and proper business methods, thought fit to address a letter, not to Miss Cooper-Willis, but to Miss Craig herself. It began: 'Under the National Trust Acts of Parliament of 1907–1937, a copy of which I enclose, the National Trust has the statutory obligation, etc., etc.' On my return I found letters, sent to my private address and marked Personal and Secret, from both Craig and St John vehemently protesting against being sent those dreadful Acts of Parliament which made no sense whatever (in ten congested pages there was not even one comma, let alone a full stop) except possibly to machines and morons; that in dealing with the National Trust they had expected at least to be treated like civilized human beings; that figures drove all true artists crazy; that they felt deeply insulted since they were artists and supposed we knew it; and that if ever a similar affront was levelled at them again they would take back the whole property, lock, stock and barrel. Would I come down at once, explain my colleague's conduct, and have some more coffee? I need hardly say that eventually they liked Christopher Gibbs immensely, but not before the secretary, MacLeod Matheson, committed another gaffe of similar dimensions.

Meanwhile Miss Craig, somewhat mollified, professed herself delighted to be acknowledged a benefactor of the National Trust. She was also thrilled with the prospect of an opening ceremony at Smallhythe. Unfortunately the outbreak of war prevented it. Providentially, before a ban on all building and repairs was enforced by the government, some very necessary work was done to the tiled roof of The Farm and the thatch of the old barn on the premises. The work was entrusted to Walter Godfrey, the architect and antiquary who was a friend of Edith Craig. Brought up in an advanced circle of socialist agnosticism Godfrey had been soused in the Arts and Crafts movement, had been author of the London Survey volumes and was to become in 1941 founder-secretary of the invaluable National Buildings Record. Miss Craig was happy to leave to Walter Godfrey and the National Trust what was necessary to be done up to £300 worth.

At first Miss Craig and her two companions intended to withdraw into The Farm in order to safeguard it against possible wartime requisition and to let the Priest's House for whatever rent it might bring in. But lack of any sort of modern conditions in The Farm and the ladies' rebarbative demeanour successively deterred all officials sent to inspect it. On the other hand Smallhythe being in the front line there were rumours in the early stages of the war that they might have to evacuate. As it was in 1940 a guard of seven men was posted at the bridge over the Rother. The ladies were rather flattered by this attention which they arrogated to themselves. When the Battle of Britain began they were disturbed by the guns at Dover and what they called the 'high-flying air army' over Kent. They were also alarmed when Irene Cooper-Willis's London chambers were badly bombed.

With the male National Trust staff away on service Matheson was left to wrestle amongst his other problems with the Smallhythe accounts, the ladies being quite incapable of coping and even determined not to make the attempt. And then befell the compounding of Christopher Gibbs' gaffe. He of course had gone to war and by 1941 was a full-blown major. Matheson was no less efficient and businesslike with an insuperable inclination to terminological exactitudes. He was not so much unsympathetic towards as un-understanding of others' lack of partiality for official documents, forms, questionnaires and demands for payments. But he made the mistake of writing summarily to Miss Craig begging for things called 'vouchers' to testify that she had paid her rates and taxes. The repercussions were fearful. The trio flew into a concerted rage. Cooper-Willis was called upon to denounce the invoker of vouchers and all his works. It was no use, she told poor Matheson, his approaching the trio on such matters. The mere mention of vouchers 'conjures up in their minds visions of Superlative Order and Method, which drives them frantic. They won't and can't keep accounts, no matter how loud and long the Inland Revenue fulminates and threatens'. But, Matheson retorted in a wounded manner, the National Trust's auditors were demanding vouchers which if not instantly produced might well land the Trust in a scandal. The public might well suppose that the Trust was an infamous device to benefit scheming rich donors at the expense of righteous impoverished taxpayers. The secretary's words fell on deaf ears. He was defeated over vouchers.

Eardley Knollys, who had in 1941 joined the National Trust staff to support the solitary Matheson, was sent to Smallhythe to sort out the War Damage Insurance contribution on the trio's behalf. He drove over with Vita Sackville-West from Sissinghurst. Whether his visit to Small-hythe resulted in the extraction of the insurance policies I do not know for I was away. It certainly had a soothing effect on the trio. They were charmed with him, discussed the theatre, painting, writing and sculpture, and plied him with coffee. St John was soon writing him letters in her wonderfully neat script. They were alarmed by the impending sale 'next Tuesday' of land on Smallhythe marsh, a stone's throw from the house, for bungalows. How could anyone want a bungalow in wartime? Would the Trust immediately buy the land and relieve their declining years from enduring misery? Somehow the threat was not realized. Then Eardley was able to be the harbinger of good news.

Vita, a consistently generous neighbour, always kept a wary eye on the well-being of what she termed 'the trouts'. (The expression was soon bandied amongst all who knew them. Indeed for a long time my wife supposed it to be their surname and that the three, somewhat alike with their cropped, straight, grey hair and mannish clothes, must be sisters, so that she even asked while staying at Sissinghurst if she might not pay a visit to the Misses Trout.) At all events Vita felt concern about Chris's digging in the Priest's House garden. Chris was already bent low with arthritis and no longer up to manual labour. Vita got Eardley to convey an anonymous offer to pay the wages of an adolescent digger to come two or three times a week. 'I should think a schoolboy,' Eardley wrote, 'well under military age, or even a girl would be best' at 16s. 4d. a week. The timely suggestion brought much satisfaction and credit to Eardley who henceforth was regarded as the blue-eyed all-provider, a compliment he did not forfeit when he left the starting-handle of his car behind. It had to be posted to him. The trouts probably guessed that Vita was their benefactor but had the tact not to mention it. A boy was engaged and his wages were duly forwarded, not to the trouts, but to the National Trust direct, for payment, on Vita's behalf.

In July 1942 I having returned to the Trust received a letter from Miss Atwood announcing that Miss Craig was 'threatened with dire consequences in red ink if she doesn't pay odd amounts to the insurance people'. Since imprisonment was looming poor Edy was posting the brutes a cheque, 'not knowing whether it would be honoured'. Furthermore the barn roof again was worn out and the temperature (it was July) below zero. 'I fear you will think this unbusinesslike and casual, but you do not know the difficulties of the situation. [I could imagine them well enough.] I hope you will come to see us again – and that we may be allowed [?by the insurance people] to minister coffee to you then and many times.' Things were obviously serious. I replied, 'I am appalled by the vision of poor Miss Craig being driven off in a Black Maria and hope she will not get any more angry notes in red ink.' This not very helpful letter was followed by a visit when I went steadfastly through all their accounts. I fear it was a case of the blind leading the blind. But I did my best.

The operation did not prevent the Tenterden Borough Council threatening to sue. Miss Craig by a curious calculation maintained that in the case of Yew Tree Cottage only the ground on which the porch stood was liable to rates. Her plea was disregarded. In desperation I asked the borough, the Inland Revenue, and all her creditors to send applications to me personally, hoping that some department of the National Trust would eventually take pity on her – and me. However by some means unremembered threats of the Marshalsea were once again averted.

In August 1943 I received an SOS from Miss Craig. A letter from me to her, unopened, had been lost. What on earth was it about? Would I come down instantly and explain? I was able to assure her it was only an enquiry about her health. In October there was another summons. Would I come and protect the property from the troops? Which troops? Our own. This seemed a little unnecessary. Smallhythe happily survived the Allies and the Germans. By the time peace was established the National Trust's Kent and East Sussex region was set up with Cuthbert Acland as area agent, and Robin Fedden the Trust's representative concerned with the historic buildings. Acland was consistently sympathetic to the ladies even when pushed beyond the ordinary limits of endurance. In December 1946 I was informed that £45 was urgently needed for repairs to the Priest's House. Underpinning of the stone foundations, 'brought to a rocky condition by the rats', a strange conjunction, was resulting in a gradual but alarming subsidence of the building. Already a year and a half had passed since a licence for the work had been applied for. It was by rights the trouts' liability. They appealed to me over Acland's head. Would I come to the rescue by the first available train? I begged Cubby Acland to get the Trust to pay for they were penniless, and I thought Edith Craig, who was becoming increasingly frail, could not last much longer. He persuaded his committee to consent. He was bombarded with grateful letters. Admiral Bevir, the Trust's new secretary, wrote, 'the dears seem to be quite pleased'.

The following February I was given a reserved seat by Miss Craig for a service in St Paul's, Covent Garden, in celebration of Ellen Terry's birthday centenary. Although a bitterly cold and foggy day it was a joyful occasion. The three trouts were prominent in a front pew, Chris St John 'wearing a fawn teddy-bear coat, man's porkpie hat, and waving a gigantic bunch of golden daffodils at her friends in the rear'. The church was crammed with stage celebrities, some of whom read lessons, while others recited from Shakespeare. Little more than a month later practically the same congregation reassembled for a sadder ceremony. On 3 March Clare Atwood wrote me a letter: 'I know how you will feel the dreadful news I have to give you. Edy Craig died this morning at 8.30. She had been ill some time with a bad heart, and died without pain. I thought that you as representing the Trust, should be told immediately.' So I went down to Smallhythe for her funeral in the tiny brick church of St John the Baptist, coeval with The Farm. The two surviving old ladies were extremely upset. Clare Atwood wrote to me that they needed no help. Beautiful Olive Chaplin, as Edy's first cousin and next-of-kin after her estranged brother Gordon, was looking after them. They had been left the right to continue living in the Priest's House. All Edy's personal things were theirs too, and the survivor would leave them to the National Trust in her will.

After a visit to Smallhythe towards the end of April I reported to the Trust that, 'the old ladies are infinitely pathetic and, if possible, worse off than they were in Miss Craig's lifetime, a situation hard to conceive'. The builders had done nothing to arrest the rats' depredations of the Priest's House and the timbers were all rotting. Yew Tree was still untenanted. I recommended that we got some retired actor or actress to live in the museum; but first we should put in a bathroom and WC. The contents of the museum were in a chaotic state and needed sorting. The two old ladies begged the Trust to manage as though they were already dead. As it happened Olive Chaplin, Ellen Terry's niece who had been on the stage, eventually became curator and trout-minder combined: but not at once.

Robin Fedden who was to be my successor at head office and then was quartered at Polesden Lacey within the East Sussex and Kent area told me he 'thought the Ellen Terry Museum quite one of the best things I have ever seen; the atmosphere exactly right and the exhibits fascinating'. He was quick to recognize that the atmosphere was of evanescent quality and if it were not to be dispelled by increasing numbers of the public who were bound to flock to Smallhythe, urgent and perhaps drastic measures must be taken. How to preserve the goose that laid the golden egg was then, as now, a paramount problem confronting the National Trust. But in the case of Smallhythe it was not one I was called upon to solve. It was clear, however, that Tony and Chris must for their own sakes be relieved of the burden of showmanship and curating. Also the organization of theatricals in the barn every year, which Edy had already ordained in her mother's memory, called for a person with special qualities.

Vita informed Robin Fedden that the old ladies had spent their uttermost farthings on keeping the museum going and that they must be reimbursed at once. Robin and I then called for a meeting with Irene Cooper-Willis, at which we readily agreed to reimburse and to take over the running expenses immediately. When we assured her that we were wrung with pity for the trouts, she disclosed that Atwood and St John were not down to rock-bottom at all; that financially they were, although not rich, quite flush; but that they never ceased to complain to all and sundry, especially at Sissinghurst, how the Trust did nothing for them. Miss Cooper-Willis's wise advice to the Trust was not to let on that we knew and to pay no attention; but so long as they remained alive, to defer the acceptance of all gifts to the museum and steadfastly stick to the *sine qua non* not to shift any of the exhibits. As for the barn theatre which had a very sacred place in their hearts in view of Edy's conviction that performances would perpetuate her mother's memory more than anything else, the Trust made it a generous donation. In this way it also hoped to curry some favour with the touchy and mercurial old ladies. Robin immediately engaged at £100 a year a charming custodian approved by them whom they quickly drove away with their carping. She was then replaced by the admittedly perfect Mrs Chaplin.

By 1948 the trouts had got their fins into the National Trust deeper than ever in spite of Robin Fedden having done wonders in helping put on a firm foundation the Ellen Terry Fellowship for the continuance of the barn theatre. In the summer of 1947 he attended a performance in which Sybil Thorndike acted in the death scene from *Henry VIII* in a very moving manner.

On 24 July 1949 Vita Sackville-West accepted officially on the Trust's behalf the contents of the museum at a formal handing-over ceremony.

It took place nearly ten years after the date first chosen by Miss Craig. By 1962 both Miss St John and Miss Atwood were dead, and the Trust could tread less warily. Nevertheless the spirits of all the trouts and that of Ellen Terry hover conspicuously over Smallhythe and their watching brief is very solemnly heeded.

Smallhythe has become an extremely popular shrine. Its appeal is deeply nostalgic. It probably contains more personal associations with a great figure of the past than any museum in the land. And of course it is not really a museum at all but a home. Its vulnerable fragility is protected by the love of its custodians and the reverential attitude of its visitors who are allowed to wander around it at will.

CHAPTER NINE

MONTGOMERY-MASSINGBERD OF GUNBY
Lincolnshire

C UT off from the rest of England by marshes to the south, fens to the west, wolds to the north, and from Europe by the German Ocean to the east, Gunby is one of those little Lincolnshire villages on a limb, dry in summer and intensely cold in winter. Standing in its own park the Hall is an Augustan squire's domain, robust, unostentatious, dignified and a trifle prim. Had it been in one of the west shires and not of the east Jane Austen might have taken it for the seat of Sir Walter Elliot, or Fielding a generation sooner for that of Squire Allworthy. However it was built, not of Bath stone but deep plum brick by Sir William Massingberd, 2nd Baronet of Bratoft, with the minimum of pretensions in 1700. The very name Massingberd, meaning in Anglo-Saxon brass beard, conjures up wild Scandinavian immigrants. But the family had been settled in the neighbourhood of Burgh-le-Marsh for generations before Sir William whose father, although he had fought for Parliament in the Civil War, became at the turn of the tide an unequivocal monarchist. Fortune favoured the Massingberds of Gunby in all but continuity of the male line. They married local heiresses and always kept the old name, becoming Meux Massingberd, Langton Massingberd (twice over) and finally Montgomery-Massingberd, before parting with the property to the National Trust during the Second World War.

Gunby was very nearly a war casualty. Like Stourhead it was threatened by the Air Ministry, and saved by the bulldog pertinacity and fighting spirit of its owner, or rather the owner's husband, who had the daunting title and name of Field Marshal Sir Archibald Armar Montgomery-Massingberd, KCMG, KCB and GCB, who until his retirement in 1936 had been Chief of the Imperial General Staff.

A long letter from the Field Marshal reached the National Trust in March 1943. It explained that in November 1941 the Air Ministry had decided to construct an aerodrome on land contiguous to the Gunby estate. What particularly annoyed the Field Marshal was that he had never been consulted and only heard about the proposal unofficially from two young officers. The scheme, he understood, would involve the felling of 800 Gunby trees so carefully planted by Peregrine Langton Massingberd in the early nineteenth century. They were then in their prime. The Field Marshal had written in protest to the Chief of Air Staff and Air Chief Marshal Sir Charles Portal who was non-committal but blandly sympathetic. Next, a rumour reached him that Gunby Hall stood in the path of a proposed new runway and would have to be demolished to allow a heavy type of bomber to rise and descend. Indeed the Field Marshal out walking had met three men in his garden measuring the height of trees with a theodolite and marking them. He immediately asked to see somebody in authority; and received no reply. So he was asking for a National Trust representative to visit the site and advise him what could be done. Matheson the secretary suggested in reply that the Field Marshal might approach the Council for the Preservation of Rural England. The Field Marshal was not going to take that for an answer and, a little piqued, wrote again. The letter was handed to me. Sorrowfully I felt obliged to point out that, strictly speaking, the Trust could take up the cudgels only when its own properties were under threat or, I added, prospective properties.

By return of post the Field Marshal wrote that Lady Massingberd who was Gunby's owner considered the soundest plan might be for her to hand over the property to the National Trust without delay. What was the Trust's view of this? Well, it made a difference. On 25th of the month I paid the first of several visits to Gunby.

I fell for the place and its inhabitants at once. Austere the house undoubtedly was outside, but not lugubrious. John Byng the diarist passing by in 1791 when it was not a hundred years old and 'had been rented to Sir P. Burrell for a shooting seat', called it 'a most melancholy place; suicide in every room'. I did not get that impression. The stark skyline without any frills or furbelows seemed fitting for the residence of a couple who epitomized the Tory axiom of Crown and Church. True there was something slightly puritanical in the economical design and, low be it spoken, the 1st Baronet had received his honour from Oliver Cromwell to whom he had 'good affection'. At any rate the baronetcy, automatically forfeited on the Restoration of 1660, was immediately granted back by the Merry Monarch. It was not an incident of which the current owners would have relished a reminder.

Behind the simple soldier ethos of wartime Gunby there lurked, if not a bohemian, certainly a very discernible intellectual and literary tradition. In the first place the ancestor Peregrine Langton who became the consort of Elizabeth Massingberd in 1802 was the second son of Dr Johnson's great friend and butt, Bennet Langton, scholar squire of neighbouring Langton Hall. Bennet's fine portrait by Reynolds, depicting a handsome young man resting a languid elbow on Clarendon's *Great Rebellion* and Johnson's *Prince of Abyssinia* (not, alas, the famous dictionary of which a signed copy is still kept at Gunby), hangs in the drawing-room. While Peregrine compiled travel diaries and jotted down copious notes about the estate his brother George made a wickedly cruel sketch of the great doctor's biographer James Boswell, now in the entrance hall. A later literary association with Gunby was that of the young Alfred Tennyson who was brought up at Somersby Rectory a few miles away. That the oft-quoted stanza from his poem *The Palace of Art*,

> ... an English home – gray twilight pour'd
> On dewy pastures, dewy trees
> Softer than sleep – all things in order stored,
> A haunt of ancient peace,

was a deliberate description of Gunby is made tenable by a framed transcription in the handwriting and above the signature of the poet and date, 1849. Certainly it seems totally inapplicable to Tennyson's exotic palace of art which he made out to be raised on 'a huge crag-platform smooth as burnished brass', with 'ranged ramparts', 'gilded gallery' and 'winding stair', whereas it suits the tree-embowered William III Gunby Hall to a tee.

Lady Massingberd had inherited Gunby from her brother Stephen whose wife Margaret, a daughter of Judge Vernon Lushington, had direct affiliations with the Pre-Raphaelites, even with Bloomsbury. During the Stephen Massingberds' reign – they unfortunately were childless – Gunby became a rural periphery of metropolitan intelligentsia, the arts and the crafts. Margaret's sister Mildred was married to a son of Charles Darwin the great naturalist, and another sister Kitty to Leo Maxse, editor of the *National Review*. Their mother had been the greatest friend of Virginia Woolf's mother Julia Stephen. On Julia's early death Kitty became a sort of surrogate elder sister to Virginia in the ways of the world. Virginia grew away from her in later years yet on Kitty's death in 1922 thought sorrowfully of her lying in a grave next to Margaret's at Gunby. She hadn't seen her but once since 1908 'and then

I cut her, which now troubles me – unreasonably I suppose.' Margaret died young to the immense grief of Stephen. The full-length portrait (painted in 1903 by Arthur Hughes) of her standing in the garden at Gunby amongst tall, sea-blue delphiniums with white doves circling overhead, dominates the dining-room. This picture evokes the very spirit of Edwardian highbrow country-house living, a spirit which if slightly dimmed, was still fostered by Stephen and Margaret's successors. For Stephen's sister Diana and Archie Montgomery-Massingberd were close friends of Rudyard Kipling, of whom there are several reminders at Gunby and at whose funeral in Westminster Abbey the Field Marshal was a pall-bearer.

The Field Marshal, though immensely distinguished, was not the least forbidding. He was tall, very handsome, with a clear complexion and bright blue eyes. His critics asserted that his promotion to high army rank was owing to his face being his fortune. Yet he was shrewd. 'Keep an eye on Pétain,' he warned Winston Churchill in 1918. And once when GOC during a discussion on military manoeuvres he noted that Neville Chamberlain did not know the difference between a division and a company, and did not bother to learn. I see him now, a dazzling figure presiding over the mahogany in a snow-white, pleated shirt-front bulging from a black velvet coat, immaculate, impeccable. Even in wartime a dinner jacket for the guest was *de rigueur*. Wharton the kindly butler, a sort of Lincolnshire Jeeves, for he was as much a gentleman's gentleman as a butler, was arrayed in black tailcoat, starched collar and white tie. Lady Massingberd was also tall, upright, forthright, no-nonsensical, jolly and just a little arch. She was intensely musical. She had studied singing with the tenor Gervase Elwes, who happened to be a Lincolnshire squire, and Sir George Herschel. She sang too with her second cousin Ralph Vaughan Williams who dedicated to her sister Margaret his well-known part song *Linden Lea*, first performed in the music room at Gunby in 1902. She was first and foremost a violinist. Throughout Lincolnshire she sponsored concerts by amateur musicians at which she played in the orchestra; and she played the organ in Gunby church.

A bond – at least I think it was – between us was my friend of long standing Peter Montgomery, also extremely musical and in peace-time conductor of the Northern Ireland radio orchestra. Incidentally he was nephew to both Sir Archibald and Lady Massingberd who loved him dearly with, I sensed, a slight reservation in that he was not of the marrying sort and thereby not destined to inclusion in their list of possible successors to Gunby, about which I was soon to be much concerned. It being time of war not a drop of alcohol was permitted to be drunk and the ration of bath water was strictly limited by a red line painted two inches above the bottom of the tub. Furthermore the 'hot water' was strictly tepid and then allowable only twice a day for one hour each time. This seemed perfectly acceptable in the circumstances and smacked of loyalty to King and country in their extremity. The Massingberds positively revelled in these patriotic austerities.

The day after I left, the Field Marshal, whether in hope or despair brought about by my visit, wrote to the King who replied through Sir Alec Hardinge that he was 'more than sympathetic' about the horrid threat to Gunby.

Having been made acquainted with the imminent inroads upon the place by the Air Ministry I wrote on my return to London to Sir Geoffrey Mander, MP, the donor to the National Trust of Wightwick Manor in Staffordshire, and a loyal friend, who was at the time parliamentary private secretary to the Minister. All the old trees in the park, I pointed out, were doomed if the Ministry were to go ahead with their project, and the house might even be demolished. I also begged F.J.E. Raby of the Ministry of Works to rouse himself to make a protest on Gunby's behalf. I do not remember what, if anything, Raby did, but Sir Geoffrey turned up trumps. Within three weeks he wrote that he had so arranged matters with the Air Force authorities in Lincolnshire that the house would not be touched and a few trees only would have to be topped. It is not insignificant that on 13 April the Under-Secretary of State for Air wrote to Sir Alec Hardinge to the same effect. The Field Marshal and Lady Massingberd on being informed were so pleased that they decided to make the property over to the National Trust there and then. They declared that once this happened it would be more difficult for the Ministry to change its mind, which otherwise it was quite capable of doing.

On 14 April I instructed Carter Jonas & Sons, land agents at Cambridge, to make a report for the Trust on the Gunby estate, with the help of the Massingberds' agent, John Langton, who was also their cousin. The Massingberds were very attached to Langton – Lincoln-shire families are close-knit – and urged the Trust to keep him on as agent until such time as he chose to retire, believing it would be a great mistake on the Trust's part to let him go. To bring to public notice the peril which had confronted Gunby and possibly lay in store for other historic houses, Christopher Hussey wrote an article on the house in *Country Life*.

In July the Country Houses Committee agreed, on the strength of

Carter Jonas's favourable report on Gunby's finances, to recommend to the Executive Committee acceptance of the property because of its undoubted merits. I communicated the news to the Field Marshal with the suggestion that perhaps the solicitors of both parties should get in touch in the customary way. 'I rather mistrust lawyers', was his retort (it was probably the only sentiment that he shared with Sir Henry Fairfax-Lucy of Charlecote Park), 'and would like to have a talk with you before you give them any instructions.' Gunby was a settled estate and the interests of different members of the family had to be considered by Lady Massingberd: the very reason, I opined, why the lawyers ought to be invoked. The Field Marshal consented that benign Mr Horne, our solicitor from ages past, might be consulted before his own. Benjamin Horne, a waffling bumble-bee of a man, had drawn up the articles of the Trust's foundation in 1895. He at once stated that the property could, unlike the majority of settled estates that came our way, easily be disentailed by Lady Massingberd.

I then went down to Gunby for a night. And the first thing I noticed the following morning through a window was a high Eiffel tower crowned by a revolving, illuminated beacon, planted since my last visit in the middle of the tennis court. This was to warn pilots to avoid crashing into the house of ancient peace. I accompanied the Field Marshal in a snail-like perambulation round the estate. Whenever he made an emphatic point he stabbed the ground with a long walking-stick and stood stock still. In July this was not so bad but in mid-winter I froze. His attitude to employees and tenants was invariably cordial yet feudal. He knocked on cottage doors always to be welcomed with a smile. He then collected from the inmates their saving funds which he took away to invest for them. In the evening conversation ensued about Gunby's future. Which member of the family should be chosen to live in the Hall after the death of the survivor of the old couple? And which member indeed would wish to live in it?

The first to be selected and to consent was a cousin of Lady Massingberd, Major Norman Leith Hay Clark, whose mother had been her aunt, born a Massingberd. For some odd reason he was the next of the family in the entail. Leith Hay Clark's name was accordingly specified in the memorandum of the donors' wishes. He agreed to the donors' condition that no future occupant of the Hall should be either a foreigner or a Roman Catholic. I foresaw some possible difficulties arising out of this proviso. What, for instance, would happen if an heir was to become a Catholic during his occupancy of Gunby? Was the National Trust to turn him out? And if not, might not, say, an elder brother who had previously become a Catholic and so been debarred from succession, feel resentment? In actual fact Hugh, an elder brother of Peter Montgomery, was already a Catholic priest which met with the tacit disapproval of the owners of Gunby. At this time he was chargé d'affaires at the British Ministry to the Vatican, and was later to become a Monsignor. The Field Marshal assured me however that in principle he and his wife had no prejudice against Roman Catholics, but the little church in the grounds and the parish would suffer were occupants of the Hall not members of the Church of England. Presumably they inferred that any foreigner would likewise not belong to the Church of England. And in any event were the Montgomery brothers' succession to come in question, for their mother Mary was another sister of Lady Massingberd, Hugh would neither want nor could he afford to live in the house as squire. It soon came to pass that the Montgomery nephews were to be in the running. The Leith Hay Clarks had two sons fighting in the Army. Both were reported missing, and then killed. Greatly distressed Norman saw little point in his moving to Gunby after his cousins' time and so withdrew his candidature. This catastrophe necessitated another visit by me to Gunby when still further consultations about the succession took place.

After my visit much correspondence ensued before the youngest of the Montgomery nephews John (for Peter besides being out of the running was heir to his father Major-General Hugh Montgomery's estate, Blessingbourne in County Tyrone) became heir presumptive to the right of residence and the patronage of several livings. This was a happy outcome in that John, like his brethren, was nephew of both Lady Massingberd and the Field Marshal. There was too the vexed question, because of the transfer of the Gunby freehold to the Trust, whether the resident should or should not take on the name of Massingberd in accordance with a clause in the will of a forebear that any person inheriting the estate should do so; otherwise the estate would lapse to the next heir under the entail. Indeed the name had already endured a number of vicissitudes which in most cases of the sort would have eliminated it altogether. In this case the name was duly revived for a fourth time.

Meanwhile an inventory of the contents of the Hall to be included in the gift of Gunby was called for. With his honourable record as past Keeper of Woodwork and Furniture at the Victoria & Albert Museum, his reputation for helping recreate and refurbish Sulgrave Manor 'as a token of friendship' between the people of Britain and the United States, his authorship of *Buckingham Palace* and much-vaunted friendship with Queen Mary, Harold Clifford Smith was readily approved as compiler. His veneration of the Queen Mother was so compulsive that like a tidal wave it overwhelmed his relations with clients and friends, whether of high or low degree. Without reciprocating it beyond a formal condescension the Queen found his enthusiasm for and knowledge of the antiques useful. Certainly his expertise covered so wide a field that the uncharitable among his colleagues deemed him a jack of all trades and master of none; which when the divergent contents of the average English country house require listing and describing is a more valuable qualification than mastery of but one trade. Benevolent though Cliffy was his slow and halting speech, prefaced by a chain of ums and ers, had so costive an effect even upon his most quick-witted interrogators that they were paralysed with impatience before he got the first words out.

The Montgomery-Massingberds had him to stay in the house. To begin with they were delighted with him. They were amused by his royal anecdotes and intimacies and edified by his information, even when irrelevant to the job in hand. After a week the Field Marshal wrote to me that Cliffy was terribly worried whether an inkpot was George II or George III. 'I can't for the life of me see that it matters.' But it did matter to Cliffy inordinately. He liked to get things right. We soon perceived that he was going beyond our mutual requirements and his report would be too lengthy. Who, the Field Marshal wrote again, was bearing the cost of this prolonged exercise? When the work was finished Cliffy's bill came only to £19. 7s., which seemed to all a modest sum. Cliffy induced the Field Marshal much against his will to write an introduction to the inventory. He then asked me if I saw any impropriety in his sending a copy to Queen Mary. I said I knew little about propriety in such matters and suggested that he should ask Marlborough House. Lady Cynthia Colville, Queen Mary's Woman of the Bedchamber, replied that he might submit it.

Here and now I wish to record that probably in the whole history of the National Trust, and certainly during my tenure of office, the transfer of a large estate to the Trust never happened more speedily or smoothly than Gunby. The Montgomery-Massingberds were amongst the easiest of donors I encountered, only vying in kindness and consideration with the Mount Edgcumbes of Cotehele. There were no wrangles and no rancour of any sort. As Matthew Arnold wrote, 'He who works for sweetness and light united, works to make reason and the will of God prevail.' There followed of course small differences which were resolved always pleasantly and often humorously.

One cause of slight embarrassment to the Trust was the Field Marshal's inclination, after the inventory had been concluded, to hand over more chattels than were strictly needed. This was an unusual attitude on the part of a donor. Some additions like the portrait of Peregrine Langton were very welcome; also some Snaffles cartoons, such as *Good Hunting, Old Sportsman!* and *Wipers*, were gratefully received. On the whole the Trust felt that only things that were works of art or had historic and family associations with Gunby should be taken by them for permanent keeping and display. The Field Marshal's valid argument was that he was as good a judge of a work of art or a relic as the National Trust; and besides who were they to look gift horses in the mouth? He had been a trifle hurt when the Trust showed a disinclination to accept some pretty water-colours of the honeysuckle-over-cottage-porch kind which he had purchased at a local sale. Such pictures adorn many bedrooms of country houses throughout the land, but do not necessarily qualify as museum pieces. The Trust had also demurred over taking two rather indifferent portraits of the Field Marshal and Lady Massingberd by Oswald Birley. They had been painted after the artist lost an eye. By all means, thought the Trust, let these things hang where they were but not for ever by binding agreement. The Field Marshal was again put out. As it happened he eventually took against the Birley portraits with loathing and one of the last wishes expressed on his deathbed was that they should be removed from the walls. When the Country Houses Committee came to deliberate upon the conundrum someone suggested that the portraits might be disposed of. Whereupon Martineau (our new solicitor), a great stickler for observing the rules to the last letter of the law, exclaimed that alienation of these portraits would be entirely contrary to clause 3 of section cxlvii of the Guardianship of Entrusted Antiquities Act of 1592 (I invent the precise statute). Whereupon Lord Esher turning to me asked casually as if in parenthesis: 'Do you have a bonfire sometimes in the kitchen garden at Gunby?' And after a pause, 'Now let us turn to the next item on the agenda.'

Needless to say no such drastic measures were taken. The portraits now hang in the gunroom at Gunby. It is curious how seen after an interval of nearly fifty years these Birley portraits strike me, not it is true as great works of art – far from it – but as perfectly decent and acceptable likenesses. Thus either portraits tend to adapt themselves to memory's impression of what persons one has known long ago looked like, or else the severe judgements of youth are leavened by the laxer standards of age.

In fine the Field Marshal, with the bit between his teeth, was inclined to give away more of his wife's possessions than she sometimes thought fitting. In her charming and modest way she asked if she might have back her Blüthner piano which her husband had made Cliffy include in his inventory of the Trust's possessions. Lord Esher had to be consulted and readily agreed.

Lord and Lady Esher were cordially invited to stay at Gunby in August 1945, ostensibly to sample the hospitality of the Trust's new property for themselves. The Field Marshal had written to me that he hoped Lord Esher 'would not advance any foolish ideas about limiting further contents to antiquity'. All went well however in that respect. The real motive for enticing the chairman of the (by now) Historic Buildings Committee was for him to experience the nuisance of the runway whose presence was an abiding affront to the Massingberds. In a letter to me the Field Marshal reiterated his determination to fight the Air Ministry 'to the bitter end'. He had no doubt Lord Esher would feel impelled to get the runway removed. 'Not only does this damned tower spoil the whole look of the lawn, but the value of the house is definitely reduced as *night and day* these heavy bombers fly a few feet above the roof of the house,' and there was 'always the chance of a bad crash'. In wartime the nuisance had to be borne, but not in peace which had just returned. As for the market value of the house the Field Marshal was overlooking the fact that now Gunby Hall belonged to the Trust it no longer had any. During this summer the Air Ministry was actually threatening to keep permanent hold of the site, and even to seek powers to purchase nearly four additional acres of the Trust's inalienable land for extensions. 'We have beaten the Boches and the Japs and now we must defeat the Civilian Element of the Air Ministry a second time,' was the Field Marshal's gallant reaction.

The visit of the Eshers, at which I was not present, passed agreeably enough. The hosts did their utmost to please and the guests to gush. Oliver Esher thought Gunby a nice little place but confessed to me that amongst the higher echelons of the Army he felt like a fish out of water. On his return he asked Lord Stansgate, the Minister for Air, and Mr Tony Benn's father, if he would remove the offensive tower, to be told that he would not until the airfield was scrapped. Instead Stansgate offered to have it camouflaged. This infuriated the Field Marshal. The very idea was damned nonsense coming from a newly inflated Labour peer. He was also displeased that Lord Esher would not press more urgently his demand for the tower's instant removal. Lord Esher had his reasons. He believed that the whole site would shortly be scrapped, and that nagging would not hasten it. The Field Marshal did not agree. He resumed his assault. And whether or not the authorities were browbeaten by his importunities, in April 1946, without warning, the whole airfield, Nissen huts, tower and all disappeared from the scene.

Before this happy issue out of their afflictions I was summoned to Gunby to discuss a domestic crisis. Lady Massingberd had written that she needed a housemaid badly and a kitchen maid if possible, 'though perhaps the Labour Government would be angry with me in wanting four servants for two people'. They never got to hear of it, and the poor Massingberds never got back their pre-war complement of staff. How therefore were they to show the public round the house without help beyond that of the indispensable Whartons? Lady Massingberd rose to the occasion. In spite of chronic arthritis she would do the showing just as during the war she had polished the beautiful barley-sugar balusters and treads of the staircase on hands and knees, occasionally enlisting, as her great-nephew Hugh relates in his entertaining guidebook, the assistance of those guests who might be lamenting the inadequacy of Gunby's central heating. Having engaged in the discussion without satisfactorily resolving the servant problem I returned to London, and developed mumps. I was terrified lest I had infected my aged hosts with this complaint so uncomfortable for adults. However they evinced no concern for themselves and much solicitude for me.

The first opening day of Gunby to the public was on May Day of 1946. A bitter east wind blew from the North Sea across the marshes. Two visitors turned up. Whereupon it was decided not worth while to pay a man to sell tickets at the gate. It was a secret relief to the anxious donors, not that they wished the public to keep away. By July quite a lot of visitors were coming and some complained with reason that there were no guidebooks on sale. The printers had gone on strike. It was reported to me that one coachload of visitors had made a successful raid on the flower-beds, even digging up bulbs. By now the Massingberds thought they had learnt how to cope with visitors and were enjoying their presence. Nevertheless they were amazed that English people could ever behave badly.

In November 1947 the Field Marshal, whose movements had been getting slower and slower, succumbed to heart failure. In thanking me for my condolences which were deeply sincere Lady Massingberd wrote that she was thinking of leaving Gunby and invited me to come down and talk it over. I went in the following January. Upright as ever and uncomplaining she did not betray her grief in any particular. After all she would stay on so long as the Whartons remained. I rather think

Wharton died in harness before she did, and yet she did not leave. We discussed the re-opening of Gunby in the summer and she then decided that house and garden must be shown at least two days a week at one shilling per head and she would somehow manage alone. In 1963 she died at the age of 91.

The Massingberd motto is : *Est meruisse satis* – 'It is good enough to have done one's best'.

John Montgomery-Massingberd duly inherited the moral right, which had been laid down by the Field Marshal and Lady Massingberd in a memorandum of wishes solemnly endorsed by the National Trust, to live at Gunby. This he did for a few years but unfortunately found the tenancy too great a financial burden, and had to sub-let. Mr and Mrs Jack Wrisdale became his tenants.

When I became an adult and visited houses known to me in childhood, such as my preparatory school which memory had engraved on the mind as an enormous place, I was amazed to find how small they actually were. But Gunby, which I got to know as a youngish adult and had not revisited for nearly half a century until very lately, has behaved differently. Both house and park look bigger than I remember. This could I suppose be explained by a painful factor, namely that in old age I am shrinking both physically and mentally, for certainly Gunby cannot have increased in bulk. On the other hand the houses most old people move into on retirement are smaller than the houses they inhabited in their prime, so possibly it follows that the criterion by which they assess size diminishes commensurably. However this may be, Gunby Hall, park and garden today seem to be enjoying a zenith of splendour. The Montgomery-Massingberds may no longer live in it but their spirit is still noticeably pervasive. All the rooms look exactly as they were in the Field Marshal's day. And yet the house is not a museum. This is thanks to Mr and Mrs Wrisdale who live in the whole house and safeguard it in the most meticulous manner for posterity. The garden too while preserving the Edwardian post-Pre-Raphaelite William Morrisy flavour, so vividly captured in Arthur Hughes' portrait of Margaret Massingberd, is superbly kept by the National Trust and the Wrisdales in what appears to be the happiest collaboration.

CHAPTER TEN

MOUNT EDGCUMBE OF COTEHELE

Cornwall

U NTIL 1947 Cotehele had descended in direct male line from
William de Edgcumbe who in 1353 married Hilaria, daughter
and heiress of William de Cotehele. Throughout the centuries
spelling of the house's name has been variant and apparently optional –
Coteel, Cottel, Cottle, Culteel, Cotele, Cothele and Cotehele. The word
derived, according to Richard Carew's classic *Survey of Cornwall* (1602),
from the Old French *cortil* meaning a little court or garth, and to the
Revd Francis Vyvyan Jago Arundell's invaluable *Cothele* illustrated by
Nicholas Condy (*c.*1840), from *coit* meaning a wood and *hel* a river in
Old Cornish. The second derivation seems the more plausible in that
whereas there are, and always have been three courts at Cotehele, the
surrounding woods over the precipitous bank of the river Tamar give
the place its distinctive flavour of russet roofs, lichened walls, ferns, rills
and sodden leaves under rain-washed skies. Cotehele house, built of
massive Cornish granite blocks and slatestone rubble, dates chiefly from
the fifteenth and sixteenth centuries. It is renowned for its contents,
mostly of the seventeenth century, and may be compared to Knole in
Kent, only in miniature, for the unusual state of its preservation, almost
suspension in time, thanks largely to its isolation and ownership by one
family.

The great-grandson of the aforesaid William de Edgcumbe was the
heroic, corsair-like Sir Richard Edgcumbe, a Cornishman of considerable stature in the reigns of Edward IV, Richard III and Henry VII.
Dissatisfied with the tyranny and impositions of 'Crooked Dick', he
enrolled under the banner of Henry Tudor, Duke of Richmond. There
followed dangerous years when he was accounted a traitor to the Crown
and a common rebel on the run. His pursuit by Sir Henry Trenowth, a
loyalist neighbour, from Cotehele house to the cliff overhanging the
Tamar, his ingenuity in floating his cap on the water, thus deceiving the

134

King's men into supposing he had drowned, and his escape to Brittany, are enrolled among Cornwall's cherished annals. Having subsequently fought with Richmond at the Battle of Bosworth in 1485 he was knighted on the field. After Henry VII's accession he became Comptroller of the Royal Household, established Tudor rule in Calais and Ireland, and helped defeat the imposter Lambert Simnel. As well as playing an important role in national affairs Sir Richard, who became extremely prosperous, had time substantially to extend the medieval structure of Cotehele house before his death in 1489. His son Sir Piers, who married a rich heiress Joan Durnford, completed the work. At the time of his death in 1539 the house looked very much as it does today but without the squat square tower at the north-west corner. This was added in the 1620s by a rather mysterious family relation known as Sir Thomas Coteel.

From 1539 Cotehele became the family's secondary seat to a new house which Sir Piers built with Joan Durnford's money on the Cornish bank of Plymouth Sound called Mount Edgcumbe. For at least three centuries Cotehele was seldom inhabited by the Edgcumbes, with one exception. Colonel Piers Edgcumbe, an ardent supporter of Charles I, for whom he fought, finding Mount Edgcumbe uncomfortably close to Parliamentary Plymouth, moved his family to Cotehele in the 1640s. In September 1644 he gave hospitality to the King on Charles's march from Liskeard to Exeter. The Charles I bedroom in the north-western tower has changed in few particulars since the King slept in it. When the Civil War was over the Colonel retired to Cotehele for the remainder of his life. To him is attributed the collection of most of the contents, including many of the tapestries which are still in the rooms. He made Cotehele habitable according to notions of domestic comfort in the Stuart age.

After Colonel Edgcumbe's death in 1667 the family again made Mount Edgcumbe their permanent residence. Nevertheless they occasionally stayed at Cotehele as the strange incident of the Colonel's daughter-in-law Lady Anne Edgcumbe testifies. In 1675 she 'died' and her body was deposited, if Richard Polwhele's *History of Cornwall* (1803–8) may be believed, in the family vault at 'Culteel'. A few days later the sexton went down to the vault and, tempted by the gold ring on her finger, tried to draw it off. In his efforts he pinched her finger. Whereupon the corpse made a movement. In terror the man fled leaving his lantern behind. Lady Anne rose and taking the lantern walked home. A year later she gave birth to a son and lived until 1729.

In the eighteenth century the family stayed at Cotehele only intermittently and rarely. The east wing was occupied throughout by farm tenants. Gradually the Georgian owners came to regard the strange old house as a specimen of antiquarian interest and virtu and the long-neglected rooms as curiosities. The 1st Lord Edgcumbe, a friend of the young Horace Walpole and discoverer of the Plymouth-born Joshua Reynolds, is thought to have rearranged the Charles II contents more or less in the setting they retain today. He added to the collection of tapestries with which he lined most of the rooms. His son, the 2nd Lord, who inherited his father's taste for the Gothick antique, cut the tapestries about just as though they were wallpapers. But he also developed an unfortunate taste for the gambling tables where he dissipated a fortune. This had one favourable consequence. Neither he nor his brother, who succeeded as 3rd Lord and was to be created 1st Earl of Mount Edgcumbe, had the wherewithal to tamper with Cotehele. The Earl, both a scientist and an antiquarian, was a staider character than his predecessor. He was a friend of King George III to whom he owed his elevation in the peerage. It was because King George and Queen Charlotte visited Cotehele in 1789 that we have the earliest description of the house in any detail. Queen Charlotte recorded the occasion in her diary. The royal pair did not stay the night but were driven from the quay where they landed up to the house to be received by the Mount Edgcumbes and given breakfast. The Queen's beady eye took in a good deal – the great hall, 'full of old armour & swords and old carved chairs of the times, the drawing room and closets hung with old tapestry, the skirting board which is straw, the chair seats made of the priest's vestments'. The chapel glass did not escape her notice or 'the decanters . . . of the year 1646', the silver forks and spoons, and the pewter plates.

In 1815 Lady Granville described how while staying at Saltram with the Boringdons she went on 'a lovely expedition, but a fatiguing one' to what she called 'Cottel' – 'six miles of carriage road, a foot's pace up and down perpendicular hills. Fourteen miles of water, rowing against the tide, a long walk' at the end. They went as trippers, and were admitted by a reluctant housekeeper. Twelve years later her niece Lady Georgiana Agar-Ellis was taken by Lord Valletort, the 2nd Earl's son, to the house where an excellent dinner had been prepared by the staff. But there was no question of staying in such a rough and ready, outlandish old place. It was a novel experience to eat off pewter plates as the Queen had found and drink out of narrow wine glasses, 'the salt cellars, spoons, forks, tankards and salvers, etc. all in complete unison'. That was then, and still is, the constituent magic of Cotehele – its complete 'unison'.

Well into Victorian times Cotehele was treated by the family as a show-place, which they might occasionally visit, with or without their friends, and eat a scratch meal on picnic lines.

The 3rd Earl commissioned Nicholas Condy, a Cornish water-colour painter, to produce a folio-size volume of coloured illustrations of the outside and the rooms of Cotehele. The beautiful plates provide an accurate and precise document of the contents, nearly all of which remain not merely in the house, but in the very same rooms and situations. He depicted the tapestries and bed hangings so that we can identify them, and the sofas, chairs, chests and tables ranged against the walls, the floor-boards mostly bare save for an occasional rug. By the mid-nineteenth century Cotehele had become famous amongst anti-quarian *cognoscenti* who flocked to see it with the 3rd Earl's easily granted permission. In a descriptive text of the book the Revd F.V.J. Arundell lamented the 'vandals of the eighteenth century who pulled down to rebuild', and rejoiced in the interest of his enlightened contemporaries in ancient buildings. As it happened the Georgian owners of Cotehele could be spared these strictures for they made no alterations to the house whatsoever. 'Happily that vandal spirit is arrested . . . in these mansions of early days', went on Mr Arundell who was coeval with Joseph Nash, the well-known compiler of four folio volumes of *Mansions of England of the Olden Time*. And he repeated the mistake of most amateur antiquarians of the nineteenth century in calling Stuart furniture Elizabethan. 'The latest is not more modern than the reign of Elizabeth,' he pronounced inaccurately.

After the 3rd Earl's death in 1861 his widow decided to settle permanently at Cotehele. Thus she was the first member of the family to do this since Colonel Piers's time. The move necessitated some structural reconditioning of the east wing for she left the staterooms untouched, apart from adding the usual Victorian clutter which photo-graphs taken in the 1860s reveal. The dowager's unmarried daughter Lady Ernestine Edgcumbe continued to live in the house until 1925. There exists a photograph group, taken at the turn of the century, of her indoor staff, numbering seventeen of whom eight were manser-vants.

The 4th and 5th Earls steadfastly refused to alter the rooms of the house. They considered that it would have been sacrilege. As Avray Tipping wrote in 1936, 'For sure, there is no actual harm in moving furniture, but when for at least a century, and, so far as one can tell, for three centuries, nothing has been touched, the place in the room of each chair and table does undoubtedly acquire a sort of sanctity. After all, such chairs have done something that no human being could do – stayed in one place for three hundred years and for that reason should be treated with some respect.' This attitude was religiously adhered to by the National Trust when it became Cotehele's possessor, and doubtless will always be adhered to.

And so we come to the Second World War and the death in 1944 of the widower 5th Earl who, having been totally bombed out of Mount Edgcumbe three years previously, sought sanctuary, like his ancestor during another calamitous war, at Cotehele. At this inauspicious date he was succeeded in his title and estates by a second cousin Kenelm Edgcumbe, a distinguished electrical engineer and President of the Institute of that profession. Although the 6th Earl and his wife had lost their only son Piers while serving with the Royal Lancers in Holland, and came into their inheritance on the approach of old age both devoted the rest of their days to the rebuilding of Mount Edgcumbe house and the preservation for all time of the Cotehele estate, house and collections.

Lord Mount Edgcumbe had three daughters of whom the eldest, christened Hilaria after her remote progenitrix, was married to Colonel Denis Gibbs, a first cousin of my colleague Christopher Gibbs. Christopher had by 1945 returned to his duties at the National Trust. In March of that year he received a letter from Lord Mount Edgcumbe explaining the complications of his family entail which prevented him from giving away the Cotehele property and enquiring whether the National Trust could help him sort them out. At the time the Trust was deeply involved with Mr Ernest Cook. Lord Mount Edgcumbe asked Christopher whether the anonymous benefactor, as Mr Cook was referred to, might be interested in Cotehele. Christopher expressed doubt (which proved to be realized) that the Cotehele estate would be large enough for him. He suggested that I should go down to Cotehele, see the place which he already knew, and discuss the whole matter with Lord Mount Edgcumbe. For some good reason I did not visit for well over a year. In the meantime Christopher invited Lord Mount Edgcumbe and me to luncheon at his club.

Lord Mount Edgcumbe was one of the most charming elderly men I have ever met. He was unassuming and diffident, yet with a sort of directness which derived from civilized upbringing, engrained sense of duty and total dedication to the path in life allocated to him by – well – the Almighty. Without appearing faintly what the French term *dévot* – bigoted is too strong an adjective – he exhaled an air of spirituality which was very impressive and heartening. I took to him in a way which

I endeavoured not to disclose. The three of us decided that the only available course by which Cotehele could come to the Trust was that of the mysterious benefactor, if the tortuous Captain Hill could be circumvented. And it would have to be initiated by the National Trust chairman Lord Crawford whose prestige among art historians and collectors was immense. Crawford agreed at once to write to Mr Cook direct, with the result that Cook referred the matter straight to Hill. This was a pity because Hill was never known to endorse recommendations which came through the National Trust. Hill pronounced that his employer was lukewarm. Nevertheless Christopher persisted with Hill who respected him, and did not respect me whom he deemed too aesthetic by half. Hill made it plain to Christopher that the chance of a favourable reception by his master would depend entirely upon his, Hill's, persuasion. He accordingly consented to make a second approach to the great man himself and see what he could do. He would submit to him Lord Mount Edgcumbe's willingness to accept £45,000 for the house, contents and 653 acres. Not that he had yet seen the place, of course, but his experience enabled him to be pretty shrewd on paper. When Hill reported that the benefactor was impressed by the *Country Life* articles on Cotehele (which I think Lord Crawford had enclosed in his letter) Lord Mount Edgcumbe and we were filled with hope. A date was fixed for the visit of inspection. Lord Mount Edgcumbe hired a motor-car (petrol rationing of private car consumption was still in force) to motor Captain Hill round the estate. But before this could take place word came through Hill that the benefactor was after all no longer interested. What unfortunately happened was that in his euphoria Lord Mount Edgcumbe nobbled his friend Ronnie Norman, who was our vice-chairman, to put in a further plea with the benefactor. When I got to hear of this I suspected that Hill already knew, and feared the worst.

We on the staff were not altogether surprised, but Lord Mount Edgcumbe was disappointed. Still he wrote, 'I would dearly like the Trust to have [Cotehele] and am *most anxious* not to put it up to the highest bidder.' He was nothing if not optimistic.

In May 1946 he wrote off his own bat to the Controller of the Estate Duty Office, suggesting that the Inland Revenue might accept Cotehele by way of payment of the duties he owed from the death of his predecessor, and then transfer it to the safekeeping of the National Trust. After all the Chancellor of the Exchequer Dr Dalton had already expressed eagerness to adopt some such course if no other means of saving an historic country house were forthcoming. Then the Chancel-

lor, suddenly getting cold feet, began nervously questioning the propriety of the Exchequer surrendering the equivalent of a capital sum
which might within a few years show a substantial surplus revenue. The
Trust's response was that this particular capital sum might on the
contrary show a substantial loss. It was anyway surprised that the
Exchequer could evaluate a property of such architectural and historic
importance in terms of £.s.d. What was the opinion of Sir Edward
Bridges, who had been secretary to the Treasury, and secretary to the
War Cabinet and was about to take charge of the Government Organization Committee? He was known to be sympathetic to the Trust's
aims – indeed he was soon to join the Council and Executive Committee
– and was treated as a sort of guru and infallible oracle by all
departments in Whitehall. Bridges's opinion was that Cotehele was a
thoroughly worthy property for the Exchequer to accept and transfer
to the National Trust. But even his weighty opinion could not immediately dispel the Treasury's reluctance to provide an endowment
for Cotehele out of its exactions from the taxpayer. It was one thing to
buy the house and land from the Cotehele tenant-for-life who was
debarred by law from donating it; and quite another for some of the
purchase value so to speak to be handed over by the tenant-for-life to
the National Trust for spending on the house, albeit the house would
belong to the nation. That was how the Treasury looked at the matter;
and that was how things rested for a time. In the long run it transpired
that the government's endowment of Cotehele turned out to be
lamentably deficient; and the National Trust has been obliged to spend
out of its general funds hundreds of thousands of pounds on the
property over the years.

The report prepared by the Trust's area agent George Senior, a dear,
rough, gruff old diamond, estimated that £1,500 p.a. was now needed
for upkeep of the house as against Lord Mount Edgcumbe's estimated
£1,000 p.a. Moreover, since the Cotehele cottages were in poor shape
and since the west bank of the Tamar running through the estate was
badly breached in places, a fairly large sum for capital expenditure was
needed in addition to an endowment, so the following question was
posed. Would the Treasury permit the Trust, after it became owner, to
sell some outlying parts of the estate deemed not to be of national
beauty to raise the cash? The Treasury's reply was that the Chancellor
was prepared to hand over the house and *enough* land as 'is needed on
this basis', i.e. to protect it (such land to be held inalienably), but 'cannot
defend a transaction of this kind', i.e. inclusion of land which might be
realized for gain. Instead the Chancellor would ask Parliament to

provide £60,000, ostensibly towards endowment, over and above what the transferred inalienable land would yield in revenue, out of some separate Exchequer fund. This ridiculously involved quibble was indeed resorted to.

The secretary of the National Trust (by now Admiral Bevir) begged the Pilgrim Trust (a charity which dispensed money to amenity societies) to give the Trust £50,000 needed for the capital expenditure. The Pilgrim Trust did not see its way to oblige but conveyed information that the Bishop of Truro might weigh in. The Bishop thought the house ideally suited to a religious community. If this met with the Trust's approval the Pilgrim Trust might well help the community with funds. Besides it sensed that Lord Mount Edgcumbe was anxious to keep the Roman Catholics out. This may well have been one of his objectives although it was not expressed to me. Lord Mount Edgcumbe certainly favoured the east and south wings becoming a home for retired clergy with a shared use by clergy and visiting public of the great hall.

On 7 December I paid my first visit to Cotehele. It was a brief one. The family were not present. I had opportunity to notice the dreadful condition of the furniture in the staterooms for the maintenance of which, when the deal went through, the National Trust would be responsible. Worm was rampant. I was obliged to report to the Finance Committee that at least £1,000 additional to the capital expenditure figure would be needed for the furniture. A week later the Executive Committee agreed to accept Cotehele because of its great importance, with or without the money needed for the capital expenditure. There were times when the Trust was delightfully Micawberish just as there were others when it was exacting and cheese-paring. This time it was definitely taking a risk in committing itself to the guardianship of objects not its own. The furniture, tapestries and armour which as tenant-for-life Lord Mount Edgcumbe could not give the Trust, the Trust, because it did not have the money, could not buy. Furthermore under the settlement Lord Mount Edgcumbe was unable to bind his successors in the entail to sell the contents to the Trust, were it somehow to come by the money, although he was very willing to pledge himself to this option. All the Trust could do was to suggest that he might persuade his next heir, a cousin Edward Edgcumbe, and great-great grandson of the 2nd Earl, then living in New Zealand, to give an informal undertaking on his own behalf. Lord Mount Edgcumbe promised to discuss the question of the contents with Edward who was shortly to pay a first visit to England with his wife. My suggestion that the Exchequer be asked to provide an *ad hoc* grant for the purchase of the contents, since it was quite ready to plunge its hands into separate funds, in other words robbing Peter to pay Paul, was not favoured by the Treasury.

In May 1947 I went for the second time to Cotehele as the Mount Edgcumbes' guest, and was given a bedroom at the top of the entrance gate-tower. Having climbed my own twisting stone staircase I felt lonely in this isolated, spooky situation. There was a thunderstorm during the night and the lightning flashed through the latticed casements to illuminate the courtyard on the far side. Next morning, Lord Mount Edgcumbe being indisposed, I was put in charge of Lady Mount Edgcumbe, who was sweet, gentle and mouse-like. I spent the day in the staterooms listing those contents which I decided ought to be on loan to the Trust and taking stock of their condition. It was necessary that should the family at some future date be obliged to sell contents and the Trust be unable to buy them the latter should be reimbursed by the family for those pieces it had spent money on repairing in the meantime. Lord Mount Edgcumbe in his usual obliging way agreed that this would be entirely right and proper. While I was busy listing Lady Mount Edgcumbe kept asking my opinion on this, that and the other. She would pause to take notes very slowly on a sheaf of loose writing-paper which got sadly muddled and then fell, scattering, to the floor. Meanwhile her Cairn puppy ate a good slice of Queen Anne's tatting from the famous needlework sofa in the Punch Room. 'You naughty little thing,' she admonished in an amused tone as it scuttled off with a mouthful. The incident made me reflect on the mutability of English furniture and fabrics like everything else throughout the ages and wonder how any treasures at all had survived past treatment by owners, not to mention children, servants, cats and dogs.

This second and more thorough examination revealed that several pieces of furniture had to be removed from the rooms without delay. I recall in the White Room a small cupboard on a stand that was practically eaten away to nothing. I was so desperately worried that when I got back to London I asked Leigh Ashton, director of the V&A, what steps he took with the museum's furniture similarly affected. He said that he took whatever drastic action seemed to him best in the interest of the museum as a whole. But his situation was somewhat different to the Trust's where all the affected furniture at Cotehele was privately, not publicly owned.

Clifford Smith offered to make an authoritative catalogue of the contents. But I thought it would be a good plan to enlist for a change the services of a different expert, and suggested Charles Brocklehurst who was then the Trust's honorary representative in what it calls Mercia to compile one. This he did admirably. He also pointed out that many of the tapestries in the house were torn and all were dirty, that the famous armour in the great hall was rusty and brittle, and the pewter tarnished. He strongly advocated fires being kept alight in the staterooms throughout the winter. On how to treat the tapestries and textiles George Wingfield Digby gave his invaluable advice gratis. In the chapel he identified the purple altar frontal, sewn with silver fleurs-de-lys and depicting the Twelve Apostles, as having been made up from parts of a medieval pall. As for the stained glass windows Dr F.C. Eeles, secretary to the Central Council for the Care of Churches, examined and pronounced them very important early sixteenth-century Flemish work and advised how they might be repaired. Sir James Mann, Keeper of the Royal Armouries, took away the worst affected pieces of armour for treatment at the Tower of London. This we thought very kind and disinterested until he so worked upon Lord Mount Edgcumbe's good nature as to persuade him to let him keep Cotehele's showpiece, a Greenwich suit of armour of a sixteenth-century boy, possibly Henry VIII, which stood prominently on a bracket on the west wall of the great hall. In return Mann graciously let us have in its place an adult's suit of no rarity or particular interest.

Eardley Knollys and I were kept busy ferrying delicate objects like footstools and stumpwork mirrors to be repaired in the V&A workshops, and back again. For general de-worming and mending of large furniture like beds and chests we employed at first local craftsmen recommended to us by the Plymouth Art Gallery and by H.W. Maxwell, director of the Bristol Art Museum. These craftsmen made periodical visits, taking away and returning the heavy pieces until their services became too expensive. The appalling furniture worm gave rise to some awkward conundrums. For instance Eardley was afraid that what was returned from repair and treatment might instantly be reinfected by its neighbours that were still riddled and like maniacs scattering dust all around them. Then there was the bogus, highly carved Charles I bed illustrated in Condy's book. It was in the last stages of decay. Should we scrap and replace it with a spare genuine bed from some other house? We decided not to. Just as someone on the estate had doubtless faked it up around 1800, so we handed it over to an incomparable jack of all trades, William Cook, who suddenly turned up as it were sent from heaven, to fake it anew.

Cook was not a Cotehele estate native, nor did he belong to the West

Country. At one time he had been working at Warwick Castle in what capacity I do not remember. He was as difficult to place as he was irreplaceable. He was ingenious, undauntable, ever ready to tackle any problem with his brain and hands. We installed him in a cottage by the quay and for several years he acted as estate clerk of the works, house steward and joiner. He dismantled and plunged the Charles I bed into a bath of de-worming solution, having first extracted and thrown away the worst infected bits. After all we only wanted it to stand up. We would never have asked it to be slept in again. Meanwhile we had the bed's original deep fringe with its heavy silk knots and devices, the valance and curtains re-backed and mended by an expert needle-woman, Sheila Breen, a farmer's wife on the estate. Once we had proved Cook we never looked back, for in him we had found our own tame craftsman.

The Trust's lack of funds was in those years so acute that I was reduced to scrounging. That so many museum keepers of departments took pity and gave their services for little or no fee showed that they thought the National Trust on the whole a good thing. But we were never able to buy the least expensive object which might once have belonged to Cotehele and which it would be nice to have back in its old surroundings. For instance, when we were offered for £3 an inscribed and annotated copy of Condy's *Cotele* I was obliged to decline it.

An enormous amount of correspondence ensued between Lord Mount Edgcumbe and myself about practical matters which bored both of us, and about the archaeology of Cotehele, by which I mean Dark Age history and twilight architectural remains, on which he was inordinately keen. As regards the practical matters there were his executors who, perhaps rightly, sought to reserve to the family mineral and china clay rights on the land. There were his lawyers who made mountains out of a strip of land bought years before by the Great Western Railway at one corner of the estate on which it intended to build a line, but didn't (Michael Trinick, Eardley Knollys' successor, got a friend to buy it back for the estate in 1977; it is now inalienable); and some troublesome stranger who claimed a piece of foreshore untrace-able on the estate map. There was Bluemantle Pursuivant who sus-pected that Lord Mount Edgcumbe had no right to a banner hanging in the great hall, and must photograph it immediately. As for archaeology as I have defined it, it never appealed to me. I have always preferred buildings above to below ground and facts to conjectures. Some of Lord Mount Edgcumbe's researches led to the enlistment of further museum experts. For instance, the pair of so-called warders' horns hanging in the great hall had to be identified and, since they were Lord Mount Edgcumbe's property, valued by us for insurance. Their owner authorized me to take one of the pair to the V&A for the Keeper of Metalwork, Charles Oman, to examine. Oman confirmed that they were very important but referred me to a higher authority, the Keeper of British and Medieval Antiquities at the British Museum and future director, Tom Kendrick, married to a cousin of mine. This eminent antiquarian and author of *The Lisbon Earthquake* pronounced them definitely Bronze Age and valued them – to my astonishment – at a mere £50 apiece. He compounded this risible figure by stating that they were 'perfect beauties'. Lord Mount Edgcumbe, who thought they were rather ugly, but very precious, was somewhat offended. Neither of us was quite sure that he was not being laughed at. Then Lord Mount Edgcumbe became deeply interested in a monstrous bed tester carved with a miscellany of shields of arms, instruments of the Passion, Welsh musical instruments, hunting scenes and a mysterious Celtic inscription which baffled everyone. Again Tom Kendrick's opinion was sought. After studying a photograph he said the tester was the work of some lunatic faker and the inscription sheer gibberish. Lord Mount Edgcumbe wasn't going to take that lying down and wrote a letter of enquiry to *Country Life*. A spate of replies were received giving eccentric and wildly improbable explanations, one correspondent claiming to interpret the inscription as the Cornish for 'Home Sweet Home'. In the end the tester turned out to have been made up of different old panels by one of the antiquarian Earls of the late eighteenth century.

We may have been poor and under-staffed, but until we were ready to open Cotehele to the public we managed very well for we were twice blessed. We had in addition to Cook the most wonderful caretaker in Mrs Down. She was one of those women who look perennially young because she was always smiling. Her pretty face under neatly parted hair radiated a placid benignity. She had worked for the Mount Edgcumbes and consented to be adopted by the Trust. She knew and cared for every item of furniture as though it were her individual child. She lived two miles away from Cotehele and in all weathers walked, key in hand, across open fields to the house where she scrubbed, cleaned and polished so that every object glittered and shone 'like her own rosy cheeks', as Eardley observed. 'Cotehele is simply the top,' he went on after one of his regular visits. 'Perhaps it was the sun. But Mrs Down's efforts made a great impression on me.' Such a wonder-worker was she that Lord Mount Edgcumbe asked to our embarrassment if he might have her back at least once a week. 'I suggest ½ a day,' Admiral Beevir weighed in diffidently. 'I know this sounds silly but very often such silly ideas provide a solution.' It did in this case.

By 1947 the Cotehele property was finally accepted by the Treasury in lieu of the estate duties payable on the death in 1940 of the 5th Earl, and at once handed over to the National Trust. It was the first property to come to the Trust by this means which was the laudable brainchild of Chancellor Hugh Dalton. Thus an important precedent was set whereby other historic country houses and estates became acceptable. Dyrham Park in Gloucestershire was one of them. Lord Mount Edgcumbe was to survive another eight years. Having saved Cotehele his next mission was to have Mount Edgcumbe house rebuilt by Adrian Gilbert Scott. On many an occasion he would call at the National Trust office or ask me to his London club to go through with him and comment upon the proposals of this distinguished architect who, I feel sure, would have been appalled had he known. Besides there never was likelihood of Mount Edgcumbe coming the Trust's way. It was none of my business. Part of the old people's mission was to induct their New Zealand heir Edward and his wife Effie into the inheritance that would shortly be theirs. Though born and bred at the opposite poles of the earth they all became the closest of friends. The old couple spoke of the younger with unfeigned affection and respect. It was not in their natures to feel superior. And it amused them when Edward took off his coat at dinner to eat in his shirt sleeves. 'Such a good idea, and far more comfortable than the usual way,' Lord Mount Edgcumbe remarked. When Lord Mount Edgcumbe died at the age of 87 in 1965 (Lady Mount Edgcumbe had died the year before) his executors agreed to leave the contents of the Cotehele staterooms on loan. A few years later nearly all were given to the Trust by the Treasury which accepted them in lieu of the estate duty claimed on the old man's death. Edward succeeded as 7th Earl and came over to live permanently in England. His nephew the 8th Earl resides on the Mount Edgcumbe estate today.

When the Trust opened Cotehele to the public they did all they could by advertising to entice visitors to this remote property. As well as needing their money they wanted to vindicate the Treasury's action in operating the 'in lieu' process and spending Exchequer funds on what was to prove a worthwhile and popular country house. In 1949, 3,500 visitors were admitted. They were not considered enough. That year, none of the family choosing to rent it, the east wing was let to a private tenant. In February 1950 Lord Mount Edgcumbe had suggested that during a forthcoming and much-heralded royal visit to Plymouth the King and Queen might be persuaded to make a pilgrimage by water and carriage to Cotehele just as George III and Queen Charlotte had done in 1789. It would be good publicity; but the idea came to nothing.

Sir Gordon Russell, director of the Council of Industrial Design and a highly esteemed furniture designer and craftsman, whom since early childhood I had known at Broadway in Worcestershire, offered to bring Cotehele to the public's attention. A big, burly man like his industrious old father, who rose from bank clerk to hotel-keeper of the famous Lygon Arms, he gave a series of BBC broadcasts on the furniture. It afforded, he said, the most valuable social history. It was remarkable because of its unbroken association with Cotehele. Though none was actually coeval with the house nearly all of it dated from but a short time after the building. It was no *period* collection. It had evolved. It remained for all to see in the rooms for which it had been made or acquired. The Stuart tapestries gave a vivid background and rendered much-needed warmth to an otherwise chill interior. Russell also talked about Elizabethan Montacute, another of the Trust's magical houses in the West Country. It had come to us nearly empty and we were striving to assemble suitable contents. Russell was encouraging our efforts. He spoke vehemently against shams and was scathing about manufacturers who sought to reproduce the antique. I do not know whether it was during these broadcast talks that he fulminated: 'There is a job for the hand and a job for the machine . . . Are we to admire things', he asked, 'because they are beautiful or because they are old? The doctrine that nothing is beautiful unless it is old has created an army of swindlers . . . And there is no reason why things made by machine should be ugly or shoddy.' No reason whatever.

Just forty-one years since Sir Gordon Russell's ardent plea to the British public to visit this precious old house, tourism has reached such a flood of numbers that the National Trust is obliged to seek means to stem it. Cotehele is not one of those properties unaffected by limitless crowds. Coachload after coachload now thrust a way down the narrow, steep-banked Cornish lanes to disgorge eager and appreciative visitors, not merely from Plymouth and Bodmin, but from Valparaiso and Port Elizabeth, Seattle and Saskatoon, Yokohama and Hakodate, places probably never heard of by Mrs Down in 1949. In 1990 the numbers reached nearly 90,000. How is the stemming to be carried out without pushing the admission fee beyond the inflation rate so as to penalize the poor visitor, or without restricting the days of entry so as to disoblige the worthy visitor (that hardy annual) who may claim to have slogged all the way from John o' Groats on foot, 'especially' to see the house? That is the Trust's huge problem of the moment. It has somehow got to be resolved, painlessly and fairly. Thank goodness it is not mine.

No wonder Cotehele has become so popular. This is very largely due to the imagination, resourcefulness and ingenuity of Michael Trinick, himself now retired, who became Cornwall's National Trust representative in 1956. Cornish by breeding and Cornish by dedication he has worked miracles of conservation in the Duchy. Not only has he saved miles of coastline but he has also reanimated those historic buildings which either fell to his responsibility or were acquired through his boundless efforts.

Whereas the rooms of Cotehele remain much as they were in my day, only better in that the tapestries, bed hangings and other fabrics have been, and still are being, repaired by the most qualified experts in this country and overseas, and the kitchen, with its high roof, utensils and implements, all bright and burnished, has been reassembled exactly as shown in Condy's illustration and added to the (unguided) tour, the gardens and grounds too have been vastly improved. Visitors are now admitted to the east garden above the Tamar and may walk in front of the windows of the wing where Mrs Julyan, widow of the Trust's first tenant, Colonal Julyan who came in 1948, still resides, apparently as contented as she is cherished. Since the 1990 hurricane which caused terrible tree havoc, a view from the formal terraces of the railway viaduct and Calstock across the valley has been opened up. Ancient grey walls enclose the upper garden, formed in 1862, where crystal-clear springs from Tower meadow feed a square pond. Adjacent to the entrance to the house the long medieval barn has been very successfully turned into a restaurant.

A further triumph has been the National Trust's rescue and reinstatement of Cotehele Quay on the right bank of the tidal Tamar. Towards the end of the eighteenth century the river became alive with shipping as a result of mineral extractions, copper, lead, silver and tin. The mines and quarries attracted many artisans until the 1880s when mechanized land transport caused the quay's decline and total neglect. Within the past thirty years the old lime-kilns, warehouses, cottages, the quaymaster's office and the Edgcumbe Arms inn have been renovated, and a quay museum has been installed. The last surviving Tamar barge, *Shamrock*, has been rescued and transported to Cotehele where it is docked on a slipway. Half a mile upstream the mill of the Cotehele estate is one of the best preserved industrial complexes attached to a country house to be found in all England. It consists of wheelwright's shop, blacksmith's forge, saddler's shop, carpenter's shop and cider house, all complete with ancient machinery kept, moreover, in spanking order. Here visitors may watch from the ground floor the pit wheel worked directly off the main drive of the great water wheel, and by ascending and descending rickety wooden stairs may follow the whole process while listening to the busy whirr and clank of machinery. Shafts, grinding stones, cogs and shutes, vats, dust-extractor and sack-hoist lead to the crusher where the apples were first pulped. And at the rear of the building Tamar's tributary, the little Morden stream, channels along a wooden conduit suspended in air, water whose fall propels the great wheel. This slowly rotating giant has a circular iron frame, spokes of oak and paddles of elm. No longer, alas, does the energy it generates grind corn or press cider for the Edgcumbe household. Although the mill, like the quay and indeed the staterooms of the house, is virtually defunct it nevertheless conveys a picturesque semblance of past reality.

CHAPTER ELEVEN

TREVELYAN OF WALLINGTON

Northumberland

I N going over the Northumberland moors near Lady Trevelyan's,
if you stop and listen, you will hear nothing but the wind whistling
– a rattling brook perhaps among some stones, now and then the
cry of a curlew, now and then the bleat of a lamb; all plaintive and
melancholy.' Ruskin's description of 1852 might well have been written
yesterday. The Border country still suggests that no world exists
beyond the wild purple horizons. Remote, unspoilt, unspectacular, but
beautiful it remains. Wallington combines everything the confirmed
agoraphobe delights to find in a country seat. The setting is nature
undefiled. The architecture is dignified, grey, unpretentious. When the
house first arose it must have looked an intrusion in its stark surroundings. Now it has grown into the landscape as an old man becomes part
of an upholstered armchair. Likewise decades, sometimes centuries
pass before houses and families integrate so that each assumes the
character of the other. In a sense difficult to define but not to identify,
Wallington and the Blackett-Trevelyan dynasty seem indivisible. Having penetrated the dour exterior of Wallington house the stranger finds
many decorative frivolities within. Peel off the rebarbative shells of the
Blackett-Trevelyan owners of Wallington and you come upon sensibili-
ties by no means apparent on the surface. However unsympathetic
some members of this family have been, few if any were stupid. To
contemporary critics of the English country gentry as narrow, obtuse,
reactionary I would point to the incumbents of Wallington. All have
displayed brain power of a high order, and most have applied it to the
nation's good. The irony of Wallington's history is that the long
partnership of family and seat has practically been broken, not by the
impoverishment of either but by the scruples of the former; whereby
the geese, one might say disrespectfully, have pickled their own golden
eggs. And another hereditary élite is dissolved.

Although the Trevelyans are of near continuous left-wing political descent, having been Radical in the nineteenth century and become Socialist in the twentieth, the early owners of Wallington were uncompromisingly Tory. The Fenwicks staked their all on Charles I and lost it. The last of that line to own Wallington, Sir John, was executed in 1697 for plotting against William of Orange. His posthumous revenge is well known. Much of Sir John's fortune confiscated by the Crown included the Wallington breed of chestnut stallions. Sir John's favourite White Sorrel was appropriated by William III. The mole or 'little gentleman in velvet' toasted by all loyal Jacobites causing the horse to stumble, threw the King who died from the fall. Before this happened Wallington was bought from the impoverished Fenwicks by a commercial potentate from Newcastle, Sir William Blackett. He was a stout Whig and supporter of 'the Glorious Revolution'. He began building the present Wallington in 1688. In the customary manner of new money he married his daughters into the aristocracy. Of the six of them Julia became the wife of Sir Walter Calverley, a Yorkshire baronet. She was an expert needlewoman whose beautiful six-folding screen in tent-stitch and a whole bedroom panelled with her work survive. Sir William Blackett's son, also Sir William, was however a Jacobite and considered by all subsequent members of his family a nonentity whose outrageous deviancy from the Whig norm forfeited him a count in their annals, and was best ignored. Sir William, 2nd Baronet, died in 1728 leaving no legitimate children.

But he had one illegitimate daughter, called Elizabeth Ord, to whom he was attached. In his will he bequeathed Wallington to his sister Julia's son, Sir Walter Calverley, on condition that he married Elizabeth and added the Blackett name and arms to his own. Sir Walter accepted the condition in the most obliging way and as far as anyone knows the unorthodox union was satisfactory. Sir Walter Calverley Blackett's reign at Wallington was marked by great splendour and munificence. He entertained Butcher Cumberland on his return from victorious Culloden in 1745 and for forty years sat in Parliament where he delivered a single speech of a few words' apology for having voted for the Radical trouble-maker John Wilkes who was the son of a malt distiller. It reduced the House of Commons to derisive merriment. Yet this blunt baronet is credited with the splendid retort to a nobleman who derided another's obscure birth, 'Every man carries his honour in his own hand. Origin is nothing; it shall have no weight with me.'

Far the greater part of Sir Walter's life was spent in Northumberland.

In the words of his descendant the late Sir Charles Philips Trevelyan, 'he converted the Wallington estate' into 'a noble and well ordered property'. He enclosed the land with hedgerows and planted hundreds of thousands of trees where none grew before. He created the park probably from his own design and not from Capability Brown's as has too often been asserted. He made the walled garden and built Cambo village. To the house he added the imposing courtyard with cupola'ed stable block, and the Wansbeck bridge as well as several other ornamental park features now disappeared. He also got one of Lord Burlington's followers Daniel Garrett (so John Cornforth has recently discovered) to remodel the house in the 1740s and '50s and engaged an Italian family of *stuccatori* to transform the staterooms in the rococo taste.

Again Wallington was to pass through the female line. When the magnificent Sir Walter Calverley Blackett died childless in 1777 the son of his sister, another Julia, inherited his uncle's fortune and his debts. Sir John Trevelyan, 4th Baronet, sprang as the name implies from a family of Cornish origins but settled since the early sixteenth century at Nettlecombe in Somerset. For just over a hundred years Sir John, his son and grandson owned the two estates and moved from one seat to the other. Through marrying heiresses they largely recuperated what the lavish Sir Walter Calverley Blackett had dissipated in making Wallington a northern paradise and repository of the arts.

The reign of the grandson Sir Walter Calverley Trevelyan, ultimately 6th Baronet, witnessed Wallington's first intellectual heyday. Walter was certainly an intellectual of a dry professional order. His interests were predominantly scientific. His studies were eclectic. Botany, geology, phrenology, mesmerism and photography were among them. He was an authority on oxygen, urine and the parasites of starfish. There was little that did not appeal to his acquisitive mind. It was however his wife Pauline Jermyn who attracted the scientists, poets and artists to Wallington where the couple went to live soon after their marriage in 1835 and which they made their exclusive home, his father the 5th Baronet remaining at Nettlecombe. Walter and Pauline had met at a conference of the British Association for the Advancement of Science in Cambridge when he was 36 and she 17. He was struck by her 'talent for languages and science', rather than her talent for art, her liveliness and abounding charm. Whereas she was small and pretty he was tall and lanky with a long lugubrious face and drooping moustaches. Although childless the marriage proved convenient for both parties. In his austere and bloodless way Walter loved her and she

BROCKHAMPTON, HEREFORDSHIRE
1. Celebration of King George V's Jubilee in 1935 at the new house built (*c.* 1760)
for Bartholomew Richard Barneby

BLICKLING, NORFOLK
2. Lord Lothian escorting
Queen Mary across the
bridge from the front door

HANBURY HALL, WORCESTERSHIRE
3. Sir George Vernon with his
adopted daughter Ruth at Hanbury
Hall

4. Lady Vernon (Doris) who virtually
saved Hanbury for the National
Trust. Portrait by the Hon. John
Collier

5. Snapshot of the derelict park taken by the author, 1936

ATTINGHAM PARK,
SHROPSHIRE

6. Lord and Lady Berwick
descending the steps of the
portico, *c.* 1920

7. Snapshot of the approach to the house taken by the author, 1936

STOURHEAD, WILTSHIRE

8. Sir Henry and Lady Hoare (Alda) with their son Harry, and 'Sweep', taken on 4 October 1912 at Stourhead

9. Bishop and Mrs Abraham
on their diamond wedding
day, 1943

10. The great hall, drawn by
John Sell Cotman in 1807

11. At the front door before hunting: (*left to right*) Ewen, Sir Henry and Lady Fairfax-Lucy, Brian and Sybil

12. Professor G.M. Trevelyan receiving the deeds of Charlecote from Sir Barry Jackson on 1 June 1946

13. Edith Craig at
Smallhythe, 1926

14. 'The Trouts':
(*left to right*) Edy, Tony
and Chris

15. Field Marshal Sir
Archibald Montgomery-
Massingberd

16. (Diana) Lady
Montgomery-Massingberd
by Oswald Birley, 1943

17. The Earl and Countess of Mount Edgcumbe by the entrance gate-tower

18. The drawing-room at Cotehele, by Nicholas Condy, from the Revd F.V.J. Arundell's *Cothele* (1840)

WALLINGTON HALL,
NORTHUMBERLAND
19. The three Trevelyan brothers with
their old nurse Miss Prestwich at
Wallington, *c.* 1910: (*left to right*) Sir
Charles Philips, Robert Calverley (the
poet) and Professor George Macaulay
(the historian)

KNOLE PARK, KENT
20. Major-General Lord Sackville and
his wife Anne before the south wing,
1936

WEST WYCOMBE PARK, BUCKINGHAMSHIRE
21. Sir John and Lady Dashwood with their children, Sarah, Francis and John, under the east portico. Photograph by Cecil Beaton in the 1930s

HATCHLANDS, SURREY
22. Harry Stuart Goodhart-Rendel, 1936

23. The south front of Hatchlands seen from astern an unidentified nautical sculpture

was content with the latitude he allowed her but of which she never took advantage among the unconventional people who assembled at Wallington.

Walter was humourless and fanatically teetotal. He would allow no liquor to be sold on his estate. Pauline was in no need of it; she was naturally high-spirited, observant, quick, magnetic and often extremely funny.

As soon as they were settled at Wallington Sir Walter, as he became in 1846, called in the well-known Northumberland architect John Dobson to contrive a hall within the open-air central court of the house. Discussions on how to decorate the filled-in spaces of the surrounding colonnade led to the employment of the artist William Bell Scott to cover them with mural paintings. Scott became a semi-permanent fixture at Wallington and drew in his train other Pre-Raphaelite painters and men of letters: John Ruskin, Ford Madox Brown, Holman Hunt, Arthur Hughes and Thomas Woolner the sculptor, all of whom contributed in some measure to the decoration of the new hall. William Michael and his sister Christina Rossetti joined the circle later, as did the young Algernon Charles Swinburne whose ancestral home Capheaton was a mere three miles away. Swinburne adopted Pauline as his Egeria. He would stride across the moors, his red hair streaming in the wind, throw himself at her feet (she preferred squatting on the floor to sitting on a chair), submit for her criticism his poems and disclose his extraordinary crypto-erotic fancies. If Swinburne worshipped her Lady Trevelyan was amused by and fond of her 'dear little carrots'. But the favourite of the circle was undoubtedly John Ruskin. To him Wallington was 'the most beautiful place possible' although he found the classical house 'ugly enough; square set and somewhat bare walled'. He became Lady Trevelyan's intimate friend and correspondent while remaining on the friendliest terms with Sir Walter. It was at Wallington in 1853 that both Trevelyans noticed with concern the ripening love between Effie Ruskin and John Millais and the apparent unconcern of Effie's husband. They dreaded his awakening.

Evidently high thinking meant in Sir Walter and Lady Trevelyan's household a degree of low living. Augustus Hare recorded that domestic conditions were very eccentric and very uncomfortable, and that the food was sparse and horrid. But then he disliked being deprived of alcohol and he objected having to barricade his bedroom door with the dressing-table in order to keep it shut and prevent the intrusion of ghosts. Artistic though 'Calverley' – as Sir Walter was called by his wife – and Pauline considered themselves to be, they made no concessions to mere prettinesses. Hare observed that, 'if Sir Walter saw his house papered and furnished like those of other people's, he would certainly pine away from excess of luxury.' He positively preferred gloom and austerity, and Pauline took care not to deprive him of them.

Pauline died in 1866 aged 52, and with her the Pre-Raphaelite association with Wallington ended. Ruskin, Swinburne and Bell Scott were desolate. 'Calverley' who married again survived her by thirteen years. To a mere acquaintance he bequeathed all his wines and spirits 'for scientific purposes'. Wallington went, not to the heir to the baronetcy (who became extremely displeased, disputed the will and removed most of the pictures – except the portraits – and the furniture to Nettlecombe) but to his first cousin Charles Edward Trevelyan on the grounds that 'Calverley' considered it wrong for one man to own two separate estates. Charles Edward on entering the Bengal Civil Service in 1826 first 'secured fame and fortune by reporting' – to quote A.J.A. Morris's biography of C.P. Trevelyan – 'the embezzlement and mal-practices of his superior.' It was not a very edifying way of starting a career. Charles Edward was speedily promoted to Governor of Madras and Finance Minister to the government of India. He was a staunch Liberal and zealous in the cause of education for the Indians and British alike. He was zealous in everything he undertook. He was married to the favourite sister of the historian T.B. Macaulay who had made their home his. The home was not Wallington because when Sir Charles Edward (he was made a baronet in 1874) inherited it Macaulay was dead; yet Wallington now contains his books and many relics in addition to the furniture Sir Charles Edward was obliged to buy in bulk from the Duveen brothers of Hull on moving into the depleted house.

With the new Trevelyan baronetcy there opened Wallington's second intellectual heyday. Sir Charles Edward, earnest and self-righteous, was a civil servant of distinction and a scholar of oriental tongues. His son Sir George Otto was even more distinguished. Historian, writer and statesman he had been a great favourite of his uncle Macaulay with whom much of his early life was spent. When an MP he was a close friend and disciple of John Bright, the Lancashire parliamentarian and reformist; and espousing the cause of the New Liberal Movement of the 1860s ardently worked for the franchise of the working classes. Author of *The Life and Letters of Lord Macaulay* and *The Early History of Charles James Fox* Sir George Otto was made Chief Secretary for Ireland and for Scotland successively. He was appointed to the Order of Merit. In between winning honours and reputation he managed to pay off death duties and mortgages on the Wallington estate, some of which dated from 1690.

Sir George Otto's eldest son Charles Philips Trevelyan succeeded as 3rd Baronet of Wallington in 1928. A chip off the old block he too had begun life as an advanced Radical MP, and then marched steadily leftwards. With his great inheritance before him he took part in a movement to make mountains and moors available to the public. In 1914 he allied himself with Ramsay MacDonald and in the First World War advocated peace by negotiation. Needless to say he made himself very unpopular with the landowning class. Losing his parliamentary seat as a Liberal in the 1918 election he joined, nothing daunted, the Labour party. In 1924 he became President of the Board of Trade where he brought about much-needed reforms. Sir Charles was a sincere idealist like his forebears and like them a man of great potential ability. In achieving positions of distinction however he fell short of his two brothers, Robert Calverley the poet and George Macaulay the historian, who following their father's example harnessed their acute intellects to a centralized objective. Sir Charles was tactless. He vociferously supported the Soviet Union and in the words of the *Dictionary of National Biography*, 'turned a blind eye on what he did not want to see', or rather he saw every cause he espoused through rose-tinted spectacles. In 1930 an embarrassed Labour government appointed him in the King's name Lord Lieutenant of Northumberland, a promotion which did not find favour in the county. In 1931 he resigned from the House of Commons and turned his activities to the large estate which was then his. He did a great deal of tree-planting on those grouse moors which he had not already made over to the Forestry Commission. To the house he summoned political conferences and debates. Wallington became a meeting place for young Socialists and a cultural centre for adult educational courses. In all his endeavours he was encouraged and at times activated by his wife Mary, daughter of Sir Hugh Bell, a Newcastle iron-master and colliery owner, and a half-sister of Gertrude Bell, author and traveller in Arabia.

On 5 June 1934 Messrs Horne & Birkett the National Trust's solicitors wrote to the secretary MacLeod Matheson submitting draft instructions drawn up by Sir Charles Trevelyan relating to the baronet's intention of transferring his Wallington estate and everything within it to the Trust. Thus do the Wallington files open. Although it may look as though Sir Charles was putting the cart before the horse he had clearly been in verbal negotiation (unrecorded) with the secretary for some time. Among his instructions Sir Charles imposed several reasonable demands: that, notwithstanding his overriding desire for the public to enjoy access to house and estate (freedom to roam all moors and woodlands was emphasized) Wallington must remain a family home; and that if after his time his son and heir to the baronetcy ceased to observe these demands then the National Trust would no longer be bound to let him reside in the house. Sir Charles directed that in the event other descendants of his or his brothers should be given the opportunity of living at Wallington. Furthermore he demanded that so long as she wished his widow Lady Trevelyan should have power to administer the estate, 'she being exceedingly businesslike and competent' (a claim which Matheson did not endorse) 'and trusted by the people on the estate'. Lastly no revenue from the property was to be spent on the family.

In submitting Sir Charles's memorandum Mr Horne warned Mr Matheson that some of the demands outlined by Sir Charles would certainly be interpreted by the Treasury as creating a legally binding benefit to his family and so would negate the donor's intention to have the estate exempted from taxation. Also the fact that Lady Trevelyan was a member of the Trust's Executive Committee would make the Treasury look upon her 'power to administer the estate' still more cautiously. On being informed of these views Sir Charles asked to see Lord Zetland, the Trust's chairman, and Mr R.C. Norman, its vice-chairman, on 21 June. He would like to bring with him his brother Professor G.M. Trevelyan who happened to be chairman of the Trust's Estates Management Committee. The meeting took place and Sir Charles was made to realize that his wishes might not be demands, but his demands might be wishes.

I have mentioned precise dates because on the following 19 July Lord Lothian made his historic speech at the National Trust's annual meeting on the need to preserve the best of England's country houses, the speech which precipitated the launch of the country houses scheme and my appointment to the staff. The dates signify that Sir Charles Trevelyan was actually anticipating Lothian's forthcoming recommendation that the Trust should take immediate action. Since he was a friend of Lothian, at least politically, it is very probable that he knew what was in his mind and had already discussed with him Wallington's future. As things turned out Wallington did not come to the Trust before Lord Lothian's Blickling estate, although negotiations to that end started well before those concerning Blickling. On 30 August Matheson sent a copy of Lord Lothian's speech, which Trevelyan had not heard delivered, to Sir Charles. He received by return a letter from

Sir Charles asking if his offer, only slightly amended in consequence of the meeting with Lord Zetland and Mr Norman on 21 June, might go before the Executive Committee at its next assembly in October; and that both Lady Trevelyan and Professor Trevelyan might be present to enlighten the members on any doubtful points.

The Executive Committee were rather overawed by the size of the Wallington estate and the inclusion of a large country house full of treasures. Such a comprehensive offer had never before come their way although it was exactly what as a result of Lord Lothian's speech they were girding themselves to grapple with. Matheson was however authorized to inform Sir Charles that the Executive Committee would be ready to accept the house and grounds but part only of the moorlands, and not the whole estate which it would find too heavy a responsibility to manage. Somewhat naturally Sir Charles was put out by the Trust's seemingly irrational and pusillanimous response to his munificent gesture. If acceptance of a large estate was to prove unmanageable how then was the National Trust going to take up the Lothian challenge? He suggested that his proposition should be referred by the Trust to Mr Baldwin, then Lord Privy Seal and leader of the Conservative party in the National Government. Baldwin would surely be sympathetic since, he added somewhat surprisingly, 'he has always shown such a markedly friendly disposition to both of us. If he were prepared to present the problem for official consideration [presumably to persuade the Treasury to forego taxation]' all might turn out favourably for Wallington. If however 'the National Trust's charter does not qualify acceptance is it not desirable that public effort be made to get the law clarified, or *altered*?' In no event would he agree to a division of the estate. Sir Charles was anxious to announce his intentions to the press and allow the public to express its views whether or not it wanted his splendid patrimony to be held by the nation for their lasting benefit. He was politely but firmly dissuaded from doing this at that moment.

At their next meeting in November the Executive Committee considered an alternative proposition by Sir Charles to leave Wallington to the Trust by will. Again the committee reached no conclusion because the taxation problem could not be resolved. Letters from Sir Charles and Professor Trevelyan to the National Trust flew back and forth. It is interesting to compare the handwriting of George, crabbed, succinct and Gothic, with that of Charles, florid, rounded, almost baroque, the one expressing reserve and caution, the other impulse and emotion.

The National Trust seems to have gone into temporary torpor. It is much to Sir Charles's credit that this naturally impatient man did not break off negotiations altogether. Such action might have scotched the Trust's country houses scheme at birth. As it was he contained himself, or was contained by George. He undoubtedly wanted the Trust to have the place because he rightly assumed that only under its protection could his descendants continue to live in the house.

Out of the blue a back-bench member of the Executive Committee who, as far as was known, had sat since the Trust's foundation in 1895 through every single meeting without once raising his voice, a sort of Rip Van Winkle, wrote to Matheson an outspoken letter. He was full of anxiety. The Trust would not accept the devise of Wallington, certainly one of the most important properties it had ever been offered, and it might well be the last. It was dreadful to have dithered for months. He suggested that the Trust present the Treasury with a hypothetical case, exactly resembling Wallington's, inferring that if only part of the property were declared inalienable, surely death duties would not be claimed on the whole. A sensible letter one might suppose. But poor Mr Malcolm Sharpe was snubbed for his pains. No useful purpose would be served by such means he was informed.

Matheson made me cognizant of the complicated issues of the Wallington case and said he was delegating it to me henceforth. But either he would not let go of the tiller or he thought I was not competent enough to control it. At any rate he did nothing of the sort for quite a time. Probably he was right because the Trevelyan family *en masse* was a formidable body to manipulate, and I was a novice. Clearly Sir Charles was determined to commit the National Trust to an acceptance which it could not very well get out of. He informed Matheson that at a forthcoming tenants' party he proposed making a public pronouncement of his intentions, having already forewarned *The Times* and a few other choice newspapers. He enclosed a draft and asked for Matheson's comments. Matheson approved the draft while deprecating the announcement at that stage of delicate negotiations. Sir Charles paid no attention.

Professor Trevelyan suggested that Mr Horne should go even further than poor Mr Sharpe's proposal by disclosing his brother's will to the Inland Revenue without any reservations and see what their reaction would be. He thought Sir Charles had been misled by the Trust into relying on hopes which might prove spurious. But Mr Horne was sure the will as it stood would invite death duties. He advocated a mere affirmative to the Treasury of the testator's intentions. It would be more prudent than submitting the will to the Treasury and getting involved in every sort of bureaucratic entanglement. Meanwhile the press, getting wind of trouble, was hinting that Sir Charles's proposed bequest of Wallington had been rendered nugatory. Reporters kept badgering the National Trust office. Sir Charles was cross with Matheson for discussing his difficulty with journalists. An article in one of Allied Newspapers' productions actually ventured that the Trust had been obliged to refuse the bequest. Sir Charles decided that he would give a broadcast talk, come what might, telling a sympathetic world what he was going to do and why. That would settle all the press's hash and speculation and commit the Trust, the Treasury and the nation to the acceptance of Wallington once and for all.

In March 1937 Sir Charles Trevelyan addressed the nation over the air. 'It became evident to my wife and myself', he began, 'that it would be a great public loss if Wallington could not continue to be open for the recreation of the increasing numbers of people who now visit it. It would clearly be a public calamity if the house were to lose the collections which make it interesting ... I made up my mind that I was not going to allow Wallington to become only a memory. I had to consider how to secure its future. There is as yet no department of State which has suitable machinery for controlling property with mansions in the interest of the public. I therefore determined to bequeath the house and estate to the National Trust.'

After assuring his listeners that the National Trust agreed with him that the interest of the place would be seriously diminished if it ceased to be inhabited by the people most attached to its traditions he concluded:

There is one great reason which makes it easier for me than for most people in my position to take this step. To most owners it would be a terrible wrench to consider alienating their family houses and estates. To me, it is natural and reasonable that a place such as this should come into public ownership, so that the right to use and enjoy it may be for ever secured to the community. As a Socialist, I am not hampered by any sentiment of ownership. I am prompted to act as I am doing by satisfaction at knowing that the place I love will be held in perpetuity for the people of my country.

It was the concluding sentiments of his speech which infuriated fellow country house owners. Many considered it an arrogation of superior motives to claim that only Socialists had at heart the welfare of their estates' future. Were not Conservative landowners just as concerned about the future of theirs? Besides the assertion that Sir Charles disapproved of private ownership of large houses was gross hypocrisy in that he wished his descendants to continue living at Wallington. The reaction of many Tory owners was borne out by Sir Charles's subsequent conduct. Some no doubt swore inwardly that they would prefer their houses to be burnt to the ground after their deaths than fall into the grasp of the National Trust. Whatever were his mixed motives Sir Charles was certainly reiterating in slightly more extravagant form the sentiments of Sir Walter Calverley Trevelyan who thought it wrong for any man to own too much property.

The situation remained static. Sir Charles held on to Wallington. Then came the war. In October 1940 at the age of 70 he began worrying again whether on his death any parts of the estate might still be liable to death duties. Mr Horne when consulted said, yes, death duties would be liable on the house and contents, but as regards the estate only on the endowment land, although the Treasury had agreed in 1937 that the greater part of the land could be held by the Trust inalienably, and so tax-free. In October Professor Trevelyan told Matheson he would try and persuade his brother either to remove from his will legal claims of rights for his family and rely on wishes being honoured by the Trust, or to hand over Wallington in his lifetime. 'Let us have a meeting here at Trinity College Cambridge [where he was then Master] and let Esher be present.' To invite Esher was a stroke of genius for 'Sir Charles is a difficult person to deal with,' Matheson informed Horne and Esher could deal with the devil himself if needs be. Sir Charles indicated in advance that he was prepared to consider – and no more than consider – handing over provided all his interests were safeguarded. He must, so his brother wrote to Matheson, be allowed to do with the estate what he should think fit. And 'He must safeguard the rights of his descendants, in order to be a bait for other donors!!' The double exclamation marks were an indication of some vestigial Trevelyan humour. Furthermore the baronet assured the professor that 'the life we lead here need be in no way affected as long as I live'.

Before the meeting at Trinity Esher wrote to Sir Charles. He agreed with him that by giving there and then or leaving the estate by will while retaining legal rights to himself and family would in either case invite taxation. On the other hand his and his family's rights could be covered in both cases in only one way, namely by taking advantage of the Trust's exemption from taxation and goodwill towards donors. 'The owner must accept the word of the Trust and believe that they [the Trust] will carry out their proclaimed policy.' In an admittedly involved letter Lord Esher had recourse to his inner wisdom which always rose to the surface when occasion demanded. The meeting took place. On 15 April Sir Charles wrote to Matheson: 'After further discussion with the Master of Trinity and my family, I have decided to give Wallington to the National Trust at once.' So that was a mighty relief to all concerned.

In May the Executive Committee agreed to accept Wallington as a gift, the donor reserving to himself a life interest 'without impeachment of waste', that familiar phrase so dear to Mr Horne and held out by him as an inducement to the reluctant. It conveyed to an owner the agreeable impression that he could do what he liked with the property after he had given it away. A formal memorandum of wishes binding on the National Trust accompanied Sir Charles's gift. In the memorandum, besides the clause recapitulating Lady Trevelyan's and the family's needs, another reserved to him subject to the National Trust's connivance and approval all the softwoods standing on the estate which might be suitable for felling in his lifetime, a reservation which was to be exercised to the full.

Sir Charles drafted yet another press announcement which he directed the National Trust to release. He pointed out that he was handing to the nation in wartime his house with furniture, china and pictures, the grounds and the woods, and an estate of 13,000 acres. The gift was indisputably a princely one. With it the interests of his family were once again emphasized, and his Socialism was stressed. So too his hopes were included that other owners would follow suit. But this last sentence was tactfully deleted by the Master of Trinity. 'Dear George,' Sir Charles wrote to his brother on 21 October, 'the Deed is now accomplished and the old place has a future if there is a future for anything.' He lived another seventeen years to eat his cake and have it. There seemed never to have been any question of his son, the present Sir George Trevelyan, living at Wallington. Lady Trevelyan died in 1966 when her widowed daughter Pauline Dower continued to live in a corner of the house. To all intents and purposes Wallington is no longer a family home, and is now a family museum, the very thing Sir Charles never wanted.

Once the deed was accomplished Matheson decided that henceforth I should definitely deal with this property. I had only just returned to the National Trust from the Army. In the circumstances of the transfer there was mercifully little I was called upon to do beyond agreeing to practically everything Sir Charles and Lady Trevelyan wanted. In September 1942 I paid my first visit to Wallington. From Newcastle station a country bus took me to Cambo village. As was usual during wartime I stood all the way and walked to the house from the bus stop. By the stables I was met by Matheson who was there to effect my induction. I sensed that he was relieved by doing so. I was dead tired and after dinner longed for bed. In my diary at the time I recorded:

> But no. We have general knowledge questions. Lady T puts the questions one after the other with lightning rapidity. I am amazed and impressed by her mental agility, and indeed by that of the [two] daughters, who with pursed lips shoot forth unhesitating answers like a spray of machine-gun bullets. All most alarming to a tired stranger. At the end of the 'game', for that is what they call this preparatory school examination, they allot marks. Every single member of the family gets 100 out of 100. The son-in-law [John Dower] gets 80, Matheson (who is also a clever man) gets 30. I get 0. But then I am a half wit. Deeply humiliated I receive condolences from the Trevelyans and assurances that I shall no doubt do better next time. I make an inward vow that there never will be a next time.

There were of course to be several.

My host and hostess were extremely cordial but alarming. He was a handsome man with piercing eyes and a mouth which turned up on the right side into a kind of sneer which was disconcerting. She, tall, poised and bustling, wore pince-nez and spoke in a brittle staccato with a North Country intonation not unlike Lord Curzon's. Both husband and wife struck me as academic, the reverse of pleasure-loving, over-political, and trailing the threadworn coat of Socialism. My aesthetic eye saw them as out of harmony with the artistic background of Wallington. But they were gracious in the way that the right – or should I say the left? – minded are with sinners from the wrong end of the spectrum.

The National Trust's role during Sir Charles's remaining years was not altogether easy. In the first place Wallington was a very long way from the Trust's headquarters; and distance gives rise to misunderstanding. In the second place Bruce Thompson, whose kingdom was strictly speaking confined to the Lake District where the Trust's properties were immense and whom I was obliged to call upon at times for help – in any case he was far more competent to deal with estate matters than myself – did not always see eye to eye with the Trevelyans. Sir Charles got to hear that Bruce complained to head office that he was selling trees on the estate right and left without informing the Trust.

He took umbrage, and then vented his wrath on Bruce. But the gentlest and most retiring of men could not understand why others should incline to brashness and autocracy. As it happened he did the Trevelyans a great service since it was on his recommendation that the whole Wallington estate had been declared worthy of inalienability in the first place, and so, with the Treasury's endorsement, free from Sir Charles's old bugbear, taxation.

Before the war ended Sir Charles warned us that the girls' school which was occupying most of the house might be leaving and the Army taking its place. This would be very unfortunate and we supported Sir Charles's objections by insisting that in that case the staterooms would have to be left out of any lease. We heard no more of the Army.

In 1946 Sir Charles posed an awkward question. Fearing senility – he was nowhere near it – he wondered whether his life interest reserved to him the legal right to sell Wallington. In the office we were far from certain what was the answer. So rather than consult the lawyers, whose pronouncements once they have been elicited are apt to be either ambiguous or downright unfavourable to the client, we wrote back to Sir Charles merely hoping that he would never wish to do such a thing.

About this time I was compiling a comprehensive guidebook to all the National Trust's historic buildings. I asked Sir Charles if Wallington might be included since owing to his life interest it was not yet strictly speaking Trust property. He replied kindly in the affirmative, sending particulars of the weekend openings from Easter to October. He asked me to mention that his woods were available to the public at all times 'subject to good behaviour'. I deliberately left out the last four words which smacked of condescension. Some of the opening arrangements were not in strict accordance with our views but we could do nothing about them. Then Bruce Thompson reported that at the entrance gate a crown had been painted on one pillar and a hammer and sickle on the other. There was no mention of the National Trust which was perhaps just as well. In reply I wrote to Bruce, 'I deplore the hammer and sickle business more than I can possibly say. I should equally deplore Conservative slogans slashed upon National Trust gate piers, or Nazi swastikas.' Professor Trevelyan to whom I mentioned the matter said that we could do nothing in spite of my objection that the world at large believed Wallington already belonged to the Trust and understood nothing about reservations of interest.

When after Lady Trevelyan's death in 1966 it became apparent that the whole house would not be inhabited by the family the Trust decided to redecorate and rearrange the staterooms which henceforth would be shown to the public and used for no other purpose. John Fowler's advice and services were sought. He painted the staircase hall apricot and white and the dining-room to which it leads a blue-grey lightly brushed, the delicate panelled plasterwork picked out in white. John Fowler tackled the magnificent saloon more drastically. When I first saw it the walls were a Neapolitan yellow beneath a high coved ceiling of which the coves were egg blue and the bold rococo enrichments white. But whereas now the coves and the flat of the ceiling have merely been cleaned so as to look a much deeper blue than I remember, the yellow of the walls was scrapped. John Fowler had the walls painted white and the enrichments periwinkle blue, a reversal of the usual Georgian treatment of white stucco-work on a coloured ground. The effect is disturbing and not a little vulgar as though a night-club proprietor and not the century's most scholarly decorator had been at work. It is a pity that the oval niches no longer contain shelves and have been fitted with looking-glass. On the other hand the incomparable John Fowler painted the walls of the needlework room a snuff brown so as to complement the background to Julia Calverley's marvellous tent-stitch panels of wool and silk. The rococo frames now white were once gilded.

If the house was found practically empty of furniture when Sir Charles Edward and his wife moved into Wallington in 1879 the Duveen brothers (uncle and father to the better-known dealer brethren who extended the National Gallery and traded in old masters on the grand Edwardian scale) did not do badly by it. Most of the furniture in the staterooms comprises very decent Georgian and Victorian pieces, in addition to Lord Macaulay's belongings and relics. The family portraits are of considerable interest and the collection of English porcelain is by any country house standards remarkable. The staterooms today look as though the dust-covers have just been whipped off and the house is awaiting the imminent return of its owners from a long absence abroad. The rather etiolated Leftish essence prevalent throughout the donors' regime no longer predominantly hovers. Their memory is evinced by a smattering of framed photographs, a striking bronze bust of Sir Charles by Gertrude Hermes in the dining-room, and Lady Trevelyan's ambitious panel of needlework depicting the equestrian founder of the Trevelyan family breasting the Cornish waves. Their younger daughter (Mrs) Patricia Jennings still occupies a few upstairs rooms of the west wing; but whether any future descendants will do likewise is open to question. It is true that Sir Charles, who passionately desired the family continuity, nevertheless conceded that after his children's generation the National Trust might be free to let Wallington to whomsoever it pleased. Let us hope the Trust will in due course encourage members of the family not to sever all ties with the home of their ancestors.

On the other hand the place is not dead. The cottages on either side of the cupola'ed clock tower accommodate employees on the estate. And during most days of the year the house is buzzing with visitors; so too are the walled, terraced, and well-watered gardens lying to the east quite half a mile away from the house in the manner of Scottish and Northumbrian country house gardens.

CHAPTER TWELVE

SACKVILLE OF KNOLE
Kent

UNIQUE is an adjective to be used sparingly. There are very few English country houses dating before the classical revival which retain their early furnishings. Drayton (like Knole with Sackville connections), Hardwick, Ham, Chastleton and Boughton come to mind. Cotehele too shares, albeit on a miniature scale, the same major attribute, namely staterooms furnished in the seventeenth century and almost completely unchanged. But what makes Knole in addition unique is its astonishing size. No medieval and Tudor house exceeds its immense dimensions, those legendary 365 rooms, 52 staircases and 7 courtyards. To go on foot from the wicket gatehouse round the outside walls and back again amounts to a respectable constitutional. There is something to be said for the house's resemblance to one of those walled cities in Tuscany. Only what in Italy would be on a hill is here on a mere hillock, or knoll. Nevertheless it is the height of Knole's situation compared to that of other great Kent houses, like Penshurst for example, that recommended it for health reasons to the cupidity of Henry VIII – 'I *will* live at Knole,' he announced – in appropriating it from the archbishopric of Canterbury at the Reformation.

Most great country houses have historic beginnings which tail off into dim if not prosaic middles, and very often sadly squalid ends. Knole however is an exception in having a perennially romantic history and seeming to be immortal. Its history is so well known from the guidebooks that there is no need to do more than summarize it here in brief reminder. The Lancastrian Archbishop Thomas Bourchier of Canterbury, Lord High Treasurer of England and poet before Shakespeare, was the house's founder in the fifteenth century. He is said to have opened it 'to literary men whose society he much enjoyed'. He may then claim to have initiated Knole into a den and cradle of poets and writers to endure throughout five centuries. In the sixteenth century a successor of Bourchier in the archbishopric, no less a prelate than Thomas Cranmer, forfeited Knole, as already adumbrated, to the Crown. In 1603 the place was acquired by the first Sackville, Sir Thomas, Lord High Treasurer of England, 1st Earl of Dorset, and also a poet of note. He altered and extended the medieval house into the great palace it is today.

Romance invests the person of the Lord High Treasurer's grand-daughter-in-law, Lady Anne Clifford, the great northern heiress. Married at 19 to Richard, spendthrift 3rd Earl of Dorset, she was summoned from Knole to Whitehall by King James I to be manoeuvred into settling her immense lands on her worthless husband. Girl though she still was she resolutely defied the monarch. No royal threats would induce her to part with an acre of her paternal inheritance. At the end of the seventeenth century the 6th Earl, himself one of the Restoration poets and patron of writers, won renown for Knole by entertaining Dryden, Pope, Prior, Rochester, Killigrew and Shadwell in the dining-room known as the poets' parlour.

Romance was not lacking in the eighteenth century. We remember prim Lady Betty Germaine, beloved by the whole Sackville family, who left an indelible imprint on her tiny bedroom, dressing-room and china closet, a ghost as it were embalmed in pot-pourri and Delft. She was no humble old maid companion to the 1st Duke and Duchess of Dorset but the widowed and childless owner of stately Drayton House in North-amptonshire which she was to bequeath to their younger son Lord George Sackville. In the late eighteenth century Madame Bacelli, famous dancer and mistress of the 3rd Duke, was arrested for all time by Gainsborough, standing on one foot on a dais, holding up her skirt and pointing a toe, with Wang-y-Tong the Chinese page-boy in the background. Then in the early nineteenth century Knole was made a house of mourning with the death of the handsome 4th and penulti-mate Duke, killed out hunting in 1815 aged barely 22. That brought about the end of the male line of Sackville owners of Knole; shortly afterwards the dukedom became extinct. The Sackville name was revived somewhat desperately in a succession of three younger sons of the 5th Earl De La Warr, who had married the 4th Duke of Dorset's sister. Of these the elder, Mortimer Sackville-West, was created 1st Lord Sackville by Queen Victoria as a sort of consolation prize for the untitled heir of a large landed property.

The romance of Knole was still by no means exhausted. At the end of the nineteenth century it resurged in a notoriety now to be assessed in retrospect. The beautiful young wife who came into Knole with a fanfare did not leave the scene with a whimper. Victoria the illegitimate daughter of Pepita, a Spanish dancer, by Lionel 2nd Lord Sackville, married in 1890 her first cousin Lionel, who became the 3rd Lord Sackville. This colourful lady contested, not without self-interest, a suit brought by her brother (like herself born illegitimate) under the Declaration of Legitimacy Act against her husband. In 1910 the petition was dismissed and the bastard Victoria emerged the triumphant and legal Lady Sackville and chatelaine of Knole.

Lady Sackville's career was interrupted by a further law case which excited much public clamour. She fought and won a suit brought against her by the relations of her lover Sir John Murray Scott. They claimed that she had inherited by devious means Sir John's share of famous French furniture from the Wallace Collection. She triumphed over this issue and raised Knole to the zenith of pre-Great War social splendour. An entertaining if erratic hostess Lady Sackville gathered together at her Saturday-to-Monday house parties the great and the not so good. A faithful though fictional picture of Knole's history of this era is recorded in her daughter Vita Sackville-West's novel, *The Edwardians*.

Lionel 3rd Lord and Victoria Lady Sackville had this one child, and the title and estate passed, to Vita's chagrin, on her father's death in 1928 to her uncle, Major-General Sir Charles Sackville-West. Charles likewise had but one child, Edward, eventually the 5th Lord Sackville. Meanwhile a strange emotional duet was played by Vita and Eddy Sackville-West. Theirs was an ambivalent, love-hate relationship in which the former element probably prevailed. Both first cousins were intellectuals and writers of rare ability. Vita was the more inventive, a poet of lyrics and georgics more Horatian than Virgilian which, though underestimated today, will surely revive tomorrow. She was also novelist and chronicler of Knole, and gardener second to none. Eddy was novelist, biographer and music critic inferior to few. The cause of the couple's underlying sensitivity was a simple one. Vita resented the fact that she had been born a girl, whereas Eddy may have regretted that he had been born a boy. Vita loved Knole with such atavistic passion that it was torture of the psyche that she would never own it. Eddy who was not brought up there as a child was bored by Knole and dreaded the responsibility of ownership and management. These two remarkable and interesting scions of a great name and domain have left their respective contributions to the annals of Knole. Unfortunately there is no portrait (other than a drawing or two) of Vita in the house. On the other hand Eddy's haunted and harassed features, painted by Graham Sutherland, are now arrayed amongst those of his

Tudor, Stuart, Georgian, Victorian and Edwardian forebears.

Impressions left by Knole on visitors have seldom been negative. Only the eighteenth-century ones were sometimes adverse. This is hardly surprising. What does surprise us is that the Georgian Sackvilles not only left the house intact but also lived in it. True, the state apartments were used for hide-and-seek and shuttlecock by children. In the age of enlightenment they were considered so archaic that nothing could be done by way of improvement other than their wholesale demolition. Nevertheless since there were plenty of rooms elsewhere in the house to be made fit for civilized beings, they were left untouched. Gradually they acquired an antiquarian appeal and were deemed suitable for house guests to amble through, admiring or mocking on wet days. Anne Rushout in 1795 pronounced the house 'extremely melancholy ... the apartments are the most dismal I ever saw, tho' very costly'. On the other hand nearly half a century earlier Bishop R. Pococke, inveterate sightseer, called it 'an exceedingly good old house'. Horace Walpole's opinions were at variance. 'The park is sweet,' an odd adjective, he wrote in 1752, although 'there are some trumpery fragments of gardens that spoil the view from the state apartments,' in other words there was no regular classical layout. 'The house not near so extensive', he went on, 'as I expected.' What can he have been expecting?

> The furniture throughout, ancient magnificence; loads of por-
> traits, not good nor curious; ebony cabinets, embossed silver in
> vases, dishes, etc; embroidered beds, stiff chairs, and sweet bags
> lying on velvet tables, richly worked in silk and gold ... There is
> never a good staircase ... sundry portraits of the times; but they
> seem to have been bespoke by the yard, and drawn all by the same
> painter ... In the chapel is a piece of ancient tapestry; Saint Luke
> in his first profession [as medico] is holding an urinal.

Observations which in a perverse way may be irrefutable if one is out to damn with faint praise.

The medieval-orientated Victorians naturally raved. Joseph Nash gave Knole a precedence in *Mansions of the Olden Time*. For a description of our own century I find Denton Welch's diary entry strangely moving. The crippled young artist-novelist lived nearby. Conversing with a friend under a fallen park tree on a dank September afternoon during the last war he found it 'a wonderful house' epitomizing English history, autumnal-like, an evanescent dream of the past, yet 'an eternal moment always dissolving which will yet re-occur a thousand times to a thousand thousand other people when *we* are dead, who will look out in the same way through the windows in their heads & see the falling rain, the bracken, the pattern of the oak bark, and wonder and go on wondering for years.' Denton was also a poet and he knew that Knole was a poem.

Nine years before Denton Welch rhapsodized over Knole in 1944 Charles, 4th Lord Sackville, was sufficiently worried about its future to invite Mr Matheson of the National Trust to discuss it over luncheon. During a long talk he complained of the appalling expense of maintaining so colossal a dwelling and explained how on his succession he had re-entailed the place on his son Edward and Edward's sons as yet unborn. Eddy's obstructive unborn sons were to become a sick joke throughout the prolonged negotiations. Matheson expatiated on the intricacies of the National Trust's forthcoming country houses schemes, explaining how at that date the law prohibited any interest being retained by a family after a property was transferred; and also how the National Trust could not hold land for purposes of endowment. Lord Sackville thought he might join our alternative scheme whereby owners of approved houses did not relinquish their possessions but banded together under the Trust's flag to bring pressure on the government to grant them relief from certain taxes in return for opening to the public on a few days in the year. In July 1936 I was detailed to inform Lord Sackville that the alternative scheme was proving disappointing. The Trust had wrung few concessions from the government. For owners the situation amounted to hand over *in toto* or do nothing.

I sometimes stayed weekends with Eddy in the Thirties when he had independent rooms over the outer wicket and part of the west front. He was frequently called upon to escort his father's and step-mother's cosmopolitan friends round the staterooms, and resented it. One summer evening we were both made to play croquet with the guests. Eddy performed with the greatest skill; I who had rashly boasted how much I enjoyed the game played disgracefully and was soundly and justly humiliated. However Lord Sackville was rather amused and entered into a sort of tacit conspiracy with me at the expense of Eddy's prowess of which Eddy was not a little proud. He put me in touch with his most operative trustee, Colonel Robin Buxton, a director of Martin's Bank with whom I was to have much commerce. The Colonel assured me that he was determined to prevent further sales of Knole's contents in order to raise funds to meet death duties on the previous Lord Sackville's death. He readily agreed to our preparing a list of those contents which in no circumstances ought to leave the house;

also to an option being given the Trust to purchase contents pertaining to Knole if ever the family should again feel obliged to raise money on them.

Meanwhile Lord Sackville asked the Trust to take 'unofficial soundings' as to the likelihood of a private estates bill passing through Parliament to enable the house and garden to be transferred; and also to consider raising an endowment fund of approximately £150,000. To the first end I went to see George Pepler, chief technical adviser at the Ministry of Planning. He was sympathetic. I also went to see A.P. Waterfield at the Treasury. He was totally non-committal. To the second end Matheson approached the Carnegie Trust and Pilgrim Trust for money which they declined to give. These advances to ministerial and charitable circles did not get us far. As for the park the Sevenoaks Urban District Council led by a conservation-minded chairman showed genuine enthusiasm for its preservation as a public open space, expressing anxiety to acquire it. Lord Sackville showed just as much anxiety to have compensation. The UDC was also laudably concerned about preserving certain vistas of the house from the park. But how was money for the park's purchase to be found? By public appeal? By contribution from both UDC and NT so long as the land was vested in the latter? We drafted a scheme to be submitted to Lord Sackville through Colonel Buxton who was as shrewd as he was deeply concerned for his friend's and Knole's best interests.

As for the private bill proposition Sir Claud Schuster, Clerk of the Crown in Chancery and Permanent Secretary to the Lord Chancellor, to whom it had to be submitted, dismissed it. He pronounced that a public bill conferring on the Court of Chancery powers to approve arrangements to meet, not only the Knole entail settlement but all future county house entails that might confront the Trust, would be preferable. On 8 August 1937 I was urging haste in view of the poor health of Lord Sackville and Eddy. I don't know why I was so concerned for Lord Sackville was to live another twenty-five years and Eddy twenty-eight. Colonel Buxton also urged haste because he always feared Lord Sackville might be tempted to sell more contents to pay for upkeep.

The endowment problem was a real worry. Matheson discussed with Lord Lothian how best to raise funds without issuing a public appeal, and even asked Ramsay MacDonald if he could recommend an obliging millionaire. He begged in vain from Lord Bearsted who already had in mind endowing his own house and collections at Upton in Warwickshire. Lord Sackville was very sensitive about his disinclination to receive charity. He would feel like living in an almshouse if Knole were helped financially by an outsider.

Letters kept flying between the National Trust, Colonel Buxton, Lord Sackville's agent Captain E.B. Glasier, and solicitors Messrs Meynell and Pemberton, the Treasury and the Office of Works when war broke out. On 29 September Matheson wrote to Buxton presuming that 'all question of Knole will have to drop for the time being'. It dropped for fifteen months.

On 30 December 1940 Matheson wrote to Colonel Buxton that the war had brought about renewed interest among owners in the surviving country houses scheme; the Trust was deep in negotiation over another settled estate, Hatchlands. 'What about Knole now?' Buxton replied that Lord Sackville was in a mood to resume where he had left off. Matheson wrote that Eddy Sackville-West, who was then living at West Wycombe Park where the Trust had moved its offices for safety, 'showed the greatest keenness'. This was exceptional because Eddy seldom showed enthusiasm and often showed defeatism over the whole project. Buxton pointed out that whereas the gross income of the Knole estate was £20,000, under wartime conditions £3,888.3s. was spendable. Yet to live at Knole in the humblest way cost Lord Sackville – he had one housemaid to keep 250 bedrooms clean – £7,900 a year. He needed reassurance concerning his family's interests if negotiations were to go ahead. Matheson warned solicitor Horne that Lord Sackville wanted to retain all management control, but was in the hands of Captain Glasier who was difficult, even rude at times and dead against the scheme – 'Jealousy I imagine'. Horne foresaw difficulties arising from that familiar bugbear, the Chancery Court. Taking refuge behind the obstructive Glasier Lord Sackville intimated that he might retain part of the park for its building value.

Matheson all alone at this preliminary stage of the war was beset by problems of every sort. Knole was only one. He lunched with Glasier who presented an unscaleable stone wall of objection to all progress. Glasier opined that after Lord Sackville's death no member of the family would consider living at Knole; therefore it had better be split up for what it would fetch. Horne had a no less unsatisfactory meeting with the Sackville solicitor Mr Leigh Pemberton who demanded that his client be refunded for past costs out of the endowment fund yet to be raised. Horne advised that the whole Knole business be dropped. Matheson's staunch comment was that after all the trouble which had been gone through 'it could not be disposed of in such an off-hand manner'.

When panic was near prevailing among all parties Lord Sackville suddenly offered to provide towards the endowment needed £4,000 a year if the Trust would find another £2,500 from legacies or general funds. Then just as suddenly he became frightened of 'joint control and interference', threatening to back out. He failed to see what advantage he could derive from the transaction. His fears were motivated by his Counsel's opinion that he could benefit only by a few hundred pounds a year, if that. Was an irreversible hand-over of his great inheritance of over three and a half centuries going to be worth the candle? His misgivings were surely understandable for there was no precedent to go by, no previous case of an entailed property of similar importance having yet been handed over and a tenant-for-life emerging blissfully happy. If he were to be the guinea-pig he might well live to regret it. When I heard from Eddy what the situation was I felt much sympathy for this charming, gentle, elegant and patrician old man who dreaded living on charity.

Matheson felt very discouraged and feared a fiasco. He appealed to that notable *deus ex machina* Dr Tom Jones, confidant of Prime Ministers, to direct his influence upon the Treasury, and even upon Mr Winston Churchill to come to the rescue and assure the future of one of England's greatest houses. Would he please wave a wand over Knole? If not, it would on Lord Sackville's imminent death (as he believed) be broken up. For once Dr Jones did not come up to scratch. When he failed Matheson appealed to John Reith of the BBC to influence the Treasury. Again there was no response. The nation's pundits had other more pressing matters to attend to. Then he thought of sending Eardley Knollys (who had joined the staff and who being an older friend of Eddy than I was knew his father better) in a last desperate bid for Lord Sackville's waning patience. Then he thought better of it. He wrote to me who was still in the Army. All I could do was to write to Eddy asking whether his father would not waive his objection to an individual coughing up the extra endowment still required. No stone should be left unturned I added portentously. Eddy replied agreeing with my letter, but 'you know how touchy my father is about charity'. And Buxton wrote to Matheson, 'We have come to a deadlock,' then conceded, 'I see no harm, if the occasion arose, in one of you with Eddy Sackville-West having a last talk with Lord Sackville.' I really believe Matheson was frightened of having one by himself.

Things seemed pretty desperate when a rich newspaper proprietor Mr W. Coker Iliffe hinted that he might buy Knole – just like that – and let Lord Sackville continue to reside. Buxton on being asked by the

Trust what price Lord Sackville would name for Knole, and whether he would countenance a high-powered meeting with the Trust, the Treasury, the Ministry of Works, the Ministry of Health and other interested parties besides, dismissed both ideas as out of the question. Lord Sackville was too proud a man to be trifled with in this way. Instead Buxton agreed with Lord Esher, who was being kept closely informed of each step in the proceedings, that we would be advised to wait until Lord Sackville died and Eddy succeeded to be faced with further death duties. Esher no more approved of purchase than did the Colonel. In any case the would-be purchaser either withdrew from the fray or died shortly afterwards.

Lord Esher wrote to me on 4 March 1942 that he believed the country houses scheme could never work 'as long as the taxation of endowment continues. I think we should use Knole as a means of getting it removed. If the prospect of the loss of Knole does not move the Treasury, nothing will.' He was of course absolutely right. With his letter he enclosed a draft memorandum addressed to the Treasury. I sent a copy of Esher's memorandum to Harry Strauss, Joint Parliamentary Secretary at the Ministry of Works and a member of our Executive Committee, by way of enlisting his benign influence upon the Treasury.

Somehow the general panic subsided as all panics eventually must. Negotiations were not broken off. I was soon inviting the highly experienced accountant Arthur Garrard of the Duchy of Lancaster office to examine on our behalf the Knole expenditure figures with Captain Glasier. Glasier did his utmost to throw spokes, and Garrard retreated discomfited. I begged Lord Sackville to intervene which he did by allowing his accountant F.M. Mason to receive Garrard. Like all trusted servants belonging to the upper echelon Mason invariably signed his letters – and dozens if not hundreds I must have received from him in those days – with his initials, never disclosing his Christian name. I have no idea what it was. On the other hand employees belonging to the lower echelon were usually known and addressed by the Christian name, the surname being as often as not unknown to the employer and even the household and his workmates. Now although Mason too began by being hostile his heart was in the right place. I was to become very fond of him when eventually he succeeded as agent, for his jolly, broad-smiling, businesslike manner and his unfeigned loyalty to Lord Sackville. But at this stage of the proceedings Garrard was not favourably impressed either with the agent or the accountant. He wrote to me, 'Any ordinary job I should give up . . . Glasier and Mason have perfected a technique of infuriating procrastination. I do not believe it possible to be more obstructive or maddening than they are being.' I passed this on to Eddy while explaining that Garrard was very disting-uished in his profession and a member of our Estates Management Committee. Matheson's observation was, 'It makes one feel the only thing to do is to shoot people who behave like that.'

Lord Sackville on the other hand Garrard found charming and helpful. This was Lord Sackville's invariable way. He always received me in the most affectionate, fatherly manner and appeared perfectly frank. Yet I came to learn that he was, if not devious, suspicious and fearful of taking decisions. Although appearing to be master of his own mind and property he would dive for shelter behind his executors and agent at the slightest sign of trouble. And his staff probably manipulated him. Mason on the other hand, while being extremely protective, adroitly induced Lord Sackville to give him instructions, whether or not they derived from his lordship, Colonel Buxton, Glasier, or himself.

Garrard's report, done for love of the Trust free of charge, did not at first satisfy Lord Sackville that he was getting much out of the deal. He protested that his income would be reduced and he would not be able any longer to make annual maintenance claims from the Inland Revenue. Mason confronted me with the outright question: did the National Trust intend to assist the owner to reside at Knole, or not? The answer was an emphatic yes *certainly*, so long as the National Trust limited its spending of tax-free monies on the fabric of the house, the staterooms, the contents and the garden and as much of the park as the public would benefit from.

After the Trust had undertaken to keep on all the family's mainte-nance staff, including Mason (who also remained in Lord Sackville's employment and gave him prior allegiance), and to supplement Lord Sackville's endowment investments yielding £3,000 a year with £2,000 a year to be derived from the surplus revenue, in accordance with a proviso in her will, of Mrs Greville's Polesden Lacey estate, lately acquired by the Trust, general agreement seemed to be reached. All that was wanting was a resolution of the Chancery Court which was still fussing over the interests of Eddy's unborn progeny and other unlikely heirs. By August 1943 with the consent of Colonel Buxton I was instructed to draft a public announcement to the press of Lord Sackville's intentions so as to forestall a garbled version through leakage. Before it came out I warned Eddy and Vita what was impending. In thanking me Vita wrote, 'You know how deeply I feel about everything that affects Knole', adding that she was bequeathing

Sissinghurst Castle to the Trust if her two sons Ben and Nigel did not marry and beget children.

The Court kept us on tenterhooks. To Raby of the Ministry of Works Matheson wrote in October 1943, 'Lord Sackville is getting very old and very frail and I only hope to goodness we can get the thing through the Court while he still lives.' Lord Sackville's latent misgivings about estate duties were resurrected. We assured him there would be none on his death. Then the German *Luftwaffe* dropped a bomb in the park close to the west front of Knole. 'The heraldic beasts on the gable finials turned round on their plinths and presented their backs to the outrage committed. What proud and noble behaviour!' I wrote in February 1944. But the consequences were worse than the heraldic beasts suggested. Lord Sackville, with whom I sympathized, wrote to me, 'There was great damage to all the windows especially in the Green Court and the great hall. Much stained glass has been broken but some can be put together again in Cranmer's rooms.' The Ministry of Works behaved admirably. They immediately sent down their experts to assess the damage and offered their services in putting things right. Vita was in agonies of apprehension.

At last the necessary papers prepared by the respective solicitors Horne and Leigh Pemberton were put before Counsel.

In October I was summoned to tea at Knole, but not as was usual to luncheon. The invitation portended trouble. 'On guard! On guard!' as the grandfather of the narrator in Proust's *Swann's Way* used to exclaim. I found Lord Sackville as exquisitely dressed as ever, in a blue tweed suit and canary-coloured waistcoat which, when his delicate build and abrupt movements were taken into account, brought to mind that domesticated bird. A gaunt pale blue nose upon a white face and a crest of white hair did not detract from the resemblance. A familiar gesture shared with Eddy was the appliance behind an almost transparent hand of a gold tooth-pick to a gleaming *ratelier*. It was the unnatural regularity of the false teeth when their owner smiled which disconcerted me. They were not in harmony with his charm and infinite friendliness. They enforced a grim contradiction in terms, which had to be recognized and dealt with. At any rate without any previous intimation Lord Sackville stipulated that a 200-year lease by the Trust to the family must be a prerequisite of the conveyance. I pointed out that this would inevitably attract the taxation which we had all been endeavouring to avert. I persuaded him, almost on bended knee, to allow the length of the lease to be limited to that term of years deemed satisfactory by the Court of Chancery. It would surely cover the lives of all those heirs in existence at the time of transfer. It was an anxious moment. With the sweetest smile Lord Sackville consented to withdraw his condition.

On 27 July 1945 I wrote to inform Lord Sackville that the judge in Chancery had pronounced in favour of Coughton Court being transferred to the Trust under the 1939 National Trust Act. I had been present in chambers at the time. The order had slipped through almost before I realized the case was under discussion. Coughton had been the test case and the entail presented problems very similar to the Knole ones. The Knole case might come up next term. The Trust was full of good hope. I also wrote to Raby asking him to send a certificate of approval of Knole as a worthy historic building for the purposes of affidavit to be made by Lord Sackville.

Precisely a year elapsed before Horne announced to us that Mr Justice Vaisey had made an order for vesting Knole in the National Trust subject to a lease in favour of Lord Sackville. It came as a great surprise to me who had no idea that the case was even pending. Within a day or two Vita made a broadcast appeal for membership of the National Trust. She wrote to me afterwards about the Knole transfer: 'Of course I cannot pretend that I like it but I know that it is the only thing to be done.' Lord Sackville was satisfied although irritated by the public ringing him up to enquire prematurely which were the opening days and hours.

A disagreement between Lord Sackville's office and the National Trust's over the dubious fashion in which part of the garden wall in a corner of the Wilderness had been repaired by his staff (Harold Nicolson was very critical) led to our appointing an architect for Knole in Geddes Hyslop, a contemporary and old friend of Eddy. Paul, as he was known, was a very suitable choice. He had an impeccable flair for doing what was right with old houses. He erected a partition at the bottom of the great staircase and another of trellis design painted French grey on the first-floor landing over the Stone Lobby, so as to separate the public from the private thoroughfares. When they were finished a stranger would not guess they did not date from Jacobean times.

The next urgent thing I had to do was to find an experienced housekeeper and staff under her to clean the staterooms and furniture and show round the public when the time came for opening the house. This was easier said than done. I could not burden Mason with it and it meant repeated day journeys to Knole to interview applicants and explain the duties required.

For an insurance inventory of the contents on loan from the

Sackvilles Leigh Ashton (director of the V&A) recommended his Keeper of Furniture and Woodwork, Ralph Edwards. After a preliminary visit the pedantic, cocky and infinitely sardonic little man said he could not possibly spare the time for a detailed inventory which was hardly surprising considering the quantity of the furniture. Nevertheless at neck-breaking speed he dictated to Mason and me in his parrotty voice rough estimates of nearly every item in the staterooms. So fast did he run and speak that towards the end I was breathless and my pencil-holding fingers got cramp. Weak on painting he begged for the valuation figures on this subject not to be quoted as his. Eventually he wrote to me as follows: 'While my heart is hot within me as the psalmist says, I send you a statement of account with the reservation that it need not be paid until you are satisfied that I have discharged my obligations. I may add, since you won't add it for me, that I hold the valuation, taking into consideration the mugging up I have done in my private time, damned cheap at the price!'

George Wingfield Digby likewise agreed to report on the condition of the tapestries and carpets. He was in most respects the very antithesis of Ralph. George was grave, shy, even reticent and spoke in a soft voice with none of the other's self-confidence and brio. He was extremely disturbed by the state of the carpets, of which several were of great rarity. They were very dirty and in need of washing. They had holes and tears. Silver fish were active in some. Pyrethrum was an advisable toxic. On no account must DDT be applied. The tapestries were in tolerable condition. The bed hangings in the famous Spangle Bedroom and King's Room were so-so. They made another story and were to be treated by regiments of needle experts after my time. George Digby recommended a retired workman from the V&A, C.W. Fletcher, for preliminary de-worming of the furniture. I was obliged to report to my committee that the general condition of the contents – all but the paintings which Lord Sackville had put in good order before the war – was that of advanced deterioration.

Fletcher, a sympathetic craftsman, but a scarecrow to look upon and with appalling manners – he told Lord Sackville to his face that he had neglected his own contents – came down from Upper Tooting and studied the furniture with a surgeon's care. He pronounced that all the woodwork must be treated with benzol-benzine, and all the upholstery with petroleum distillate, horribly inflammable fluids. He would have small missing parts made up if the Trust would allow him to enlist a fairly young man under his supervision. Joyfully I engaged Fletcher at 5 shillings an hour and the fairly young man at a good deal less. Where the fabrics on the furniture were irretrievably decayed Mrs I. Ray, living in Sevenoaks, an accredited needlewoman late of the V&A, and strongly recommended by Wingfield Digby, consented to repair and make them up.

I was slightly perturbed to receive letters of second thoughts from both Ralph Edwards and George Digby who had compared their notes and impressions. The first had paid another visit to Knole off his own bat. It convinced him that the state of the furniture was definitely worse than he had originally imagined. Piles of dust from woodworm lay on the floors. To treat the furniture alone was beyond the services of one experienced man and an inexperienced boy. More craftsmen must be engaged. My friend, Matley Moore, living at The Greyfriars, Worcester (which he and his sister were to bequeath to the Trust), gave me the names of a cabinet-maker and a young joiner in Worcester city who would think it a privilege to join the team at Knole. George Digby advised that the Anglo-Persian Carpet Company should clean and repair the two rare carpets (one English Jacobean) from Lady Betty Germaine's rooms. This they admirably did for £6 and £8 each. He also counselled that Lady Smith-Dorrien of the Royal School of Needlework be invited to inspect the textiles. I motored this distinguished lady down from London. A year later her school at Knightsbridge was deep in the long process of repairs, having begun with the Venetian Ambassador's bed hangings, one chair and some embroidered cushions from this room.

By November 1947 I knew that I simply lacked the time to search for staff and visiting craftsmen and arrange quarters and buy furniture for them at Knole, which though immensely important was one only among a number of historic buildings in the Trust's ownership and in my guardianship. The last straw which (nearly) broke my back was the difficulty of procuring utility furniture at all. Oddly enough there seemed to be none to spare in the attics and out-buildings of the vast house. I was obliged to beg the officer in charge of the Utility Furniture Office at the Board of Trade for authority to purchase the bare minimum required in beds, tables, chairs, linen and blankets to accommodate a resident staff of five. The Board of Trade refused. So I told them that the opening of Knole to the public who were clamouring for admission would in consequence be postponed indefinitely, until they did give consent. It was as simple as that.

I was fortunate to enlist Robin Fedden in taking over the practical jobs relating to the staterooms and contents of Knole by means of Mason's office in the Stable Court. He was a very gifted man, cosmopolitan (having been brought up in France), much travelled, an intrepid mountaineer, highly literary and a writer of brightly polished prose. His books *The Enchanted Mountains* and *Chantemesle* are minor classics. His syntax is clear as morning dew; his style crisp as hoar frost on an autumn leaf. He had joined the Trust staff in 1945 as curator of Packwood House in Warwickshire, soon moving to Polesden Lacey in Surrey where he took charge of the Trust's historic buildings in the south-east of England. He had a fine flair for period and a sure aesthetic eye. In 1951 he succeeded me as secretary to the Historic Buildings Committee for the next twenty-two years. What was the secret of Robin's extraordinary success as administrator?

He did not claim to be a specialist in any one branch of the arts. Although his horizons were broad he recognized his limitations. He was essentially an eclectic connoisseur in the eighteenth-century tradition. This was his strength. Above all he knew which experts to approach for opinions. In a trice he picked their brains and immediately acted upon his own assessment of their (often conflicting) advice. I think this particular gift is a shining example to all aspiring National Trust representatives.

Other worries at this time were how to pay for all the repairs being done on the contents, and how to ensure that the Sackvilles would not sell more and, if they did, how we could purchase them. To take the first worry. Luck came to the rescue. The Ministry of Works in handsomely carrying out repairs of the bomb damage had done more than was strictly needed on the roof. All this was free of charge. It meant that we therefore could dip into the £4,000 capital sum put aside for the structure, and spend it on the contents. Any expenditure over and above could be met from the surplus funds of Mrs Greville's legacy.

And now for the second worry. I was firmly of the opinion that Lord Sackville's agreement not to sell heirlooms from the staterooms without giving the Trust three months' notice to raise the money for them had been obtained. Apparently this was not so in spite of my production of past correspondence to prove it. Horne & Birkett had either forgotten to insert the clause in the contract or the judge in Chancery had struck it out. On the other hand there was a contractual obligation on the Trust to insure everything on loan. Martineau our new solicitor on the staff asked Leigh Pemberton for the names of all persons (apart from Eddy's unknown offspring) in succession under the entail. I had to approach them individually and ask if they would give a written undertaking to grant us the three months' notice should they ever feel like selling. Eddy Sackville-West and Ben and Nigel Nicolson at once agreed. I don't remember asking Lord Sackville's brother Bertrand and his sons. But if I did I am sure I had a friendly and co-operative response.

Far the most qualified person to write the guidebook of Knole was Vita. This she consented to do so long as I would carefully check that any pieces of furniture and pictures she might mention in her text were still in the same places where she remembered them. She had not been to Knole since her father's death in 1928 and could not bear to return. It did not mean that she had broken with her uncle – far from it – although she intensely resented his second wife Anne because of her offhand attitude to Knole, which she regarded as a sort of antiquated white elephant without the American mod. cons. Lord Sackville had given Vita a key to the garden which I believe she used once only for a stroll by moonlight, and which she cherished as her most sacred possession. Indeed it symbolized a means of re-entry to the scenes of her gilded childhood when she saw herself as rightful heir to the enchanted palace of her ancestors, an image to be transmuted by Virginia Woolf into Orlando, the handsome and gallant, androgynous and perennial, young duke of their conceptual fancy. Nevertheless, although she had not entered the house for a quarter of a century, every stick of furniture and every picture was accurately recorded in Vita's prodigious memory. Few objects had been shifted since her self-exile from Knole and I do not recall questioning a single reference to the contents in her text.

Over Easter 1947 there were 1,082 visitors and over the spring holidays a further 2,090. Mason was worried about the numbers, chiefly because of the bottle-neck passage up and down the great staircase (a problem which baffles and alarms the National Trust today) and the deficiency of staff to cope. At times it was touch and go whether the three ladies whom Robin Fedden had engaged to look after the staterooms could manage until Mason himself took over control. In its eagerness to supplement the endowment funds the Trust was surely mistaken in over-encouraging visitors and over-publicizing the house. I waged a perennial battle against the publicity department whose interests were intrinsically the opposite of mine. And I managed to thwart their desire to stage an official handing-over ceremony. Lord Sackville was likewise dead against it. He did not see himself in the role of willing benefactor of the National Trust to be accorded grateful thanks on a public stage. He saw himself as the inheritor of a glorious palace the burden of which he had been forced by a disobliging new world to shift on to the shoulders of an alien organization while retaining, as far as it were possible, the status granted him by the old world. A BBC television unit filming Knole in May, and promising wide publicity, was in Mason's words to me adding salt to Lord Sackville's wounds. Yet Lord Sackville liked and praised our resident staff and appreciated Robin Fedden's tact and civilized demeanour. One of the three ladies, Barbara Tate who had worked for Lord Sackville before 1939 and returned to Knole after war service to work there for the National Trust, retired only a year or two ago and lives in the house today.

On the whole the opening of Knole did not start off auspiciously. The geography of the rooms caused overcrowding, delays and irritations. The staff got worn out and somewhat browned off. Besides large numbers meant few tips for their pains. There were letters in *Country Life* complaining that crowds of people were being turned away. An old woman of 84 was knocked down by a car at the entrance. Did the National Trust have a comprehensive policy to cover it against further contingencies of the sort? Impatient visitors passed the time carving their names on the gatehouse door. Mrs Hugh Dalton, whom I accompanied to Knole more than once, considered quite rightly that special facilities should be provided for serious students of the works of art, and suggested a connoisseurs' day. I agreed that we must arrange this as soon as we could.

Towards the end of the season I wrote to Robin: 'There must be something wrong at Knole. A great number of grumbles from visitors this year at having to wait hours and then ill manners of the wicket-gate people. When we [Mrs Dalton and I] were there everything seemed to work very smoothly, but I suspect that the dragoness at the gate, and that extraordinary *gauleiter* figure with a walking-stick are probably extremely dictatorial with the public – at least they frightened us to death.' Robin agreed that 'the pre-Trust inhabitants of Knole still feel, and sometimes show, that they are doing the public a great favour in admitting them to My Lord's house at all.' This was unfortunately the attitude in evidence at Knole and some few other country houses where the Trust and the donor's staff worked both for the old master and the new. We learned from the experience that divided loyalties were regrettable and must somehow be prevented in future. So when Lord Sackville asked us to allow our stateroom staff to look after the north wing for him if he paid them we declined. We also learned that in the following season we must have more opening days at Knole, and that special coach parties must be restricted to one mid-week day.

In December 1948 John MacGregor wrote me a warning letter about the appalling condition of the stonework in the Stone Court and Water Court. He advised immediate SPAB treatment of brushing down and applying silica seal, followed by lime-washing over the stonework. Mason, adopting the traditional view of Knole retainers that the house's condition 'had always been like that' ever since they and their forebears could remember, considered that MacGregor was too pessimistic. But Robin and I meeting MacGregor on the spot, or rather spots, for most of the house proved to be affected by spalling, soon appreciated the serious deterioration of the stonework, and took alarm. The consequence was that for several decades the whole house was at the cost to the government in special grants of over a million pounds subjected to drastic treatment of the Kent rubble walls and, in many instances, total renewal of ashlar window mullions and surrounds.

We both concluded that the National Trust ought to employ an itinerant craftsman plus mate with a van of tools and instruments perpetually on the road from one Trust house to another. Little did either of us foresee how an enormous army of experts of every description would by 1992 be marshalled in each region to deal with instant emergencies as well as the everyday demands of maintenance. Thanks to this army Knole is now better kept than it may ever have been in the past. The vexing problem of visitors is controlled by a system of booking ahead which seems to be accepted as essential by both the public and the gate-keepers.

The present holder of the Sackville title still inhabits parts of the south front and his brother parts of the north wing. Half a century ago Lord Sackville told me that certainly no successor after Eddy would live at Knole. But judging by conditions there today it seems likely that every successor but Eddy, who even before his father's death preferred to live in Ireland, will want to do this very thing.

CHAPTER THIRTEEN

DASHWOOD OF WEST WYCOMBE

Buckinghamshire

THE Dashwood family has lived at West Wycombe since Queen Anne's reign. It enjoys the distinction of holding the first baronetcy granted by the Crown after the union of the two kingdoms of England and Scotland in 1707. Thus the present holder of the West Wycombe title is the premier baronet of Great Britain, and takes precedence over his distant Dashwood cousin of Kirtlington who derives his baronetcy from Charles II in 1684. Whether or not there is merit in a Christian name is a moot point; but of the eleven Dashwood baronets of West Wycombe to date the three most outstanding have all been baptized Francis. Sir Francis, 1st Baronet, a rich merchant of silk from Smyrna, alderman of the city of London, and MP, was the purchaser of his elder brother's half-share of the West Wycombe estate and the builder of the present house's nucleus. Sir Francis, 2nd Baronet, rake, hoaxer, politician, inheritor in 1763 of the medieval barony of le Despencer by right of his mother, was the overall creator of the present house and park. Sir Francis, 11th Baronet, besides being entrepreneur of numerous business ventures, is the renovator on a splendiferous scale of the seat of his ancestors.

The humorous and often scandalous exploits of Sir Francis Dashwood, 2nd Baronet, have given him an exaggerated reputation for folly and dissipation. In actual fact he was a man of very considerable parts and achievements, which the voyeurs of the Hell-Fire Club exploits have done their best to minimize. Besides being Chancellor of the Exchequer and Postmaster-General in successive governments he was a Fellow of the Royal Society and the Society of Antiquaries, and a co-founder of the Dilettanti Society. In an age of hidebound social conventions he was liberal-minded and humane. Above all he was an amateur and connoisseur of architecture, painting, furniture and the decorative arts. He was the friend of artists, poets, writers and statesmen. But he was a cynic whose mockery of the establishment's sense of decorum transgressed into blasphemy. He had himself painted as Pope Pontius VII and as a monk raising a full chalice to the genitalia of a statue of Venus; and while on grand tour in Italy with his ghastly show-off friends he was drunk from morning till night, behaving like those beer-bellied yobs from the 'inner cities' when abroad today. How he came to produce a shortened version of the Book of Common Prayer which was to be adopted by the Episcopalian Church in America, is a mystery. It can partly be explained by the co-authorship of the patriot-philosopher from Philadelphia, Benjamin Franklin, and partly by the baronet's ostensible compassion in wishing to relieve those 'whose age or infirmities will not suffer them to remain for hours in a cold church, especially in the winter season'. Sir Francis remains an enigma, deeply serious and perennially frivolous. Yet I do not wholly like him.

His best memorial is the house and grounds at West Wycombe Park which took shape between 1724 when he succeeded and 1781 when he died. Not a great seat as English seats go, West Wycombe is in the Italian sense a *villa* in that the word embraces both house and appendages and grounds. Too far from London to be an eighteenth-century surburban retreat like, say Marble Hill or Pope's toy house at Twickenham, nevertheless West Wycombe evinces metropolitan elegance and neatness. It does not accord with the rough and tumble of a true English country house. Hunting and shooting do not seem pursuits appropriate to it. Foxes and pheasants somehow seem far removed from its trim lawns. Top-boots, whips and guns would look out of place in its precious hall. Yet the encroachment of subtopia is only too much in evidence today. The tentacles of High Wycombe, a horrid town, are fingering the very skirts of the woods and glades. From the drive as one is approaching the west portico some strident modern development is distressingly visible across the landscaped valley to the north.

If one can turn a blind eye upon these intrusions the immediate surroundings are an almost perfect exemplar of the age of the Picturesque. I say *almost* because one can justifiably criticize the superfluity of ornamental buildings within a rather confined area. The place fairly bristles with temples to a whole hierarchy of pagan deities, in shrines, follies, grottoes and a cascade. Humphry Repton when called upon to 'improve' the landscape by Sir Francis's successor, remarked that 'many of the designs, although perfect in themselves, were rendered absurd, from inattention either to the scale or situation of the surrounding objects.' For one object of his disapproval he instanced 'the figure of a man in a brown coat and a broad-brimmed hat, representing the great Penn, of Pennsylvania, which Sir Francis placed on the top of the saw-mill in the park. Being much larger than the natural proportions of a man, it yet gave the appearance of a giant on the roof and diminished the size of every other object within sight.' Repton instantly had it removed. Happily nearly all the other clutter was suffered to remain.

As for the house the exterior is very engaging, being like everything to do with Sir Francis the Creator, a mixture of the absurd and the sublime. There is the joyous, two-tiered colonnade of the south front, the west portico, a replica of the Temple of Bacchus at Teos in Asia Minor by the neo-Greek architect Nicholas Revett, and the correct Palladian east portico by the architect John Donowell (whose name might well have been invented by his eccentric patron). All three appendages were jammed on any old how so as to appear preposterously unrelated to their respective fronts. Moreover all three, which are exposed to the elements, were frescoed after Guido Reni's more Paphian ceilings in baroque Rome. Whatever Sir Francis had in mind he certainly had his tongue in cheek. For over two and a half centuries he succeeded in shocking the purist and delighting the complaisant connoisseur.

In 1937 Sir John Dashwood, 10th Baronet, was one of several country house owners to inform the National Trust that when the National Trust Bill of that year became law he might take advantage of what it had to offer. Evidently I went down to talk to him for the first sheet of paper on the West Wycombe Park files contains the jotting by me: 'Helen [Lady Dashwood] would hate the scheme, Johnny less so.' The words were to be amply borne out during the future negotiations.

The house was at this date rather dilapidated although a bold front was maintained by the Dashwoods who regularly entertained weekend guests from London. Nevertheless I remember it being extremely attractive and unpretentious owing to Lady Dashwood's natural good taste. In the 1920s and '30s chunks of the estate between West Wycombe and High Wycombe were sold piecemeal for building development, and even the 'Adam' bookshelves of the upstairs library went in order to raise provision for a dowager. Yet the beautiful village abutting the north boundary of the park was spared. Sir John sold nearly the whole of it in 1929 to the Royal Society of Arts. After spending large sums on reconditioning and modernizing the cottages under the care of the great craftsman-architect William Weir of the

SPAB, the Society handed the property over to the National Trust. In 1935 Sir John generously gave to the Trust Church Hill, the top of which is conspicuous across the valley from the north front of the house, minus the church and family mausoleum. Therefore to part with the house and grounds on favourable terms to his family was not an inconsistent sequel in Sir John's eyes. The alternative was sale in the open market to which Lady Dashwood would by no means reconcile herself and on which she imposed, I firmly believe, a decisive veto.

At first Sir John cherished a hope that if he were to give the house outright the National Trust might pay him some part of the commercial value (which was considerable) of the park. This the Trust was in no financial position to do. During the ensuing months of peace negotiations dribbled on through an intermediary, the egregious Captain John Burrow Hill, who was Sir John's agent as well as the National Trust's agent for the village, and the right hand of the Trust's benefactor Mr Ernest Cook. Hill was to play a very ambiguous role in the future negotiations in that he did not seem to act in the interests of the Dashwoods and was often at loggerheads with the Trust's staff (with the exception of one member) although claiming to act in the interests of both parties. However, soon after the outbreak of war in 1939 the National Trust by arrangement with the Dashwoods moved its headquarters, and very reduced staff, to West Wycombe Park. The Wallace Collection was already stored for safety in the music room under the auspices of the Office of Works. The Trust's offices were accommodated in the brown (now red) drawing-room and Sir John's study. When I rejoined the Trust in January 1942 Florence Paterson, chief clerk, and Winifred Ballachey, filing clerk, were lodged upstairs as I too was to be in the pretty 'Adam' bedroom with green wallpaper and Thomas Daniell's eighteenth-century views of the house overlooking the south colonnade. MacLeod Matheson the secretary and Eardley Knollys commuted daily, the former from an Ouspensky colony near Staines where with his sweet and self-effacing wife Enid he was living, as did one typist and a 'junior' aged 15, from the village. That was our full complement of staff. We all ate at two tables in the saloon which was then the dining-room.

Sir John, who had served in the Army during the First World War and afterwards in the Diplomatic Corps, was away most of the time as Counsellor in the Foreign Service. Lady Dashwood was left to cope with the household and the paying guests, most of whom were old friends, Nancy Mitford, Eddy Sackville-West, Sir Alfred Beit, MP for St Pancras, then stationed at RAF headquarters in High Wycombe, his wife Clementine Mitford, and myself. In spite of extreme winter cold because the radiators seldom worked and a chronic lack of domestic staff (the National Trust ladies were enrolled as willing helpers) our spare time was spent in much hilarity. Nancy, engrossed in the study of Captain Scott's Antarctic expedition, could not read enough books on the subject. She compared a nightly walk along the upstairs passage to *The Worst Journey in the World* and referred to the lavatory when she got there, with its window which did not shut and let in the snow, as the Beardmore Glacier. Lady Dashwood was not amused. In the long evenings before going to bed we huddled before an inadequate fire in the tapestry room, Eddy and I labouring with our knitting while the others read ghost stories aloud or made bad-taste jokes. Clementine, who was not impressed by my knitting, referred to it as 'the True Sock' which in emulation of St Januarius' liquifying blood would unravel whenever our hostess examined it too closely.

A year later negotiations between Sir John and the National Trust were resumed. By that time the Trust had moved its headquarters back to London. The venerable doyen of estate agents Sir John Oakley of Daniel Smith, Oakley and Garrard in St James's Street was engaged by the Trust to prepare a report on the West Wycombe property. Old and grand he was informed that there were no taxis at High Wycombe station and few buses running to West Wycombe. So he took a train to West Wycombe station and in his grey spats, patent leather shoes and kid gloves splashed a way down the main road and up the drive through thawing slush. On arrival he was made to accompany first Sir John Dashwood and then Captain Hill round the estate on foot because of the petrol shortage. Sir John Oakley was to estimate that annual maintenance of the house would amount to £620 p.a. and income from farm rents to £612.14s., just £7.6s. short. He made the mistake of recommending that to save expenses the tower of St Crispin's Cottage, one of the Creator's favourite follies, and the Sawmill House, where Penn formerly stood on the roof, and both prominent landscape adornments, could well be disposed of. For his services which extended over at least ten months he consented to receive payment of £34.17s.2d.

When the Oakley report was submitted to him Sir John Dashwood considered the figure of £620 p.a. rather steep although the wages of one odd man (at £162 p.a.) were included in it. In giving me luncheon at the Travellers' Club he advised that the Trust had merely to sell thirty acres of the park to raise the whole endowment required for house and grounds. Somewhat piously I replied that he did not seem to realize the Trust would have to declare all the parkland inalienable.

The Country Houses Committee asked W.A. Forsyth, their architect member, if he would visit West Wycombe and give his opinion on the Oakley report, the conclusions of which Sir John Dashwood was questioning. Sir John wrote me a friendly but impatient letter. He might be called abroad at a moment's notice; and the National Trust did not appreciate his offer to redeem 'the land improvement charges' (a new revelation to me implying some form of money-raising) on the home farm. They could be reckoned the equivalent of an endowment, 'but *tant pis!*' (Unfortunately the committee did not see them in that light.) He hoped Forsyth would be given clear instructions as to what was required of him, 'so that we don't get any more recommendations to destroy some of the more attractive architectural features, such as the sawmill house. Please also get him to move quickly. I must know fairly soon one way or the other in order to get things square.' His frequent missions which were dead secret and mysterious were probably also dangerous, and like many other people charged with hazardous duties he could not look far ahead.

On receipt of Forsyth's opinion of the Oakley report I sent a copy to Lord Esher. Forsyth had cast an oblique eye on the redundant service wing to the south-west of the entrance portico, and the connecting subterranean passages to the house. He said there was much disrepair of the structure, and many signs of damp, although the roof was in tolerable shape. In fact he did not overstress the deplorable condition of the whole place. He did suggest some demolitions in the service quarter. The temples, well! They needed drastic attention; the lake needed dredging, and the private roads mending. He estimated capital repairs at £4,095.

Captain Hill wrote to me mischievously enquiring whether Lord Esher, whom he hated because he dared to tease him, had not endorsed Oakley's suggestion to demolish St Crispin's useless tower. I was able to reply that on no account would Lord Esher consent to the demolition of any useless building if it were beautiful.

Sir John thereupon offered to hand over with the house and park £2,000 in 3½% war stock, to accumulate a reserve fund for capital repairs in anticipation of the day when the government might give permission for landowners to spend money. And he stipulated that work on the house and temples should take precedence over the cottages on the estate so long as no threat of danger to life or limb of his workers and tenants was incurred. For its part the Trust agreed to provide another fund of £1,000 for expenditure on practical improvements like the heating system, re-wiring, new boilers and new drainage.

On 29 September I wrote to Sir John Dashwood that the Country Houses Committee had on Esher's recommendation authorized the transfer of West Wycombe to be immediate. 'I feel very happy about it all and I hope you do too.' I was really pleased for although I fully realized how dilapidated, how under-endowed and how likely to pose problems of maintenance in the future West Wycombe was, I also knew it to be one of the most fascinating amalgamations of mid-Georgian culture, a very quintessence of the English architectural, decorative, cabinet-making and landscaping arts met happily together. Of all the country seats evolved or influenced by members of the Dilettanti Society it was the most comprehensive and bewitching. Nor was I then aware how a third Sir Francis, in the fleeting presence on the scene of a bright young schoolboy with a precocious flair for a bargain, would one day revive West Wycombe Park almost to its original splendour.

Deterioration of the frescoes about the house, notably those on the exposed south colonnade walls and the two portico walls and ceilings, was a worry. I got a very skilled craftsman called Shearsby to do some minimal patching; and I asked John Summerson, then director of the National Buildings Record, if he would have photographs taken of the worst affected areas pending the time when they could be properly restored. If they were left much longer it would be impossible to guess what they originally looked like. Summerson was very co-operative. It was important, he wrote, 'that we collaborate on every possible occasion'. I asked that the photographer might visit when Sir John Dashwood was at home for he alone knew which frescoes were which. In a letter to Sir John about this matter I must have referred to the windows of my little Chelsea house having been blown out for the third or fourth time because he replied, 'What a bore the doodle bomb is but I hope you have not suffered more than inconvenience.' Five months later one of these tiresome Nazi flying pests landed at West Wycombe. The explosion shook the house and broke two windows of the blue drawing-room, causing cracks in the ceiling of Bacchus and Ariadne Triumphant, part of which collapsed to the floor. It also caused a further crack in Sir John's and the Trust's relations with Captain Hill.

Sir John had omitted to mention the doodle-bug visitation to Hill who was after all his agent. He told me and asked me what the Trust would do about it. Hill on learning weeks later about the incident second-hand was furious. On 4 April 1945 he sent to Hubert Smith, the Trust's newly appointed chief agent whom he regarded as his only ally, a catalogue of complaints of his shabby treatment by the Trust and Dashwood alike and their lack of support, ending, 'I have been refused the moderate amount [of petrol ration] I asked for to deal with Coleshill and Charlecote and the extra work entailed on Cook's estates and I have informed Cook of this. As a result I fear Cook may defer making any further contribution towards the preservation of historic estates.' This was more than a veiled threat that the Trust might no longer expect to inherit the several estates and historic houses acquired by their benefactor through Hill's medium unless they came to heel and treated him with the recognition and deference he considered his due. Sir John on the other hand thought that his agent was not behaving as it became him. Five days later he wrote a long letter to Hill remonstrating about Hill's expenditure on West Wycombe village of monies from the West Wycombe Park reserve fund to which he, Sir John, had largely contributed. The letter showed his keen concern for the house and the temples, and a businesslike grasp of estate management. He did not understand why Hill had raised with the National Trust the question of moving the wall separating the village from the park further back into the grounds:

I wrote to Lord Esher on September 19 1944 after you yourself had started this hare saying that the proposal was 'personal to my agent and entirely contrary to my wishes and views' . . . I dislike the idea intensely. My intention, as Lord Esher and Lees-Milne know full well, has all along been to preserve the mansion house and grounds as nearly as possible in their present state and an alteration, such as is apparently contemplated, would be entirely contrary to this principle.

I think it desirable to put on record that it is the preservation of the *beauty* of the place and not necessarily tidiness and efficiency which should be arrived at. In other words, trees should not be felled because they are not good forest specimens, nor cottages pulled down or drastically altered because they don't have modern sanitation, etc. Obviously trees will have to come out if they present a potential danger to buildings or people, but if they are worth it from the aesthetic point of view the trees should be lopp'd or topp'd or otherwise treated so as to render them safe and those cottages which are not fit for a developing family should simply be reconditioned in such a way that they would make good homes for people of advanced years whose dependents have gone out into the world, or for some other purpose than a dwelling house. It must be remembered too, as Lord Esher so aptly remarked when examining the property, that so long as I and my family continue to reside on the place the general public could hardly expect the standard of maintenance to be raised to the same point which might be required in respect of a property which was little more than a museum combined with a public park.

Good stuff, typical of the traditional English squire's common-sense attitude towards his inheritance half a century ago, though its sentiments might not meet with total approval today. To show his good faith Sir John promptly agreed to the 'throwing', i.e. felling, of three trees which he admitted were dangerous.

When I confirmed in writing that Lord Esher strongly supported his and Lady Dashwood's opposition to Hill's proposed demolition of the wall Sir John wrote, 'I sometimes begin to wonder what say the National Trust and I are to have in running West Wycombe.' Hill's attitude to the village was singularly proprietory and he utterly failed to understand the Dashwood point of view over the park wall. He also seemed not to understand that the Trust made a principle of consulting donors and seeking their agreement to changes on their ancient properties. Again he wrote to Smith caustically, 'There is naturally certain resentment against any interference with Dashwood's control of the property, and he has not yet appreciated that the bargain he made with the Trust must be adhered to. He would, I know, like to carry on as if the estate were still his property.' Hill's attitude towards his employer was the very opposite of Mason's towards Lord Sackville.

On the contrary Sir John Dashwood tried his best to be co-operative with the Trust. He was always ready to keep us informed of impending developments in the neighbourhood likely to affect West Wycombe adversely. In November 1945 he notified me that the High Wycombe Rural District Council were seeking powers to build on the north escarpment which in his view would seriously mar our own property. In suggesting to the RDC other land more suitable for their purposes he advised them that they ought to consult the Trust's interests, and the Trust that they ought to demand to be kept informed by local authorities. Captain Hill on the other hand advised the National Trust not to intervene.

Meanwhile I was harassed by the usual business of guidebook compilation. In those days National Trust guidebooks – I speak of my own – were pretty basic, unscholarly and often, I fear, inaccurate. In the course of my elementary researches I received a letter from a Flight-Lieutenant H.M. Colvin about the respective contributions to West Wycombe's architecture by Henry Keene and John Donowell. The house's architectural history seemed to him nearly as complicated as that of any medieval church or monastery. It demanded a very careful examination of the structure with all the attributions in mind. The flight-lieutenant was kept six days out of the seven in the week by his duties in the RAF at Marlow, but could manage to pay a visit on the seventh. When I met him the flight-lieutenant was just 25 and looked about ten years younger. I sent a copy of his letter to Clifford Smith who was busy with an article on Henry Keene for *Country Life*. Cliffy was greatly impressed and wrote that he would be interested to know who this H.M. Colvin was. He and all students of architectural history were soon to learn. Howard Colvin, Fellow of St John's College, Oxford, was in 1954 to publish the *Biographical Dictionary of British Architects 1660–1840* (of which an amplified edition appeared in 1978), a pioneering work as momentous in its way to architectural historians as Dr Johnson's *Dictionary* was in 1755 to students of the English language.

The actual opening of the house gave rise to problems. The house is not so commodious, nor so planned that the public can pour through rooms without making life for the family uncomfortable, to say the least. Nearly all the important rooms are downstairs which means the family either retreating upstairs or quitting the house altogether on opening days. When towards the end of 1945 the secretary proposed to Lady Dashwood that the house might be shown every Wednesday and Thursday throughout the year at one shilling a head, and the grounds every Saturday and Sunday without charge, she was so appalled that it took her over a month to reply. She strongly objected to the house being opened more than fifty days in the year, quoting Lord Esher and myself as having committed the Trust to this term, and demanding that we abide by the decision. We were now demanding 156 days in the year. As for the grounds she would have to prohibit access to the park walk for 'that is where all our pheasants, such as they are, gather, and we should not want anyone walking there in August, September or October'. Also there would be difficulty in keeping gates shut. Instead she suggested opening the house and grounds every day from 1 July to 3 August, plus once a fortnight on Thursdays between those dates. That would make more than the fifty days required by the Trust. She supposed too that the Trust would provide someone to prepare and clean the rooms, and push back carpets. 'When I showed the house during the war for the Queen's District Nursing Association I found it needed at least three people, one of them a very strong man, to control the public who came to see it, and who pushed and struggled in the most extraordinary way. I do not imagine this will occur when it is opened at regular and frequent intervals for the National Trust.'

Now Lady Dashwood was a clever and astute Canadian who knew her position in the world and her rights. She had struck a shaft at the Trust's Achilles heel. For it is true that in issuing the pamphlet outlining the Trust's proposed country houses scheme in 1936 by way of enticing owners of historic houses to join, Lord Esher and I had vaguely suggested fifty opening days within the year as about adequate and had skated altogether over the number of helpers required to deal with the showing and cleaning, and who was expected to supply them. But that was nearly ten years ago and during the interval of war and the social upheaval the world had moved on and democracy was asserting itself. After a deal of bargaining with Lady Dashwood a compromise was reached whereby from May to September West Wycombe house was to be open every Wednesday at a charge of one and sixpence and the grounds on Wednesdays and Thursdays, plus the first Saturday of each month, without charge. The Trust was barely satisfied but felt obliged to put up with the compromise in the hope that things would work out more generously for the public in the long run, which I believe now to have been the case. Nevertheless the family was mightily put out when a rich sub-tenant in the Regent of Iraq failed to come up to scratch.

The daunting prospect of opening the house allied to straitened circumstances induced the Dashwoods to consider letting. For some reason Mrs Dalton, who was very thick with the Iraqi royal family, had suggested West Wycombe as a suitable asylum for them in the event of a crisis in their homeland. She motored down with an Iraqi representative to inspect the premises. I laid on luncheon for them at the Apple Orchard, an excellent little restaurant in the village run by a friend of all of us, Irene Donald. Miss Donald sent me a word of warning: the Chancellor of the Exchequer's wife was a stickler for etiquette. 'Mrs Dalton has lunched here before and is adamant about "meals in restaurants" restrictions. So I remind you that if you elect to have bread with your soup, you have had two of the three courses permitted you.' However, to the disappointment of Mrs Dalton and the Dashwoods the Iraqis ratted, ostensibly because the obligation to open the house would contravene their security arrangements. Incidentally His Royal Highness also hinted that the bells in the house functioned inadequately, which was a polite euphemism for not functioning at all. And whose liability to have them mended was that? The donors' or the National Trust's? The Regent, a most civilized man, was to meet his death in the ghastly massacre of the royal family by their unspeakable countrymen in 1958. Did he ever regret, I wonder, turning down a carefree sojourn at West Wycombe, bells or no bells, the gentle British public or no British public?

Relations between the Dashwoods and the Trust were not made easier by Sir John declining to interfere with his wife's authority inside the house. While Lady Dashwood was abroad in 1947 Sir John wrote about a commercial company's request to have a film taken of the rooms, 'I have sent the film correspondence to Her Ladyship recommending acceptance. But you will realise from what you saw when you were here that the house is in "curling papers" and so she won't want films before her return. At least I guess so!!'

Somehow we muddled through the 1946 showing. In April of the following year Lady Dashwood wrote to the secretary, 'I hope the arrangements for opening West Wycombe Park to the public will work better this year and not be in such chaos as last year. I am told Knole is efficiently arranged, and also Cliveden . . . With regard to Captain Hill, I never communicate with him; and you know, my complaints come direct to 42 Queen Anne's Gate!!!' They certainly did. Although she was usually mellow with me because we had known each other for a long time she often let fly at my colleagues with that asperity which is sometimes evinced by the intelligentsia of the New World. Yet she had the good grace to make amends. To Carew Wallace, who from head office was to take over the management of West Wycombe from Hill and whom Lord Esher congratulated for his singular calm and tact in face of assault, she wrote, 'I am afraid I was very cross to you yesterday and I am awfully sorry. I realize how helpful and kind you always are, a great ally in fact. But I am so terribly upset over this hideous tree hacking . . . Please forgive me.'

The tree hacking was the final episode in the prolonged warfare waged between the Dashwood family and Captain Hill. Hill took it upon himself to fell the strip of woodland between the park and village in order to augment the site of a proposed new village hall and car park. Sir John promptly sacked him. Nevertheless Hill kept on his office in the village and continued acting on behalf of the National Trust in matters concerned with the village, as though nothing had happened. To say the least it was odd of the Trust to permit this anomalous situation. But as I have indicated elsewhere Hill to some extent flourished the whip-hand over the Trust because of his authority with Mr Ernest Cook. The Trust knew that with a flick of the lash he could prevent several desirable estates from being bequeathed to them under Cook's will. But the situation was intolerable for the Dashwoods. There was the hated enemy firmly encamped in the village on the other side of their park wall which he was doing all he could to demolish. In vain the Dashwoods asked for the management of the village to be taken out of his grasp. Poor Admiral Bevir the secretary bemoaned the bad relations: 'I wish we could get affairs at West Wycombe on a better footing,' he pleaded. Sir John Dashwood who by then was residing permanently at West Wycombe protested to Bevir, 'I think it is now clear to most of us, except Hill, that so long as he continues to mess about with West Wycombe things are bound to be uncomfortable and difficult, and I cannot for the life of me understand why he wishes to go on thrusting himself in where he is so very clearly not wanted.'

Johny Dashwood was fundamentally an easy-going fellow, wishing well to mankind, perpetually bubbling with laughter and eager to exchange rather schoolboyish smutty stories with all and sundry. But Captain Hill had got his goat. The Admiral, feeling obliged to raise the Hill issue with the Estates Committee of which Hill was a member, warned him. Hill wrote the Admiral a very truculent letter in reply. 'Please leave out all those other people [members of the staff concerned with West Wycombe, i.e. Carew Wallace and me] at the next meeting. I do hope as regards West Wycombe I can deal direct with Smith', his one ally on the staff of the Trust. And he reiterated his role in the drama as self-appointed champion of the village against the alleged reactionaries in the big house. Whatever transpired from a secret session of the Estates Committee, of which no minutes were kept, Hill emerged unrepentant.

The sparring of the triumvirate reached a climax almost funnier than it was deplorable. Lady Dashwood wrote to Wallace in London, 'Would you kindly *instruct* Captain Hill to remove a large notice *someone* has put up at Kitty's Lodge [on the main road] . . . It was put up without Sir John's or my permission . . . The [felled] tree on the lawn is still there. It is over a month since I asked you to have it removed, and this Saturday we *specially* wanted the lawn to be cleared of it for the fireworks and the dance.' Her letter was forwarded through London to Hill sitting tight at his desk 300 yards from Lady Dashwood sitting at hers. The tree was ultimately removed by Hill, but not until the fireworks and dance were over. Lady Dashwood commented, 'The lawn will not recover for at least a year.' And Hill wrote to Wallace, 'Dashwood can leave the trees that we do not want provided he pays for them, and I should be grateful if you would make that clear to him.' Then Sir John wrote to Wallace that since Hill was charging the Trust £5 odd for the hire of his auto-scythe, he, Sir John, proposed to charge the Trust for the use of his tractor, gang-mower and his man at a rate of

£20 a year. Young Francis Dashwood wanted the use of Kitty's meadow for occasional rugger and cricket playing with the villagers; and why not? Hill opposed it vehemently. The Admiral, hearing of the dispute, counselled Hill that he ought to advance a better *modus vivendi*. Hill retorted that a better *modus vivendi* could easily be reached, 'if people would not work behind my back'.

Finally Sir John, driven to distraction, accused Hill in June 1948 of flagrantly disregarding the arrangement reached between himself and the National Trust that he was to be consulted before the felling of any trees whatsoever. He resented Hill's persistent hostility and suggested that 'the care of the property were to be entrusted to another person'. Sir John wrote to the Trust that he had received an impertinent reply from Hill demanding his withdrawal of criticism in a simple statement. On the 11th of the month the National Trust at last took courage. It issued an edict transferring 'the responsibility from Captain Hill to Mr. Wallace of the management of the property to be let [a technicality at a peppercorn rent] by the Trust to Sir John Dashwood as soon as the lease is signed.' That, one might well conclude, would be that, better late than never and none too soon. But not a bit of it. On 14th Hill wrote to Sir John,

> My experience in the treatment of the class of woodland (Kitty's walk and yew trees) is considerable and I have been a member of the Estates Committee of the National Trust for very many years and I think I know how the National Trust wish their woods treated. Also I have known you for many years and I cannot believe that you can seriously find fault with anything I have done ... You have made statements [unspecified] which I consider defamatory and I have asked you to make a very simple reparation. I still hope you will do this. Yours truly, John Burrow Hill.

During a discussion of the unfortunate West Wycombe case the General Purposes Committee encouraged its members to air their views on the attitude to be adopted towards donors by the Trust. The general opinion expressed was that in the administration of properties full respect should be paid to donors' wishes so long as they involved no detriment to the property or the public interest. This pious resolution is, I like to suppose, still observed by the staff today. Hill's reaction was predictable.

> I am disgusted [he wrote to the Admiral] that the National Trust

have not supported me over the last episode, and I shudder to think what is going to happen in the future if the National Trust cannot be more firm with Sir John Dashwood. It seems to me with my intimate knowledge of the property and of the Trust's obligations, that you are going on entirely wrong lines. I have always put the National Trust's interests in front of my own.

He ended by requesting support of his demand for reparation from Dashwood. Indeed to Sir John he wrote, 'Much as I should dislike to cross swords with you, I shall be compelled to do so if you do not see the reasonableness of my request' – to withdraw his statement, whatever it was. Alarmed, the Admiral told Sir John that the Trust was not going to be involved in his personal dispute with Captain Hill. Sir John retorted that already the Trust was directly involved, 'and may well be drawn into the quarrel if Hill pursues it'.

Whether Captain Hill did pursue his threat of sueing Sir John for defamation or Sir John capitulated (which seems unlikely) history does not relate. Nor does it much matter. Before retiring from the scene Hill had a last fling at getting his own back. He asked Hubert Smith to let him know when the formal lease of house and grounds to Sir John was signed so that he might stop the men under his control from working 'on the area which I am handing over [to Wallace], that is the house, lawns, and the woods round the lake'. To Hill's reference to the National Trust's 'lack of courage in giving way to the Dashwoods in every particular', Smith replied, 'I deprecate the National Trust allying itself with the Dashwoods in their childish machinations.' In thanking Smith for his sympathy the Captain assured him that, 'My beloved village is almost as depressed about the situation as I am . . . Bless you.' However less than a year later the blue-eyed ally informed the Admiral, 'I do think we must get across to Hill somehow that he is not the lord of creation at West Wycombe.' A keen bird and plant conservationist Hubert Smith was shocked by the other's refusal of access to a harmless botanist who had begged permission to study a special kind of primrose on the West Wycombe property. The Captain may have retreated from the field but he still made a feint of brandishing the whip-hand after his habitual fashion.

In the middle of the 1950 season Helen Dashwood wrote to the Admiral's successor, secretary Jack Rathbone,

to warn you that I do not think we can have the house open next summer on the same terms as this summer as it is turning out to be

quite the most awful imposition I have ever dreamed of! . . . I find
that constant supervision from me is daily necessary as the guides
and cleaners do not seem to be able to work on a system and carry
on sensibly unless always directed, and, as you know, the preparation for opening (due entirely to the lateness of the arrangements
made by the N.T.) necessitated my being here almost every single
day this summer and working extremely hard, sometimes for eight
hours and sometimes more, lifting and cleaning furniture. So I do
not think we could possibly go through this again.

For her trouble and exhaustion she was being paid a mere £64 subject
to tax. To the desperate appeal Jack Rathbone, who was unaware that
the opening necessitated Lady Dashwood's presence at all (he had only
just been appointed secretary), expressed heartfelt sympathy and
besought her to offer suggestions how to improve her wretched lot. He
hated to think of her trundling heavy furniture about, and enclosed a
benefactor's card which entitled all donors of Trust properties to
special privileges denied to ordinary members. He apologized for not
having sent one before. On the same day the bemused new secretary
received a letter from Sir John reluctantly agreeing to his wife's
alteration of a date he had fixed for a gymkhana in the park. 'For some
reason or another she seems to think it will interfere with the duck
shoot. For your private information I think this is sheer nonsense.'

Lady Dashwood thought the showing of the house to the public
unsatisfactory. The public thought so too. Critical reports of the *de haut
en bas* way they were treated reached head office. It was all rather
disturbing. *The Cabinet Maker* referred to much local dissatisfaction that
four only out of sixty-four rooms were shown at a charge of three
shillings per person. 'Once in you can hardly move for the number of
uniformed guides who are in the four rooms.' Moreover some guides
barked at those visitors they thought might misbehave. Others had a
habit of darting out of corners to tell them how horrible they were, and
how much they wished they would go away. One person even described
the experience as like being in a penitentiary. I suspect that these
complaints were much exaggerated.

It is nice to confirm that the sad conditions have long since changed.
They were after all but teething troubles before a novel system of
showmanship evolved through experience. Today visitors are conducted in small parties round virtually all the downstairs rooms by the
most courteous of guides, starting from the hall every twenty minutes.
And if large numbers cause delays they may sit on chairs in the south

colonnade while admiring the straight ride recently opened up with a bold equestrian figure (in fibreglass) astride the distant skyline. This interesting feature was commissioned by, but does not, I understand, represent the third Sir Francis Dashwood, the Renovator, who still lives at West Wycombe with his family. To him is due the spanking new look of the place. And if the English Heritage memorial fund (disbursed by the government on essential improvements to monuments in public ownership) has contributed to the cost, he most certainly has borne the brunt of it. He has had all the temples and the cascade, which on his succession were in near ruin, restored to a pristine condition. He has even raised a column carrying Britannia in honour of our Queen's sixtieth birthday. He has cleared the Broad Walk with its eastern vista across the lake towards the park.

To the exterior of the house the Renovator has given a much-needed face-lift. Apart from repairs to ceiling and wall frescoes of the east portico he has disguised the clumsy irregularity of this front by planting clumps of trees at either end, as indeed one of the Daniell views shows to have been done by the symmetry-loving Creator. The rendering of the north front has lately been painted a rather startling yellow which certainly thrusts into relief the sculptural stonework of a fine Palladian design previously obfuscated by a prevailing greyness. As for the interior it has been transformed. The marbled staircase hall – the stair-tread inlay is of the very highest quality – with porphyried dado and bracketed busts has been reinstated and even the original floor of different polished stones revealed and repaired. Beneath the painted Palmyran ceiling, supported by Tuscan columns, the room shimmers in cool browns, purples, pinks and creams.

The dining-room when the Trust took over had been partitioned into a warren of small offices. Sir Francis has brought it back into the use for which it was intended, namely dinner parties on grand occasions. With the original Georgian marbled walls, patterned ceiling and new chequered floor, it is now the richest in the house. No apartment of the size – it is not colossal – except Robert Adam's ante-room at Syon, is more decoratively colourful and opulent. From the walls Sir Francis the Creator masquerades and grins as a sultan surrounded by sultanas and courtesans – in reality his respectable female relations – as Pope Pontius and, more soberly, as the unfictional Postmaster-General.

What became the dining-room in the nineteenth century was reconverted in 1953 to the saloon. It used to be a melancholy room and for me has melancholy memories. In it I listened to the wireless news of 1942, always bad, like the fall of Tobruk and the German occupation of

Vichy France. But Sir Francis the Renovator has judiciously kept inviolate the three high windows of 1854 which afford an idyllic view of the lake and Temple of Music below. The walls have been painted a Neapolitan yellow. The old brown drawing-room (in which we of the Trust slaved over our files and typewriters) has become the red, the walls rehung with crimson damask. The study walls are now crammed with the Georgian architects' working drawings for house and temples. They present a tantalizing feast for the serious architectural student were he to be given a ladder and torch. Long may they survive that north light against which George Wingfield Digby seriously cautioned me. It was, he said, more prone to fade fabrics, water-colours and ink drawings than direct sunlight from the south and west. The exquisite seventeenth-century *verre eglomisé* 'chimney glass' bearing the Dash-wood arms over the fireplace and the two bookcases with marquetry inlaid door panels, sold from the house in 1921, have been bought back and put where they so handsomely belong. The blue drawing-room and the lofty music room, both with coved and frescoed ceilings and superb marble chimney-pieces, complete the series of rococo staterooms restored to life and glory by Sir Francis the Renovator.

CHAPTER FOURTEEN

GOODHART-RENDEL OF HATCHLANDS

Surrey

ATCHLANDS has enjoyed no very long association with one particular family. It was built from scratch so to speak in the 1750s for one of England's naval heroes, Admiral the Honourable Edward Boscawen, with money from spoils of his country's enemies. Its construction and decoration were shared by the Admiral with his adored and adorable wife Fanny, whose spirited letters to her spouse when overseas and her bluestocking friends like Mary Delany and Elizabeth Montagu describe some of the problems and delights of making a home in mid-Georgian England. But the Admiral's long-anticipated retirement to the house of his dreams was cut short by early death in January 1761 after a bare two years of settling down. For a while Fanny struggled on alone with her children. Then in 1769 she sold Hatchlands to the Sumner family. The Sumners lived there the longest of any family and sold the property in 1888 to Stuart Rendel 1st and last Lord Rendel of Hatchlands. He was the son of a distinguished engineer and one of several brothers who worked for Lord Armstrong's famous engineering firm in Newcastle.

Unlike his boss Lord Armstrong, who commissioned a well-known contemporary architect R. Norman Shaw to create for his dynasty a rambling mansion of gables and ingle-nooks called Cragside in Northumberland, Lord Rendel acquired one of the first country houses to which the great neo-classical Robert Adam has a distinctive claim. He was proud of Hatchlands although he lived in it only a few months of each year. He was enlightened enough to respect Adam's rooms. He certainly coloured and gilded ceilings. He also embellished the great staircase, by no means badly, with Edwardian rococo panels in fibrous plaster. For this and other minor alterations he employed a nephew by marriage, Halsey Ricardo, until they fell out and Halsey fell by the wayside. He may be said to have aggrandized the house, notably by getting Sir Reginald Blomfield to add a portentous music room, not in the style of Adam to be sure, but of Sir Christopher Wren. Blomfield in protesting that it was a shame Hatchlands had been designed in 1760, a time of architectural decadence, rather than 1710, set about rectifying the mistake in so far as he was able. Blomfield was to become known by the budding Georgian Group in the 1930s as an arch-reactionary and philistine architect whose presumptuous proposal to rebuild Carlton House Terrace they resolutely and successfully opposed. I well recall how, having sat next to him at a tea party and enormously relished his old-world manners and learned conversation about Sebastian Le Prestre de Vauban, of whom I had never heard, to discover too late who my neighbour was, I felt ashamed that I had neither reviled nor ignored him. On the contrary I was charmed by him. Lord Rendel's choice of Blomfield had largely been due to his precocious grandson, young Harold Stuart Goodhart-Rendel then aged 15.

Hal Goodhart-Rendel, born in 1887, was the only son of Lord Rendel's daughter Rose Ellen by Harry Chester Goodhart, a lecturer in classics at Cambridge University, who had died when his son was barely 8. On the grandfather's death in 1913 Hal inherited Hatchlands house and estate, and most of the village of East Clandon, having already tacked on the name of Rendel to his patronymic. After Admiral Boscawen he was to become Hatchland's most notable owner.

As a child Hal was extremely delicate. Throughout his life he suffered from asthma and constant pain. He survived only one year at Eton, his mother removing him to be privately educated. She was a woman of forceful personality to whom he was absolutely devoted. She had great influence upon his upbringing, directed his tastes and virtually supervised his lessons. As early as 1894 Mary Monkswell, a guest of the Rendels at Hatchlands, described the recently widowed Rose Ellen at the age of 28 as 'rather too bright for every day, apt to exercise her wit upon her near relations – very handsome and with one handsome, dark-eyed, most attractive little boy of 7'. Mrs Goodhart's anxious care of the little boy's health and his apparent inability to take more strenuous exercise than bicycling leisurely over to Munstead Wood to have tea with Miss Gertrude Jekyll and sit at her feet, rendered Hal something of a mother's darling and, because of his greatly superior education to most of his contemporaries', rather a cocky child.

The boy's two absorbing interests were architecture and music. His grandfather's Adam house where he spent much of his youth was to have profound influence upon his ultimate architectural style. But not at once. At first he found inspiration in Lutyens's Chinthurst Hill near

Guildford, a house rented by his mother. He was drawn to the Art Nouveau and Beaux Arts movements, and the Art Workers' Guild. He made it known that he wanted new things and had no use for Chippendale and Hepplewhite: very healthy in a young architectural aspirant. Instead he steeped himself in *The Studio* and *The Architectural Review* magazines. Early influences were contemporary architects A. Beresford Pite, Halsey Ricardo and J.F. Bentley (designer of Westminster Cathedral), men who having reacted sharply to the exclusive High Victorian Gothic were experimenting with eclectic continental styles. However, at Trinity College, Cambridge, Goodhart-Rendel thought fit for a while to make music composition his career and studied under Donald Tovey. But taking against his teacher's enthusiasm for Brahms whom he detested he dropped the idea and, while still an undergraduate, designed a commercial building for Calcutta in a bold, almost Byzantine style. Thereafter architecture was to be his career.

When the First World War broke out he managed to get a commission in the Grenadier Guards but was not fit for active service. The war was, he claimed, the happiest time of his life. He developed a new passion for the Brigade of Guards which transcended that for music and architecture, and was subordinate only to the Roman Catholic Church which he embraced in middle age. It was the discipline, the order and the camaraderie of his regiment which he loved. In the years of peace he still kept in touch with the Grenadiers and every summer hired their band to play at a garden party on the lawn at Hatchlands.

Immensely erudite, Goodhart-Rendel was better informed about the progressive styles and issues of Victorian and Edwardian architecture than any scholar of his generation. When such buildings were much out of favour he amassed a collection of data on nineteenth- and early twentieth-century architects, especially ecclesiastical, that has proved of inestimable service to students. He bequeathed the data to the Royal Institute of British Architects. Goodhart-Rendel's brilliant book of essays, *English Architecture since the Regency*, was a mere compendium of the knowledge committed to his card indexes. Although a lucid and extremely witty lecturer, his tendency to parody made him difficult at times to follow. In conversation likewise his thoughts were often too quick for his words, and he was apt to trip up over them.

His own buildings, chiefly churches, have not received the recognition this imaginative and innovative artist deserves and may one day yet attain. In his lifetime they were considered by the general run of critics too eclectic and too wishy-washy. Nor did contemporary architects take kindly to his patrician attitude towards their profession. The avant-garde of the '20s, '30s and '40s, when he was active, judged their fellows from a biased political standpoint. So long as architectural design answered 'the needs and desires of our own time', to quote one left-wing critic of the age, in other words, so long as it smacked of Lenin and Stalin, was without ornament, was functional, puritanical and anti-élitist it was taken seriously. Goodhart-Rendel's architecture was not so positive or forceful as to overcome the current inter-war prejudice and make itself heard and widely respected. Though intellectual and often brilliant it was traditional. It had not the daring of great genius which overcomes all blinkered opposition. Besides when all is said and done, although Goodhart-Rendel reached the pinnacle of the architectural hierarchy – as Slade Professor of Fine Art at Oxford in 1933–6 and President of the Royal Institute of British Architects in 1937–9 – he remained in the best sense amateur. He was other things than an architect, namely owner of an historic country house, squire of a picturesque village, and devotee of arcane callings which eventually transcended even those of the profession.

Hal Goodhart-Rendel was a friend of the Eshers and it was natural that he consulted Oliver on what he should do to preserve Hatchlands. I was detailed to talk to him in June 1938. He received me in his elegant Regency drawing-room at 13 Crawford Street off Baker Street, a tall, stooping, narrow-headed, all-profile, pop-eyed man with an absurd Hitlerian moustache and a complexion such as I had never seen at close quarters before. His face was green as an unripe olive caused, so it was said, by mercury or some therapeutic drug administered during the war. He was extremely voluble and fidgety. He thrust his face into mine in the earnestness of his talk as though that were the only way to make his words penetrate. He was affable yet distant, uninhibitedly communicative and withal highly sensitive. After delivering a monologue he sank back into a chair and waited politely for approval. The message I had received was plain. He was 'very anxious in my last years' – he was then 50 – to 'restore the Hall for the sake of the Trust to its appearance as I remember it before my grandfather's last operations.' He was not to deviate from this determination. He never questioned the Trust being the only suitable holding body for his beloved Hatchlands when he was gone. Not that he did not vacillate in the coming years over how this was to be brought about.

The estate was entailed upon several cousins, all of whom fortunately were of age. Unlike Eddy Sackville-West this bachelor was not encumbered by unborn offspring. Nevertheless it was necessary to await the outcome of the 1939 National Trust Bill in Parliament. A year elapsed before Lord Esher told me that Goodhart-Rendel was anxious to hand over immediately, and advised that the Trust should have a report on the property prepared. The very last letter I wrote from the office before the next war broke out was to tell Goodhart-Rendel that the Bill had become law and the Office of Works had agreed to add Hatchlands to our supplementary list of most important country houses. He replied that he was pleased and would consult his cousins and his trustees. On 5 September Matheson wrote that I had gone off on war service. In October Goodhart-Rendel told Matheson that his cousins and trustees all supported his intentions; and that Hatchlands was already let to St Anne's College for Girls at Sanderstead for the 'duration'. He was just as concerned about East Clandon village as the house, he said. He would like to reserve some outlying land then ripe for development in order to ensure that it was developed properly.

In November Matheson asked the ineluctable Captain John Burrow Hill to prepare the required report with help from the prospective donor's agent, H. Mitchell of the Rendel Estate Office, Brighton, for Goodhart-Rendel also owned urban property at Kemp Town. To some irrelevant comment by Hill about possible financial interests, since the estate was heavily mortgaged, Matheson retorted sharply: 'It doesn't matter a rap what the building value of the land is if it is to be held for preservation.' Having asked Raby of the Office of Works for a certificate of approval of Hatchlands and receiving the reply that Works would first of all have to make a formal inspection of it, he warned Raby, 'Relations with Goodhart-Rendel are a bit touchy ... and as P.R.I.B.A. [he is] unlikely to relish his judgment questioned.'

In March 1940 Hill reported that Hatchlands was an excellent house in every respect and very lettable. It was in very good repair, and generated its own electricity. The village of East Clandon was charming and the whole estate delightful. One could never be sure in what light Captain Hill would assess a prospective country house especially if it were Georgian and had not been introduced to the Trust by him in the first place. When Matheson informed Goodhart-Rendel that the Office of Works man was prepared to grant a certificate for Hatchlands under section 4(B) of the National Trust Act of 1939 he added that Goodhart-Rendel would be interested to learn that Works might even certify houses built by Lutyens. This was not very tactful of Matheson for it implied that a house by the sensitive PRIBA might not be so favoured. A little huffily Goodhart-Rendel replied, 'I imagine because his work has been the quarry for all the mechanical building design done in their own building department. If they actually did such a thing whilst cold-shouldering Norman Shaw or Nesfield, I must confess that I should feel extremely petulant. This however merely by the way.'

Petulance was one of Goodhart-Rendel's venial foibles. When his agent Mitchell was summarily dunned by the National Trust for payment of 6/7d. to clear a debt unspecified, he protested on Mitchell's behalf irritably. But it was a mistake, Matheson quickly wrote back; the demand was meant for 'our warden on the Calf of Man of the same name'. G-R was not instantly appeased.

When the Country Houses Committee discussed the offer of Hatchlands some members questioned whether it was architecturally important enough to accept. Lord Radnor for instance thought it was not. Lord Gerald Wellesley, Lord Brocket and Mr Robert Holland-Martin were in favour. And so at their meeting in November the Executive Committee were recommended to accept.

By October 1941 the solicitors of both parties were jointly satisfied that after all there was no need to make application to the Court of Chancery in the Hatchlands case since no problems concerning minors and unborn children had arisen. Nothing happened until January 1942 when Goodhart-Rendel wrote to Matheson an agitated letter from the officers' mess, Guards Depot, Caterham, where to his joy he had been recalled to duty at the age of 55 with the rank of captain. He was very much concerned with other matters than Hatchlands. Moreover Mitchell had presented him with a précis of the negotiations 'with the disagreeable result that I feel I must postpone the ratification of all our work until the end of the war or such time as I can decide better than I can now . . .' It was plain, he continued, that he would never again be able to inhabit Hatchlands. The Trust's terms were not as favourable as he had hoped and his financial position had lately worsened. Whose indeed had not? He was greatly distressed. Nevertheless the house must somehow be saved.

Matheson took the turn of events on the chin. Goodhart-Rendel was not the first owner of a country house to change his mind during the blackest period of the war and to be near despair. Matheson calmly told Horne & Birkett to drop the case altogether.

Back to work in 1942 I though fit to write to Goodhart-Rendel that Captain Hill had a client – Mr Ernest Cook again – who might buy Hatchlands for the National Trust and that a scheme to suit him might be worked out because to our surprise Mr Cook really did appear to be interested in Hatchlands. Could this be a solution to his financial difficulties? Goodhart-Rendel did not reply. In my absence he had got used to dealing with Matheson. To Matheson he wrote on 7 February in very pessimistic vein ignoring Mr Cook's advances. It was East Clandon village's future which now weighed heavy on his mind although he was never to make an outright offer of it to the Trust.

If the cottagers who have claims could be accommodated in new cottages to their liking (I suppose costing £1000 apiece after the war!) East Clandon would go all Broadway – tho' with genteel heads nodding out of all the windows I doubt if I should think it worth keeping. Still I suppose there's likely to be more money than ever in sweet little places unless Stalin packs us all into concrete bird cages.

Round both stations [Clandon and Horsley] a Tudoresque hell must be let loose. And we can have lots of unspoilt acres closed to the public at six in the evening winter and nine in the summer. What I feel now is that the whole place as a living thing is mortally sick and that what we must do is to save what ought to be saved at face value. The house has architectural claims, the village pictur-esque and archaeological claims, the park possibly has claims as background [it was laid out by Repton]. But once there isn't somebody established there the whole exhibit seems rather a large specimen to keep in a bottle of spirit.

Do you think there is anything to discuss in all this?

What Matheson with his permanently stiff upper lip and disinclina-tion to sentiment and fantasy made of this effusion I can only guess. It was indicative of the temperamental, prima-donna side of Goodhart-Rendel. Yet G-R's prognostications were more or less realized within thirty years or less. 'Sure enough the village has now been sold to various bidders, at remarkable prices, the old cottages have been tarted up and few if any of the ... original inhabitants remain,' Maurice Wiggin, a former resident, was to write in 1972.

Matheson ignored the contents of Goodhart-Rendel's letter, merely replying that he had a partial scheme in mind for the house and park. When he knew the views of the Country Houses Committee, etcetera, 'I would like to suggest that Lees-Milne should meet you one day and have a talk with you.' Goodhart-Rendel probably didn't want anything of the sort and parried the idea. But soon he wrote to me that he was having an exceptionally busy time with his soldiering; however, as soon as the Trust had a practical scheme to submit which would leave the future tenants for life with sufficient realizable land to supplement their meagre incomes, he would be delighted to discuss it with me. In November he saw me. He said that the National Trust must accept less endowment than they were then asking for; and begged me to work out some modified scheme by which Hatchlands' future could be assured. He was by no means the first donor to remonstrate in this way; and there was little doubt that he was hard-pressed for money.

I duly went cap in hand to Hill. There seemed no other way out of the impasse. I asked whether the philanthropic Mr Cook might purchase for the Trust the house and park only, leaving Goodhart-Rendel the rest of the estate for him to live on the rents over and above his captain's pay. Hill, in spite of his report that the house was easily lettable, replied that the proposition did not appeal to Mr Cook who would have the whole estate or nothing. So this little plan came to naught.

In due course the Executive Committee duly accepted a revised offer of house, park and 420 acres of farmland to be rented by Goodhart-Rendel at £375 a year. Over the details of the transaction I dealt, not through the solicitors, but direct with Goodhart-Rendel's amenable and very co-operative agent, Mitchell. Through him I extracted his master's consent to allow public access to the house on 52 instead of 30 days in the year. I recommended to the Executive Committee that all the land of 420 acres should be held inalienably.

By February 1944 I was sending a draft press announcement to Goodhart-Rendel for comment and approval. Inevitably several further points about the deal arose for settlement. My chief trouble was how to winkle Goodhart-Rendel out of the Guards depot at Caterham, which then held his exclusive allegiance, in order to attend to our mutual business. I was particularly anxious to know whether he intended living in the house, or sub-letting. At the time he was actually busy writing a drill manual for the brigade. By a happy chance I was dining alone one evening in March at my London club. So too was Goodhart-Rendel dining with Willoughby Cooper, his stepfather and principal trustee. After dinner we drifted together over port, G-R protesting that his soldier-chauffeur was at the door waiting to take him back to Caterham and he could not linger. Nevertheless the three of us spent an hour resolving some outstanding knotty problems in detail.

Next day G-R wrote me a long letter giving particulars of the contents of Hatchlands, some of which were in the house when Lord Rendel bought it. For instance all the crystal chandeliers had been made up from pieces of old glass under his grandfather's directions. The curtain pelmets brought by him from London were 'quite out of style with the house'. Lord Rendel also took several pictures out of the original fitted frames and put them into new fitted frames made of *carton pierre* enrichments by Ricardo so as to look part of the Adam decoration; he also added 'frightful' doorheads to the mahogany doors which Goodhart-Rendel always longed to remove. The fine console tables in the drawing-room and the insignificant side-table in the entrance hall were his grandfather's importations. The bookcases in the library were part Adam, part new, and ought to stay as having belonged to the Boscawens. In the music room Reginald Blomfield's organ case had also better stay because though disagreeable it might one day have a period appeal. If G-R were to hand over the house to the next heir under the entail then he would take away the organ while leaving the case.

The inset looking-glass over the drawing-room chimneypiece ought, he said, to be painted out or removed from the frame which was a fixture of the room and deserved a painting or stucco relief (which is what from Adam's design seems to have been originally intended). Lord Rendel put in the glass plate which looked silly because it was far too high. G-R wrote: 'I want everything of antiquarian interest to be firmly attached to the house – but the things accidently happening to be fixed that have nothing whatever to do with anything except my family must continue with the rest of the furniture to be mine.' Consequently he erased several items of fixtures on the list of the contents which I had made.

G-R's attitude to the Trust throughout was friendly, generous and trusting. He thought a memorandum of wishes 'cuts little ice' and he had complete confidence in the Trust carrying out his wishes without one. A year later he actually asked for the memorandum which his solicitors had drafted to be withdrawn. Furthermore he did not want the Trust to create a reserve fund for expenditure on Hatchlands exclusively; any surplus which might accrue from his donated estate should be spent on other National Trust houses in need. But he was prone to contradiction, changes of mind, caprice and impetuous storms of peevishness. In November 1944 he completely lost his temper with the estate lawyers and instructed his personal solicitors to take over and finish off the legal transfer. Horne & Birkett greatly disapproved of this heterodox behaviour, beseeching me not to incur his disfavour likewise so as to cause a break in our cordial relations, but to continue dealing direct with him over the terms of the lease with extra caution. This amused me no end. After a lapse of six months I was abusing Horne & Birkett with equal petulance for failing to reach agreement with G-R's personal solicitors. We ran a real risk of losing this property, I warned

them, for it was two years since we had released the press announcement of the Hatchlands acquisition and Captain Goodhart-Rendel's
patience was running out. Why could the lease not be settled? And why
on earth, I failed to understand, could the conveyance of the property
be ante-dated and yet the lease not be ante-dated?

And what precisely was to happen to the house when it was
de-requisitioned from the girls' school? Before the war was over G-R
had considered letting it, on the recommendation of the enigmatic Dr
Kurt Hahn, headmaster of Gordonstoun School, to the Caldecote
Community, an academy for normal children from abnormal backgrounds. Mercifully this scheme came to nothing. Would the National
Trust object to his re-letting the servants' wing to some brother officers
'screaming for quarters', who would be company for him too were he to
decide to live in the house. Far from objecting the National Trust gave
this scheme their blessing. Almost anything rather than normal children of abnormal parents.

By February 1946 we were arranging to open to the public on
Wednesdays between 11 and 7 o'clock or dark when earlier, at one
shilling to the house and no charge to the grounds. G-R wrote to me in
distress, 'Dear Lees-Milne' – for after eight years we had reached that
degree of intimacy; and I was invited to omit the Mr or Captain – 'my
domestic duties are acute'. Could we keep the public to the ground floor
to start with? I said we might. Was it all right his bashing two doorways
through partitions in the servants' quarters? Yes it was, so long as he
was satisfied with the way it was done. And would the committee agree
with his plan to do away with the ribbon beds in front of the house? The
committee agreed. Anything to save labour.

In August I called at Hatchlands while he was away to find Brewster,
his faithful butler, gallantly coping by himself with the visitors who were
enchanted by him. G-R had always been fortunate with his servants who
were very fond and protective of him. A previous butler had taught him
as a gangling boy how to bicycle in the gravelled forecourt, which
conjures up a quaint spectacle. Then Goodhart-Rendel wrote an
excellent and telling history of Hatchlands for a guidebook. He
included descriptions of rooms not open to the public just 'in case he
went under a bus'. When the proofs came he was very upset by the
printers' flagrant omission of two genitive apostrophes and their
rejection of as many extremely indifferent snapshots taken by himself
for illustration.

I deliberately refrained from nagging him with questions; and he did
continue living at Hatchlands. After a decade, however, he had had

enough of the struggle all on his own. His health was declining. In 1957 he decided he must move into the parsonage in the village and sub-let the big house. An obliging tenant was found in Francis Mathew of The Times Publishing Company. G-R fairly dreaded the sorting and packing involved, not to mention choosing what to take with him, what to dispose of and what to leave behind. The interests of the big house were the first consideration: in fact what should belong to it, and what to him and his heirs, notwithstanding the definitive correspondence on the subject of twelve years back. This was the cause of much further correspondence between us. 'What I would like to do', he wrote to me on 20 October, 'is to leave the rooms shown to the public still appropriately furnished, if not so profusely as at present, and with substitute pictures and ornaments in all places that removals might make bare.' This sounded very well and straightforward but it gave rise to dreadful complications and heart searchings and nearly drove him wild with worry. On the bedroom floor curtains in the three principal rooms should be left, he directed; also the velvet curtains in the big staircase window. What to do with the organ, in spite of the previous decision to take the instrument and leave the case, was a recurring problem. And then he changed his mind, saying he could not afford to leave any furniture at all in the showrooms. Robin Fedden, who seven years ago had succeeded me, tried to get the Ministry of Works to buy it, the pictures having already been catalogued by Christie's for sale on 7 March 1958. Goodhart-Rendel, giving further thought to the furniture, declared that after all he would be prepared to sell at any figure the Ministry of Works might offer for the lot. But neither of paintings nor of furniture did the National Trust want the lot. Of the former St John Gore the Trust's adviser on pictures made a selection of what might suit the Trust; of the latter Ralph Edwards, the V&A expert who whisked round the rooms at Knole, Gore and I made a selection. Little of either category was of great value. But we did not want to be landed with an empty house. Even when G-R was living at Hatchlands it was sparsely furnished and rather bare. The Trust rightly thought that through his museum status Ralph's influence with the Ministry of Works would strengthen the Trust's need for bulk rather than quality. The picture problem was resolved by Works quixotically buying all of them at Christie's. The furniture problem seemed at first more vexed. Works put a limit of £4,500 from government money which they could properly spend on the furniture. We were faced with their bidding for, let us say, one exquisite commode by Jacob or a great deal of rubbish. After a certain amount of persuasion by Ralph and much prevarication on the part of Works, they did neither.

Goodhart-Rendel decided not to sell the furniture after all. The very idea of a sale in the house was repugnant to him. On the contrary he would be content to lend all the furniture to Mr Mathew the tenant, provided it was properly insured and cared for, with the proviso of course that he might remove pieces from time to time whenever he thought fit. Then he changed his mind again. He would lend the furniture to the National Trust for them to do the caring. And this is what happened. Perhaps he had discovered how many children Mr Mathew had, and envisaged their treatment of it.

All the while Mr Mathew, his wife and quiverful were patiently waiting to take up residence.

My colleagues, all very intelligent men who by now were concerned with Hatchlands, admired and appreciated Goodhart-Rendel's splendid brain, but found him difficult. And this I understand for they had to bear the brunt of the equivocations, revocations and contrarieties of his declining health and old age. But I, most of whose dealings with him had been during his prime, was perhaps more privileged to experience his charm, his astonishing knowledge, his willingness to impart it to attentive ears, and his generosity of spirit. He was a very devout man, and although extremely reticent about his inner beliefs, was voluble in expressing ethical opinions which were clearly guided by them. In conversation he did not so much shout one down as take over. I found his monologues wonderfully rewarding, and sometimes spell-binding. Occasionally they excited irreverent mirth for he would become seemingly oblivious of other people's presence. There was a day when he was holding forth with break-neck enthusiasm in the drawing-room while Ralph Edwards on hands and knees beside one of the pair of Lord Rendel's console tables beckoned me to join him. Together we crawled underneath the table and in dumbshow Ralph explained to me how most of it was fake. All the while G-R, pacing up and down the room, was declaiming on the table's remarkable merits. Ralph, who saw the funny side of every situation, started giggling, and I joined him. Choking with laughter, the tears pouring down our cheeks, we both realized the ridiculous spectacle we must be presenting, our heads buried out of sight, our posteriors quivering like jellies within view of our host who halted and turned his fish eyes upon them. 'What are you doing?' he asked, for we were then stuffing our mouths with handkerchiefs, unable to speak a word. When we emerged it took several minutes before we could utter. And even then we could not very well explain what we had been doing. I am not at all sure that G-R cottoned on to the cause of our merriment. That was the last time I saw him. He died in 1959.

On Mr Mathew's death Hatchlands was sub-let by the Goodhart-Rendel heirs on a succession of short leases, one to a school again, and none entirely satisfactory. Hatchlands became a problem house. No heirs wanted to live in it. The situation was saved by a chance solution which promises to be the perfect one. Alec Cobbe, picture restorer and decorative painter by profession, man of property (former owner of a family seat in Ireland), collector of works of art and musical instruments, gifted pianist, and connoisseur of extraordinarily sumptuous tastes, offered to translate his collections, with wife and children, to semi-empty Hatchlands. In 1987 he collaborated with Christopher Rowell, representative of the National Trust's southern region, in redecorating the principal rooms. Whereas the Charity Commission allowed the National Trust to spend from its funds on this major operation, Alec Cobbe with his assistants has carried it out with his own expert hands, in return for the loan of his rare early keyboard instruments by makers known to Haydn, Mozart, Beethoven, Schubert and Chopin, his high-quality French and English furniture, bronzes and marbles after the antique, and his baroque paintings crowded on the walls in a manner that conjures up Pyne's coloured engravings of Carlton House. Alec Cobbe organizes concerts of chamber music in the house; and on opening days visitors may well see him flitting from one instrument to another and hear him playing on a harpsichord by Kirkman, or the pianoforte reputedly made by Erard for Queen Marie Antoinette. Part of the deal has been the lease of a flat to the Cobbes on the upper floors.

The result of the transmogrification of the Hatchlands rooms is amazing. The former rather austere and chilling walls and ceilings of Robert Adam's chaste decorative youth have become warm, colourful and extremely opulent. Cornices have been painted in deep blues and crimsons, and skirtings in porphyry. Fabrics of silk and damask specially woven for walls and curtains and chairs have been substituted for stuffs of pale and neutral tints. Traditionalists may be shocked that the house which Goodhart-Rendel left to the Trust should almost overnight be enriched so drastically, and in a flavour Regency rather than Adam. They may say with some degree of truth that the Trust's vaunted policy has always been to preserve the continuity of family tradition and that when, as in the case of Hatchlands, that tradition came to an abrupt end with the demise of the last of the Rendels, the Rendel ethos should have been encapsulated for all time. Instead of

Harry Stuart Goodhart-Rendel lecturing. Caricature by H. de Cronin Hastings, *c.* 1926

which the Trust has allowed a tenant to impose upon the donor's family taste an alien exotic gusto. But the Trust also argues that its country houses should be, whenever possible, living, that is to say changing homes, and that what has happened at Hatchlands in a patently successful and beautiful manner is justified. Certainly the changes at Hatchlands have been brought about with the wholehearted approval and co-operation of the National Trust's staff of experts. Alec Cobbe's reinterpretation of the Georgian spirit strikes me as acceptable. His touch is not that of the fashionable commercial decorator. It is that of an inheritor of an historic country house in the eighteenth-century tradition, who is also an artist and craftsman. Gervase Jackson-Stops has claimed that Cobbe's decorative upmanship is extenuated by the fact that the Hatchlands rooms, unlike those, say, of Osterley and Syon which are unadulterated Adam complete with original contents, had been overlaid and blurred by 'layer on layer of history'; and that today they give the impression of a great Adam house 'remodelled by a great connoisseur'. It is not irrelevant to add that Hatchlands' case is different to Hanbury's. Hatchlands was never a warm, cosy, knock-about squire's dwelling like the other. It was built for an eighteenth-century noble-man's son in the grand manner, albeit on a modest scale. Its bedizen-ment, if that is not too strong a word, is not out of keeping.

Anyway no basic alterations to the structure have been perpetrated or grave solecisms committed which a future generation could not undo, were it to be so philistine and idiotic, or, which is always on the cards, were Mr Cobbe to decide to remove his splendid collections elsewhere.

What Goodhart-Rendel, if he could revisit Hatchlands, might think of it is not difficult to guess. He would surely gasp at the opulence and be a trifle resentful that a successor should have improved upon his own sober handiwork. He might even exclaim in one of his outbursts of petulance, 'Why on earth did I sweat blood and money to preserve my grandfather's house for the National Trust, in which I had implicit confidence, to alter out of all recognition?' And, after a pause, add in his generous way, 'I have to allow that it has been done by a scholar with sensitivity.'

EPILOGUE

AND now I cannot help wondering why I chose to write about the houses I did, and not the several others that came my way and the National Trust's – besides the quite considerable numbers which were tentatively offered by owners and came to nothing. In the latter category the one I most lament was Westwood Park in Worcestershire. I had cherished it for a long time. The owner Lord Doverdale, a sympathetic and delicate man, loved the weird Jacobean house planned like a starfish with a detached gatehouse, all turrets and spikes. He kept it in apple-pie order and bequeathed it to the Trust in his will. All was signed and sealed and poor Lord Doverdale had only to die in peace. Then his relations disputed the will and the family solicitor supported their objections in discovering some paltry flaw in the testator's wording. And so the Trust never got the property which was immediately sold, the house in separate freeholds and the splendid park trees for felling.

Among some favourite houses that did come to the Trust during my time is Robert Adam's masterpiece Osterley where until the outbreak of the last war Lord Jersey entertained large weekend parties of his young friends. In ambling around the garden and park on hot summer evenings one felt in those anxious years no nearer to London than one would feel today in remote Radnorshire. Another is Lyme, Cheshire, likewise standing in a capacious park contiguous to industrial Stockport. Lord and Lady Newton were the most harassed owners I ever encountered. He sighed from morning till night while she lay prostrate on a sofa. Indeed their predicament was the sad but not singular one of deciding what to do with a vast ancestral white elephant. Red-brick Owletts in Kent was a joy to visit. Sir Herbert Baker, eminent architect with Dominion connections but vilified by the fans of his pre-eminent rival Lutyens, and Lady Baker, both immensely charitable and both crippled with arthritis, were the most welcoming of donors. Petworth on the contrary was not a cosy establishment. Lady Leconfield, pursued by harmless fantasies, was conspicuously absent in London where she charmed luncheon parties with her unconventional behaviour. Lord Leconfield ('I'd sack your man if I were you'), the most blimpish peer imaginable, was on the other hand omnipresent. He knew his position – and yours – in the social hierarchy to a tee. 'I am told they give very good snacks there,' he said, pointing to Priscilla's Pantry across the street from his back door. 'Put yours down to me.' It had an enormous notice, 'Closed', in the window. His secretary Miss Harris, burly and jolly, was overflowing with banter and fun. I was struck by the contrast with her employer in everything but breeding. For there was something endearingly patrician about her nonchalance. Loyal and discreet, she yet managed by silent glances to convey her irrepressible amusement with pomposity.

Lacock Abbey may have been very down-at-heel like its saintly owner, Miss Matilda Talbot. Nothing could restrain her delight in entertaining. Miss Talbot's 'hops' in the great hall on winter evenings – *thés dansants* they may have been called – were not easily avoided without causing offence. Where she collected her young ladies from it is hard to say. All were exceedingly plain and utterly speechless. To an ancient gramophone which required winding every two minutes we danced the Roger de Coverley while the fog swirled against the Gothick windows and indoors a green yule log emitted such dense smoke that the guests were literally blinded and choking.

Sedater households were Oxburgh, Norfolk, and Coughton, War-wickshire, both belonging to Papist families of Norman descent and presided over by dowager mothers of rather errant baronet sons. I can see Lady Bedingfeld enthroned very upright like a benign Byzantine empress in a stiff chair beneath Mary Queen of Scots' needlework and Lady Throckmorton reverently fondling Catherine of Aragon's embroidered purple cope. Lady Throckmorton may not have been handsome nor for an elderly matron well dressed, being always in non-descript black, yet she was beyond others distinguished and in moral fibre splendid; and when you won her confidence even affectionate. Furthermore this zealous protectress of Catholic Coughton's traditions remained what she had been born, a staunch Anglican.

A very different establishment was kept at Anglesey Abbey by Huttleston 1st Lord Fairhaven who insisted on being served at meals before his guests, according to medieval precedence, in a vaulted crypt. Everything – food, drink, comfort, service and even the temperature –

was precisely regulated. No owner can have surveyed his good fortune more complacently than Huttleston as he lounged in a deep armchair, cigar in mouth, port glass in hand, while gently flicking invisible specks of dust off his immaculate trousers. Not that there was no justifiable cause for satisfaction with the house which he had filled with much high-class furniture from London's top dealers as well as some very considerable works of art; and also the grounds laid out *à la* Versailles to his own design and peopled with statuary. The most eccentric of owners was undoubtedly Charles Wade of Snowshill Manor. Wearing square-cut, shoulder-length, Roundhead hair and dressed in trunk and hose this magpie collector would, while showing visitors over the house, suddenly disappear behind a tapestry panel to emerge through a secret door on a different floor level. The sweetest perhaps was Mrs Henry James, Ruth Draper's sister, who took me one summer afternoon to Rye to inspect Lamb House. It had recently been badly damaged by a flying bomb which totally destroyed the early Georgian garden-house where the incomparable novelist Henry James, her uncle by marriage, wrote *The Wings of a Dove* and *The Goldon Bowl*. All the windows of Lamb House had been smashed and boarded up and what Jamesian contents were left strewn about the floors. But far and away the most congenial owner to me was Wyndham Ketton-Cremer of Felbrigg where in winter, even inside the house, one felt in one's bones the spume of the cold North Sea which buffeted the coast two miles away. Ketton-Cremer, squire, historian, man of letters, model guardian of his Wyndham ancestors' treasures, and recondite conversationalist lived alone in the immense rambling mansion, the very acme of a civilized country house not too luxurious – the bathroom and WC were about 300 yards from the bedroom – but isolated, tranquil, electricity-less and infinitely old-fashioned.

It is a fact that the National Trust concentrates far less on historic country houses than formerly. Admittedly the dwindling countryside and the coastline of Great Britain cry aloud for immediate protection and are given precedence in so far as the Trust can raise the funds. Nevertheless I sense that the Council of the Trust is of the opinion that the acquisition of country houses has had its day. It conveys the impression that it now possesses enough architectural specimens of the distinctive styles and dates, and therefore need not bother about the rest which may be in jeopardy; that the smaller ones can look after themselves; and that certainly they are all a hideous expense to run. I sense too that the Council is slightly embarrassed by them as symbols of élitism. But surely their immense popularity with the public discounts this coy attitude. It is anyway strange to me that the word élitism should have a pejorative meaning. I would suppose that all bright and ambitious people from no matter what backgrounds aspired to a condition of life aesthetically, intellectually and morally superior to the one they were born into; and that it was not shameful and snobbish to cast aside ignorance, prejudice and philistinism. Not of course that the country house way of life today represents an exclusive means of escape from these shortcomings. On the contrary it is little more than a lingering anachronism. It is doomed not merely by economic and social changes but by the spirit of the age as well. A pity one may be allowed to think because it was the very flower of the British Renaissance, having risen phoenix-like from the rubble of the monasteries which the Reformation had brought to ruin. And we have to remember that throughout the dreadful Dark and the mystic Middle Ages the monasteries, as well as being communities of holy men were the sole seats of learning, the arts, the humanities, the sciences and medicine. The country houses that took their place did not of course fulfil inclusively the role of the monasteries because the universities were likewise promoted by the Reformation. But in Tudor, Caroline and even early Georgian times they were the principal suppliers to the universities of both teachers and taught as well as being the local centres of authority and influence. They were also the refuge, often for years on end, of learned divines, professors, poets, painters, creators all, sometimes in the role of chaplains and tutors and usually just friends like Tyndale at Little Sodbury Manor, Bishop Ken at Longleat, and the writers Pope, Swift and Fielding at Prior Park, men who before the Reformation would probably have entered the monasteries.

It was in late Georgian times that the professional and in Victorian times that the industrial classes first aspired to the ranks of the squirearchy. No one disputed their right and no one considered it either presumptuous or preposterous, not even the old families who behind their sniggers approved. Deep down the old families took it for granted that the territorial status was the goal of civilized existence. And so in many senses it remained until the turn of the present century. The gentry old and new ruled from their country houses the counties just as from the Palace of Westminster they ruled the state. And so long as they were able to retain their responsibilities and, generally speaking, behave themselves, they retained the respect of those of us born with spoons of the baser metals in our mouths. At all events their houses are as much part of our history as is our constitution.

During the short Edwardian reign and aftermath the country houses of Britain, large and small, reached the crescendo of their prosperity and prestige from which between the two great wars with Germany they started to plummet. Lord Lothian – I come back to him – with his prescience paid heed to the rumbling landslide before the majority of his fellows. He was quick to discern that without some sort of help from on high these houses were doomed; and also that the most likely means of preserving their links with the families to which they belonged as by right divine was through the compromise offered by the National Trust scheme. But despite 'the most likely means' the compromise did not work, and fewer and fewer families live in their old homes. The *Zeitgeist* was, and is, against them. It is no use battling against the *Zeitgeist*. However, notwithstanding this condition which has to be accepted, posterity is at least lucky to have and be able to visit, even as museums, the domains of the defunct regime, so lovingly and adeptly preserved in aspic by the National Trust.

INDEX

Berwick, William Noel-Hill, 3rd Baron, 54, 63, 67
Betjeman, (Sir) John, 43
Bevir, Vice-Admiral Oliver, 82, 119, 141, 145, 196–8
Bexon, J.D., 109
Birkbeck, Christopher, 30, 33–5, 38–9
Birley, (Sir) Oswald, 130
Blackett family, 151
Blackett, Sir William, 151
Blenheim Palace (Oxfordshire), 35
Blessingbourne (Co. Tyrone), 128
Blickling Hall (Norfolk), 14; bequeathed to NT, 28–9, 156; described, 30; history, 31–3; decoration and furniture, 33–7; library, 38; restoration, 39; post-war access and occupation, 40–2
Blomfield, Sir Reginald, 87, 203, 210
Blunt, Anthony, 77
Boleyn family, 31
Bond, Nigel, 6
Bonham Carter, Sir Edgar, 8
Boscawen, Admiral the Hon. Edward, 202
Boscawen, Fanny, 202
Boswell, James, 124
Boughton House (Northamptonshire), 166
Bourchier, Thomas, Archbishop of Canterbury, 166
Bradenham Hall (Buckinghamshire), 40
Bramshill (Hampshire), 12
Breen, Sheila, 144
Brewster (Hatchlands butler), 211
Bridges, Sir Edward, 140
Bright, John, MP, 154
Bristol Museum, 70
Brocket (Hertfordshire), 12
Brocket, Arthur Ronald Nall Nall-Cain, 2nd Baron, 12, 207
Brockhampton (Herefordshire): described, 19–20; ownership, 21; transfer to NT, 22–7; access to public, 27
Brocklehurst, Charles, 17, 63, 82, 143
Bromyard (Herefordshire), 20, 23–5
Broughton, Sir Delves, 12
Brown, Ford Madox, 153
Brown, Lancelot ('Capability'), 21, 152
Browning, Robert, 57
Buchan, John (1st Baron Tweedsmuir), 108
Buckingham Palace Gardens (London), 4–5, 13
Buckinghamshire, John Hobart, 1st Earl of, 32

Buckinghamshire, John Hobart, 2nd Earl of, 32
Buckinghamshire, Mary Anne, Countess of, 30–1
Bulwer, Lilian Mary, 38
Burlington, Richard, 3rd Earl of, 32
Burrell, Sir P., 123
Butler-Thwing, Lady Minna, 33
Buxton, Colonel Robin, 170–5
Byng, John, 123
Byron, George Gordon, 6th Baron, 54

Calverley, Julia, Lady (née Blackett), 151, 164
Calverley, Sir Walter, 151
Calverley, Sir William, 151
Calverley Blackett, Elizabeth, Lady (née Ord), 151
Calverley Blackett, Sir Walter, 151–2
Cameron-Ramsay-Fairfax-Lucy, see Fairfax-Lucy
Carew, Richard: Survey of Cornwall, 134
Caroline (Murat), Queen of Naples, 54, 58, 62–3
Carter Jonas & Sons (land agents), 126–7
Catherine II (the Great), Empress of Russia, 32
Cecil, Emma (née Vernon; later Sneyd; then Phillips), 44–5, 52
Cecil, Henry (later 10th Earl and Marquess of Exeter), 44
Chamberlain, Neville, 6, 12, 125
Chantrey, Sir Francis Legatt, 43
Chaplin, Olive, 119–20
Charlecote Park (Warwickshire): owners, 93–4; negotiations for transfer to NT, 94–9, 102–3, 108; contents and furnishing, 104–7; rebuilt, 105–6; 1946 opening, 108–9; brew house, 109; access to public, 110
Charles I, King, 83, 135, 151
Charles II, King, 32
Charlotte, Queen of George III, 136, 147
Chastleton (Oxfordshire), 166
Cheere, Sir Henry, 80
Cherlecote, Thurstane de, 110
Chesshire Gibson & Co. (land agents), 96–7
Chettle, George, 8, 96–7
Chinthurst Hill (Surrey), 203–4
Chippendale, Thomas, the younger, 69
Church Hill, West Wycombe, 187
Churchill, Sir Winston, 125, 173
Clandeboye (Co. Down, Ireland), 35

Lyminge, Robert, 31, 41
Lyttelton, Oliver (Viscount Chandos), 41

Macaulay, Thomas Babington, 1st Baron, 154, 164
MacDonald, Ramsay, 29, 155, 171
McGregor, John, 75, 87, 182–3
Mackintosh, Colonel, 109
MacQuoid, Percy, 36
Madresfield Hall (Worcestershire), 43
Maintenon, Château de (Eure-et-Loir), 3
Mander, Sir Geoffrey, 126
Mann, Sir James, 143
Marble Hill, Twickenham (Middlesex), 32, 185
Marlborough, John Spencer-Churchill, 10th Duke of, 35
Martineau, Anthony, 130, 180
Mary II, Queen, 44
Mary, Queen of George V, 25, 129
Mason, F.M., 174–5, 177, 179, 181–3, 192
Massimo, Countess Visconti di, 76
Massingberd, Diana, 125
Massingberd, Margaret (née Lushington), 124–5, 133
Massingberd, Peregrine Langton, 123–4, 130
Massingberd, Stephen, 124–5
Massingberd, Sir William, 2nd Baronet, 122
Matheson, Donald MacLeod, 2, 4, 13; and Brockhampton, 22–3; and Lothian, 29; and Blickling Hall, 30; and Stourhead, 68, 72–5; leaves NT, 75; Knollys assists, 76; and Little Moreton Hall, 89; and Charlecote, 94–100, 103; and Smallhythe Place, 115–17; and Gunby, 123; and Wallington, 155–62; and Knole, 170–3, 175–6; commutes to West Wycombe in war, 187; and Hatchlands, 206; and Goodhart-Rendel, 207–8
Matheson, Enid, 187
Matheson, Hilda, 2, 29
Mathew, Francis, 212–14
Max, Burgomaster (Brussels), 12
Maxse, Leo & Kitty, 124
Maxwell, H.W., 143
Merrill Trust (USA), 51
Methuen, Paul, 4th Baron, 6, 11, 82
Meynell & Pemberton (solicitors), 172
Millais, Sir John Everett, 153
Miller, Gordon, 56
Milner, Alfred, Viscount, 28
Mitchell, H., 206–7, 209

Mitford, Clementine (Lady Beit), 188
Mitford, Nancy, 187–8
Monkswell, Mary, 203
Montacute House (Somerset), 2, 24, 81, 102, 147
Montagu, Elizabeth, 202
Montfort, Henry de, 110
Montgomery, Major-General Hugh, 128
Montgomery, Hugh, 128, 132
Montgomery, Mary, 128
Montgomery, Peter, 125
Montgomery-Massingberd, Field Marshal Sir Archibald Armar, 122–3, 125–32
Montgomery-Massingberd, Diana, Lady, 123–5, 127, 131–2; death, 133
Montgomery-Massingberd, John, 128, 133
Moore, Elsie, 26
Moore, Matley, 26, 179
Moreton, Edward, 85
Moreton, Sister Elizabeth, 86, 89
Moreton, Geoffrey de (born de Lastock), 85
Moreton, Richard (born Taylor), 85
Moreton, William, 85, 90
Moreton, William, Bishop of Kildare and Meath, 85
Morris, A.J.A., 154
Morris, William, 7, 87
Mortimer, Raymond, 76
Mount Edgcumbe family, 129, 136–7; see also Edgcumbe
Mount Edgcumbe house (Cornwall), 135, 138, 146
Mount Edgcumbe, Edward, 7th Earl of, 141, 146
Mount Edgcumbe, Effie, Countess of, 146
Mount Edgcumbe, Ernest Augustus Edgcumbe, 3rd Earl of, 137
Mount Edgcumbe, George Edgcumbe, 1st Earl of, 136
Mount Edgcumbe, Kenelm Edgcumbe, 6th Earl of, 138–46
Mount Edgcumbe, Lilian Agnes, Countess of, 142
Mount Edgcumbe, Piers Edgcumbe, 5th Earl of, 137–8
Mount Edgcumbe, Richard Edgcumbe, 2nd Earl of, see Valletort, Viscount
Mount Edgcumbe, Robert Charles Edgcumbe, 8th Earl of, 146
Mount Edgcumbe, William Henry Edgcumbe, 4th Earl of, 137–8
Müntzer's (of Albemarle Street, London), 37
Murray Smith, Mrs, 14